The Story of World War II

Future Books is an imprint of Future PLC
Quay House, The Ambury, Bath, BA1 1UA

A catalogue record for this book is available from the British Library.

ISBN 978-1-83648-295-6 hardback

The paper holds full FSC certification and accreditation.

Printed in China by C&C Offset Printing Co. Ltd. for Future PLC

GPSR EU RP (for authorities only)
eucomply OÜ Pärnu mnt 139b-14 11317
Tallinn, Estonia
hello@eucompliancepartner.com
+3375690241

Interested in Foreign Rights to publish this title? Email us at:
licensing@futurenet.com

Editor
Charles Ginger

Senior Art Editor
Stephen Williams

History of War Editor-in-Chief
Tim Williamson

History of War Senior Designer
Curtis Fermor-Dunman

Head of Art & Design
Greg Whitaker

Editorial Director
Jon White

Managing Director
Grainne McKenna

Production Project Manager
Matthew Eglinton

Global Business Development Manager
Jennifer Smith

Head of Future International & Bookazines
Tim Mathers

Cover images
Getty Images

FUTURE
Connectors. Creators. Experience Makers.

Future plc is a public company quoted on the London Stock Exchange (symbol: FUTR)
www.futureplc.com

Chief Executive Officer **Kevin Li Ying**
Non-Executive Chairman **Richard Huntingford**
Chief Financial Officer **Sharjeel Suleman**

Tel +44 (0)1225 442 244

MIX
Paper | Supporting responsible forestry
FSC® C008047
www.fsc.org

STORY OF WORLD WAR II

STORY OF WORLD WAR II

WWII. The name alone conjures images of chaos, destruction and death, nations grappling in a bitter struggle for supremacy. Yet while the deadliest conflict in human history both scarred and shaped the world and the millions of people who endured its horrors, its roots and legacy remain a source of both debate and fascination to this day.

In **Story of World War II**, you'll discover how the seeds of this devastating clash of arms were sown by the rise of the Nazi Party and its charismatic leader before delving into what drove Italy, Japan and Germany to form the Axis powers. You'll then plunge into some of the greatest battles ever fought, meet the key figures who led the Allies to victory, and examine the downfalls of Hitler and Mussolini. It will then be time to explore the legacy of this catastrophic event and how it ultimately set the stage for the Cold War that followed in its wake.

CONTENTS

ORIGINS

KEY MOMENTS

BATTLES

KEY FIGURES

END OF AN ERA

ORIGINS

© Alamy, Getty Images

HOW THE NAZIS SEIZED POWER

The Nazi Party's rise was not a sudden snatch of power but a slow, methodical, manipulative climb to the top

It would be easy to assume Hitler's rise to power happened like something from a fantasy story. An evil lord rises from the darkness, slaughters his opponents and enslaves a population. But the true tale of the Nazis is one of variable factors, of events where one difference could have altered everything. It is a story of a hidden threat, one that others believed they could control and didn't realize they couldn't until it was too late.

Since 1929 Germany had been suffering greatly under the grinding, relentless heel of the Great Depression. Unemployment was rife, rising from 8.5 per cent to nearly 30 per cent by 1932, and industrial production had plummeted by 42 per cent. The struggling German people were looking for radical change. The government coalition of pro-republican parties had broken, and in the elections of the 1920s the democratic parties lost their majority in the Reichstag. It was an opportunity that the National Socialist German Workers' Party (NSDAP) – better known as the Nazi Party – and their rising star, Adolf Hitler, did not intend to let slide.

Hitler had risen quickly through the ranks in the earliest years of the party. He was an incredibly skilled speaker, and he was aware just how valuable his oratory skills were to the NSDAP. Sensing an opportunity, he gave them an ultimatum: make him leader or he'd leave the party. Realizing what they could lose, party officials acquiesced. Hitler then surrounded himself with men like him, men who were willing to use violence in order to achieve their aims, and this resulted in a party that was ruthlessly driven to succeed no matter the cost.

Hitler knew that fear and uncertainty was rife within the German population and he capitalized on this. The Nazi Party unleashed an aggressive slew of propaganda to appeal to the working class. It promised that Hitler was the strong, stable leader needed to guide their country to power and prominence once again. Simply put, people wanted change and the Nazis offered it.

By fair means or foul

However, the party did not experience immediate success, with only a small gain of 12 seats in the 1928 elections. But as the country declined further into economic poverty, the party gained more support. In the 1930 election its votes increased eightfold, and in 1932 Hitler ran for president against Paul von Hindenburg. He was defeated, though not drastically, polling 30.1 per cent in the first and 36.8 per cent in the second round to Hindenburg's 49 per cent and 53 per cent.

Meanwhile, the streets of Germany became combat zones. The Nazis' paramilitary, the SA (Sturmabteilung), engaged in battles with its communist and social democrat counterparts. Although it was his party unleashing mayhem,

Hitler's captivating oratory performances attracted vast and devoted audiences

THE CHANCELLOR

How a personal revenge quest led to Hitler being placed in the role of chancellor

Franz von Papen was a sleeping threat whose ultimate entwinement with the Nazis played a major role in their ascent to power. Previously a professional soldier, von Papen entered politics after the end of WWI, during which he was accused of sabotage and espionage. He served as deputy to the Prussian state parliament, the Landtag, as part of the ultra-right wing of the Catholic Centre Party. He only became chancellor thanks to the efforts of Hindenburg's adviser Kurt von Schleicher (von Papen's best friend), much to the surprise of pretty much everyone in German political circles.

Eager to gain the support he lacked, von Papen lifted the ban on the Nazis' paramilitary and deposed the Social Democratic government of Prussia. Schleicher was understandably unhappy at this development, and he worked quickly to turn the tide against von Papen, slamming him publicly and forcing him to resign.

Licking his wounds, von Papen planned his revenge against his former friend by plotting with Hitler to find a way to oust Schleicher. He managed to convince Hindenburg to appoint the Nazi leader to the position of chancellor, with von Papen serving as vice-chancellor. Von Papen foolishly thought this would give him the power to hold Hitler back, but during Hitler's purge he only narrowly escaped death.

Thanks to his reckless revenge plot, which had been fueled by his bruised ego, von Papen had placed the most dangerous man in the world in a position of terrible power. As for his former friend-turned-rival, Schleicher would be murdered during the chaos of Night of the Long Knives in 1934.

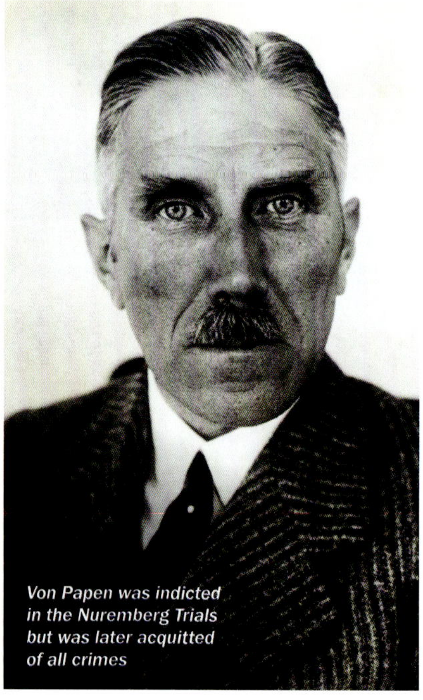

Von Papen was indicted in the Nuremberg Trials but was later acquitted of all crimes

Hitler appealed to a terrified middle class, pledging that he would restore law and order. Hatred was always bubbling away within the Nazi rhetoric, but Hitler actually sold himself to the German people by promising to provide stability and revive a floundering economy.

Clearly the German people believed him, because in the July 1932 election the NSDAP won 37.3 per cent of the popular vote. This meant it became the largest party in the Reichstag with 230 seats out of a total of 608. But it wasn't enough. Hitler didn't have a majority, and none of the other parties wished to form a coalition with him. If the other parties had been able to put their differences aside and form a coalition against Hitler it may have slowed his rise. But the communists rebuked the social democrats, splintering the opposition to the Nazis and forcing the country into another election. This time Hitler planned to win on his own terms – and he did not intend to share power.

Due to the NSDAP being the largest party, it was able to select Hermann Göring to serve as president of the Reichstag. Hitler asked to be made chancellor. Chancellor Franz von Papen instead offered him the role of vice-chancellor. To Hitler that was a slap in the face. He didn't want to play second fiddle; he wanted to rule.

But even for Hitler things were not so simple. The resulting November 1932 election actually saw the Nazi Party lose 35 seats. Although this still meant it remained the largest party in the Reichstag, this was a massive disappointment for the Nazis. Yet again they failed to form a coalition, with none of their rivals willing to team up. This election would be the last free and fair all-German election until 1949. Hitler was getting agitated – fair elections were not providing him with the results he needed.

A fatal mistake

The government, meanwhile, was in disarray. Chancellor von Papen had been governing with no support and relying mainly on legislative decrees from Hindenburg. It was an unsustainable situation, and everyone knew it. He recognized that a vote of no confidence was coming, and he knew it would pass, so on September 12 he asked Hindenburg to dissolve parliament. With the subsequent November election providing no clear majority, things became desperate. Von Papen, knowing he still held some sway over Hindenburg, promised Hitler that he could be chancellor as long as von Papen could serve as vice-chancellor.

Hindenburg, despite the drastic political situation, was understandably wary of Hitler and didn't wish to give him any great power, but his hands were tied. The election had not provided a majority government, and he couldn't deny Hitler's rising popularity. Hindenburg received a letter from 22 esteemed representatives of industry, finance and agriculture, all imploring him to make Hitler chancellor. Hindenburg caved, agreeing to appoint Hitler to the post and forming a coalition government with the NSDAP and his own party, the DNVP – the German National People's Party.

The new cabinet was sworn in on January 30, 1933, with Hitler as chancellor, Wilhelm Frick as minister of the interior, and Hermann Göring as minister without portfolio. The SA and SS poured onto the streets of Berlin in celebration.

The other politicians were not blind. They knew that Hitler was vying for more power, and they knew the extreme right-wing leanings of his party. Their mistake was underestimating the Nazis. The conservatives were convinced that by being in a coalition with Hitler they would be able to control him and tame the wild whims of his party. Hitler would be the popular face, but they would be the ones truly in charge in government. Hitler was a crowd favorite, but he was all talk and no action. Foreign ambassadors branded him "mediocre" and a "bad copy of Mussolini". Many demoted him publicly to merely a mascot or piece of furniture of the government. All of Hitler's extreme views and lust for power were played down. The newspapers stated that his hopes of forming a dictatorship would be impossible to fulfill because of the German nation being so proud of "the freedom of speech and thought". Even the Jewish community, which was well aware of Hitler's anti-Semitic views, was not particularly worried, believing that nobody would dare to threaten its people's constitutional rights. It simply would not happen. Not in Germany. Not in the modern world. Hitler was a wild dog, but he was on a leash.

However, not everyone was easily convinced that Hitler was so simple to tame. Sir Horace Rumbold, British ambassador in Berlin, acknowledged that Hitler was hardly a statesman but he was "uncommonly clever and audacious […] fully alive to every popular instinct". Rumbold warned the foreign office that the Nazis were "here to stay".

Another senior British diplomat, Robert Vansittart, believed that if Hitler was able to twist his circumstances and gain the upper hand, even for a second, he would exploit it and another European war would be upon them. Their quiet voices of doubt, however, were not loud enough, and it is always easier to ignore the beast than confront it.

Devil in disguise

None of the Germans who opposed Nazism acted quickly enough, and by squabbling over their own differences and divides they failed to unite against it. Underestimated and dangerously ambitious, Hitler plotted a path to absolute power under the noses of those who purported to hold him in check. He just needed a spark, a lick of flame to light the powder keg he had been building for the last 20 years. Hitler was the ultimate opportunist, and the very chance he was waiting for fell right into his lap on February 27, 1933.

Four weeks after Hitler was sworn in as chancellor, a literal fire tore through the Reichstag. The fire was first reported after 9pm,

This 1930s poster has Hitler stating, "We take the fate of the nation in our hands"

Hindenburg was opposed to Hitler but caved in and appointed him chancellor to satisfy his demands

© Alamy, Getty Images

A huge amount of money was invested in the Nazis' 1930 campaign, with over 1 million pamphlets produced

and the main chamber was already engulfed in flames by the time the authorities arrived. One man was found near the building, Marinus van der Lubbe, and he was arrested on suspicion of starting the blaze. For Hitler this was a huge moment – not because the government had been set on fire but because the alleged perpetrator was a communist.

Hitler could use this information to his advantage. He could twist it and claim that such a dangerous attack was the result of communist agitators seeking to wreak havoc. Although a German court would later decide that van der Lubbe had acted alone, the Nazis used this attack as evidence that the communists were plotting against the German Government. They were the rebels, they were the agitators, they were what Germany needed to rid itself of to have any hope of stability. Hitler urged Hindenburg to pass an emergency decree suspending civil liberties and to undergo a "ruthless confrontation" of the Communist Party of Germany. Faced with a literal blaze Hindenburg could hardly disagree. The decree was passed.

This gave Hitler free reign to conduct mass arrests of communists, not excluding the delegates in parliament. For so long the Nazis had been engaged in bitter fights with the communists, their biggest rivals. Now they were gone. Their seats were empty and the Nazi Party eyed them hungrily. Another election was coming in just a few days, and this time Hitler did not intend to let a majority slip through his fingers.

Enabling evil

Thanks to the Reichstag Fire Decree suspending most civil liberties, Germany became a nation ripe for the Nazis to exploit and bend to their will. The act suspended habeas corpus, freedom of expression, the press, the right of free association and public assembly, and even the secrecy of the postal service and telephone lines. Hitler used this to ban any publications that were not friendly to the Nazi cause and proclaimed that the only way to stop the communist plot was to vote for the Nazis during the impending election.

Nazi stormtroopers unleashed a wave of violence against not only the communists but also the trade unionists, left-wingers, social democrats and the Centre Party. Nazi newspapers sent the population into a panic and, with thousands of communists imprisoned, their vote swelled from 33 per cent to 44. Even with Nazi organizations monitoring the vote process, this still wasn't the majority Hitler needed, but with the DNVP's eight per cent added on, Hitler's party gained a majority of 52 per cent. It hadn't been easy and it was not a runaway victory, but finally he had done it. Now Hitler's real plan for consolidating power came into effect.

Hitler knew that the president would always be the thorn in his side, for the president had the power to remove the chancellor at any point. He couldn't hope to operate freely with one man able to stop him at a moment's notice. What he needed to do was pass an enabling act. This would give him the power to pass laws by decree without them having to go through the troublesome Reichstag. This would last for four years before his new powers would be up for review, certainly enough time for Hitler to set his plans into motion. He could do a lot in four years.

An enabling act would afford Hitler the power of the president – the power to rule by decree. Such an act was almost unprecedented and passed only in situations of extreme

The true blame for the Reichstag fire remains the source of much debate

"AN ENABLING ACT WOULD GIVE HITLER THE POWER TO PASS LAWS"

emergency. There was one problem: Hitler needed a two-thirds majority vote in order to pass the act.

Hitler knew that the Social Democratic Party would be his biggest opposition, so he used intimidation and arrests to prevent many of them taking their seats during the vote. Hitler promised that, with his new powers, he would not threaten the Reichstag, the president, the states or the churches. He was, of course, simply doing what needed to be done to set the country back on the straight and narrow after those nasty communists messed everything up. He gave parliament a choice: "It is for you, gentlemen of the Reichstag, to decide between war and peace." Convinced by Hitler's rhetoric and likely terrified at the prospect of going against it, the remaining politicians passed the Enabling Act on March 23, 1933, without offering much in the way of opposition, essentially giving Hitler all the powers of a dictator.

The Führer rises

All the promises Hitler made fell away almost immediately. Without any parties to oppose him, he abolished the power of the states and eliminated any non-Nazi parties. He also stripped the Reichstag of its democratic responsibilities. He allowed Hindenburg to continue ruling, and it was only until his death in August 1934 that Hitler truly consolidated all his power. However, he did not waste time, and on the very day of Hindenburg's death he commanded all soldiers to swear the Hitler Oath, a vow of unconditional obedience to their new leader.

Hitler didn't set the world ablaze on the road to securing power. Even at the height of voter intimidation and opposition arrests he failed to achieve a majority, his brutish disciples unable to scare enough people into obeying their demands at the ballot box. In fact, unconvinced by Hitler's fiery rhetoric, most actually voted for another party. But it didn't matter. He was able to seize every opportunity that fell into his lap, manipulated the law and convinced his fellow politicians that he was no threat and was in fact determined to help them.

Hitler deftly slipped under the radar, and by the time the mistakes were realized by those who could have stopped him it was too late. Now Germany was Hitler's to do with as he wished. The rest of Europe would soon follow.

RUPTURING THE LEAGUE OF NATIONS

To the German people, the League was not a union but a tool of oppression

When Germany announced its withdrawal from the League of Nations in October 1933, it was the result of a storm that had been brewing for 14 years. Still licking their wounds from the Treaty of Versailles, the German people believed that the treaty had labeled them a pariah state. The treaty placed full blame on Germany for the war, while the common Germans believed their actions to be that of defense. However, the biggest humiliation to Germany by the League was the failure of other countries to disarm as they had been asked to.

Hitler leapt on this negative sentiment and held a referendum on withdrawing from the League of Nations. He intentionally timed the vote to take place close to the 15th anniversary of the Armistice of Compiègne, a bitter memory for most of Germany. Even so, such was the support for leaving that Hitler knew that he wouldn't have to use any coercion tactics to achieve his desired result. It was a landslide, with 95.1 per cent of voters favoring leaving.

Nine months after Hitler was appointed chancellor, Germany left the League of Nations. It marked the start of a rapid period of rearmament that eventually led to the seizure of Austria, the annexation of Bohemia and Moravia, and, fatefully for the rest of the world, an invasion of Poland in September 1939.

The League lasted 26 years, disbanding in 1946

REARMING GERMANY

The road to WWII was paved with chaos, ambition and hubris, with Germany's rearmament campaign a dangerous cocktail of all three

As the Great War drew to a close in 1918, the Allied powers forced the Germans to sign the Treaty of Versailles, imposing a crushing set of punitive provisions designed to permanently neuter Germany's military capabilities. Aside from paying hefty reparations, Germany would have to disband its military leadership, restrict its army to just 100,000 men and its navy to 15,000 and limit its stocks of weapons, ammunition and naval vessels.

The treaty also stipulated that Germany could only produce armaments at Allied-approved factories in limited amounts, and it strictly forbade the importation of weapons and the production of armored cars, tanks and military planes. Moreover, conscription was banned and the 31-mile Rhineland stretching west of the Rhine was demilitarized.

By signing the treaty the Weimar Government was seen by most Germans to have committed the ultimate betrayal – one designed to forever place the great German nation beneath the yoke of its European neighbors. As Chancellor Scheidemann proclaimed, "What hand would not wither that binds itself and us in these fetters?" However, throughout the 1920s the Weimar Government secretly defied the treaty, reintroducing military training for police, creating the Abwehr military intelligence organization and reorganizing the supposedly disbanded military hierarchy.

The country also saw a rise in paramilitary organizations, vaguely disguised as innocuous youth, labor and athletic groups. Despite being banned, the air force covertly maintained a bare-bones number of pilots and staff, supported by the legitimate aero industry – with airfields hidden from prying eyes. Ships comparable in size and type to those banned were also produced, with the naval fleet disguised as a civilian one.

Meanwhile, Adolf Hitler's star was on the rise, and with him came a dangerous new paradigm to which warfare would be central. In an environment of chaos and mass unemployment, by the time the Nazis rose to power in 1933, the Nazi paramilitary group, the SA, and its subsidiary, the SS, numbered around 500,000. Once elected chancellor, Hitler's priority immediately shifted to re-establishing Germany as Europe's pre-eminent superpower – one he had long dreamed of leading to war.

A giant begins to stir

In June of that year, Reichsbank president and future minister of economics Hjalmar Schacht agreed to finance an eight-year rearmament program through a company underwritten by the Reichsbank. The country would spend four years building up its defensive capacities and then another four developing an offensive strike force. To bolster public support and stave off foreign criticism, the Nazis exaggerated their sense of vulnerability by fabricating a story about foreign bombers dropping communist leaflets over Germany.

While in attendance at President von Hindenburg's funeral, Hitler claimed to be pursuing a path of peace; this was at odds with his bold assertions of the inevitable oncoming great war prophesied in *Mein Kampf*, and the French were growing wary. The Nazis had already launched the Replacement Shipbuilding

Program, designed to create a new fleet by 1949, and in another show of strength, the Nuremberg rally of 1934 was accompanied by a parade of 100,000 marching soldiers, with numerous military officers in attendance. The event culminated in a showcase of military tactics and equipment, with 130 anti-aircraft searchlights forming a 'cathedral of light'.

In 1935, Hitler decided to step up his rearmament campaign, authorizing the formation of the Luftwaffe air force and publicly declaring its existence. With the country just beginning to recover from the throes of economic depression, it still had 5.5 million unemployed. Killing two birds with one stone, the Nazis created the Reich Labor Service, rolling out conscription with a view to having 700,000 soldiers within the Wehrmacht (German Army) by 1939.

A deadly deception

Despite the elaborate display of German military might at the Nuremberg rally, rearmament remained a pipe dream. While the army had grown beyond its Versailles limitations to boast half a million men, as economist Rolf Wagenführ wrote, "Public views of the scale of armament were very much exaggerated."

Steel production had slowed down and rubber factories were operating with just two

ALBERT SPEER'S ARMAMENT MIRACLE

With the rapid defeat of the USSR having failed to materialize and Allied bombings decimating Germany, by 1942 the situation was becoming desperate for Hitler. However, his appointment of his architect Albert Speer as minister of armaments and war production did offer hope, kickstarting what would later be dubbed an 'armament miracle' as production apparently tripled in two years. In the first half of 1942 alone the armaments industry doubled its output, and the production of locomotives rocketed from 1,918 to 5,343 in two years.

Speer boosted productivity by limiting the types of weapons being made, which helped to streamline mass production, and scaling back minor design adjustments to save time refining production equipment. Moreover, aesthetics were stripped back in favor of faster manufacturing. Speer also forced companies to share technological secrets to improve efficiency across the country. The government renegotiated with its suppliers, moving from cost-plus contracts to fixed-price contracts, thereby incentivizing them to lower their production costs (these measures had already been rolled out in the aircraft industry before Speer's appointment).

Some argue that Speer overstated his contribution to these improvements, using indices based on particularly low 1941 figures. However, having previously masterminded both the Nuremberg rallies and 1936 Berlin Olympics, Speer worked with Goebbels on a propaganda campaign centered around the slogan 'The best weapons bring victory'.

Due to a chronic lack of fuel and rubber, the Nazis relied heavily on horses, taking up to 750,000 into the USSR

months' supplies. However, Hitler was more than happy to let his foreign counterparts overestimate his abilities. Winston Churchill claimed that German rearmament expenditure stood at 12 billion Reichsmark (RM), when in truth it was closer to 5 billion. Eager to maintain the illusion of power, the Nazis painted fleets of civilian aircraft with military patterns and put on air shows. While the Germans were not ready to mass-produce military planes, they showcased bombers such as the Do-17 'flying pencil', seemingly faster than any of its French or British counterparts.

Meanwhile, the commercial He 111, used by Lufthansa, which had been built with a large smoking compartment, now revealed its true purpose – the smoking room had been converted into a bomb bay. Legendary American aviator Charles Lindbergh was invited to tour German facilities and fly the country's aircraft and left proclaiming "Germany is undoubtedly the most powerful nation in the world in military aviation, and her margin of leadership is increasing with each month that passes."

Risks in the Rhineland

The Nazi rearmament campaign crossed a critical juncture in March 1936. With Britain and France in disarray over how to deal with Mussolini's colonial incursions into Abyssinia, Hitler sent 22,000 men into the demilitarized Rhineland. The 19 infantry battalions, 13 artillery groups and 54 planes joined local police for a combined force of 36,500 that the French incorrectly estimated as standing at 295,000.

Hitler justified the move by pointing to the Franco-Soviet pact ratified the month prior. Having previously espoused the Nazi desire for international friendship and peace, Hitler declared "in accordance with the fundamental right of a nation to secure its frontiers and ensure its possibilities of defense, the German Government have today restored the full and unrestricted sovereignty of Germany in the demilitarized zone of the Rhineland."

Once again the British and the French failed to create a united front – the former favoring appeasement and the latter too weak to mount a military response alone. As Mussolini left the League of Nations and Spain descended into civil war, lines were beginning to be drawn in the sand.

Hitler had made the ultimate gamble – had Britain and France met the Germans with force the Nazis would most likely have been routed and forced from the Rhineland with, as Hitler's interpreter Paul Schmidt said, "our tail between our legs". Instead they missed their last great chance to nip the German threat in the bud. The Nazis had instead shattered the Treaty of Versailles' military manacles and thrown down the political gauntlet, setting in motion a deadly series of events.

Emboldened, the Nazis secretly sent scores of 'volunteers' to fight in the Spanish Civil War, directly in contravention of the Treaty of Versailles, which prohibited Germany from sending armies abroad. Armed with fraudulent papers, Spanish money and uniforms, more than 14,000 Nazi pilots gained almost three years' experience in Spain as they tested out the military capabilities of the Messerschmitt Bf 109.

While the Nazis produced a public 'white budget', where military spending stood at 360 million RM in 1936, the secret 'black budget' stood at more than 3 billion RM. That spring, increasingly concerned about the Red Army to the east – whose numbers had swelled to 1 million – and the rearmament of France and Britain to the west, Hitler instructed Göring to ready the army and economy for war within just four years. Pursuing a path of self-sufficiency, Göring would be in charge of investing in the synthetic production of rubber, iron, petrol, industrial fats and textiles.

Upon announcing the second four-year plan, Hitler asserted that war was inevitable, that it was Germany's task to "defend Europe against

THE INTERNATIONAL RESPONSE

While Germany began rearming itself under a cloak of secrecy, Hitler publicly declared his intent in 1935 by formally announcing the Luftwaffe and rolling out public conscription. However, Germany's defiance of Versailles went unchecked, with the British even ratifying a naval treaty that included battle-ready submarines in a bid to appease Hitler.

The previous winter, American journalist William Shirer wrote there was "much talk here that Germany is secretly arming, though it is difficult to get definite dope, and if you did get it and sent it, you'd probably be expelled". Winston Churchill went so far as to speculate the German air force had grown to match Britain's, a fact Hitler was more than happy to reinforce when visited by British politicians Sir John Simon and Anthony Eden.

The real turning point was Hitler's remilitarization of the Rhineland. While France was equally outraged and terrified, it could not mount armed opposition without the help of Britain, who instead opted for a path of appeasement. Though Churchill warned in 1936 that "the era of procrastination, of half-measures, of soothing and baffling expedients, of delays, is coming to a close", with the United States in isolationist mode, Hitler emerged from his most vulnerable state emboldened and ready to march into the German-speaking territories and beyond.

Bolshevism" and that "a final solution of the food problem only can come through an expansion of living space" – a reference to his policy of Lebensraum.

Geared for war

The army began to dramatically scale up its expectations, building a field army of 3.6 million men by 1940, even larger than the Kaiser's army in 1914. The strongest infantry divisions would be given around 600 trucks, 400 cars and 400 motorcycles. Alongside the 120,000 trucks would be 630,700 horses, enough for one in four soldiers. With more than 35 billion RM set aside for the army from 1937 to 1941, only five per cent was marked for land vehicles – almost a third was set aside for artillery, guns and ammunition, and just nine per cent allocated for fortifications.

By 1938, approximately 80 per cent of goods and services purchased by Germany were procured for the Wehrmacht. Half of the Nazi military budget was spent on the Luftwaffe, with monthly aircraft production rising from 30 in 1933 to 425 in 1936, before rising by a further 60 per cent. The country shifted its tank production to the Mark III in 1938 and the Mark IV in 1939, producing 247 tanks in three months alone.

In the six years leading up to 1939 Hitler boasted of spending 90 billion RM on rearmament. Conservative estimates suggest a more accurate figure of around 55 billion RM – just over half of all public expenditure and ten per cent of gross GDP. The country now enjoyed full employment, and subsequent rearmament had helped lift production 25 per cent higher than 1929 levels.

At the dawn of WWII, as the Nazis prepared to invade Poland, they were producing 500 aircraft a month – boasting a powerful fleet of 1,000 bombers and 1,050 fighters. Britain and France had a combined 1,800 bombers and 950 fighters. That year the Nazis embarked on a program to build six huge battleships, 249 U-boats and eight long-range cruisers, with a budgeted 33 billion RM being set aside for almost 800 ships.

Though it appeared Hitler was more than ready to wage total war, all was not as it seemed. While the Germans were now spending 15 per cent of their GDP on military expenditure, so were the British, and the Americans were spending ten per cent. For Germany, with tax rates already high and the country reluctant to borrow more funds, rearmament on such a massive scale was

In March 1936, Hitler marched 22,000 men into the demilitarized Rhineland, essentially crossing the Rubicon, to no response

"55 BILLION REICHSMARKS WAS SPENT ON REARMAMENT IN THE SIX YEARS LEADING UP TO 1939"

unsustainable. The country was also spending heavily on highways and public works. Having approved a final 3 billion RM for rearmament in 1938, the Reichsbank president, Schacht, was dismissed the next year for refusing to offer any more. Following his departure the country overhauled the economy, rolling out cost control on all public contracts and abolishing the gold standard, thereby giving the Wehrmacht access to a black budget of 21 billion in 1939 alone, with roughly half given to the navy and Luftwaffe and half to the army.

A doomed investment

Hitler's strategy had been to expand his Lebensraum piece by piece with a series of brief blitzkrieg wars. With America on the sidelines, Germany would slowly annex Western Europe and draw upon its resources to prepare for a greater war with the Soviet Union in the future. In truth, Germany only had enough crucial resources – fuel oil, iron ore, magnesium and gasoline – to sustain a few months of fighting. The Germans had just 2,439 tanks in 1940 with which to face 3,254 French tanks and a combined total of 4,200 Allied tanks. While Göring announced plans to expand the Luftwaffe to 21,000 planes, they never far surpassed 5,000. Meanwhile, at their peak Britain and the USSR would boast 8,300 and 17,000 respectively, and the US 21,000.

Having prioritized the navy and Luftwaffe, after some initial success and a doubling of production in 1940, in the second half of 1941 army production dropped by 30 per cent. As Hitler's series of brief conflicts unexpectedly blossomed into total warfare, the inept scale and manner of the Nazi military investments were eventually revealed – especially once the Soviets began to turn the tide on the Eastern Front and begin their advance on Berlin.

In a telling move, as the Americans poured resources into the development of the atom bomb, the Nazis decided to seek out more cost-effective solutions to their problems. Ships were confined to the coast and fjords of Norway as planes were recalled to defend the Fatherland in the face of sustained bombing. Even after the catastrophic failure at Stalingrad, Germany only stepped up its war production in a meaningful way toward the height of Allied bombings, tripling from 1942 to 1944 – but it would prove too little, too late. Rather than expanding, Germany would be forced to push its war machine into top gear, battling all the way back to Berlin, sustaining itself just enough to drag millions to their graves along the way.

AXIS OF EVIL

In the wake of WWI, ruthless ambition, dark determination and lust for power drove three men to plunge the world into an era of death and terror

GERMANY

One man's quest to reclaim Germany's honor

Everything was perfectly aligned for Adolf Hitler's rise to power. The army veteran had tasted the bitter pill of German defeat in WWI and witnessed the once great nation become a broken land that could barely feed its own people. Determined to rebuild the country, he joined the German Workers' Party and his charismatic speeches soon caught the nation's attention. He was saying everything the struggling people wanted to hear – he promised them food, employment, and, most importantly, reclaimed pride. The ranks of the Nazi Party swelled and the people spoke; in July 1932 many voted for Hitler and he was duly appointed as chancellor.

In control of all of German life and having banned all other political parties, Hitler and his Nazi Party focused their efforts on unravelling the Treaty of Versailles. The Führer legitimized his actions by claiming the treaty denied Germany adequate 'living space'. One by one, Hitler broke the post-war agreements. He withdrew the country from the League of Nations, built up the military and began to flex Germany's muscles, occupying the German Rhineland, annexing Austria and invading Czechoslovakia. He was testing his enemies. He had already angered France and Britain, who promised to declare war if he invaded Poland, and he was well aware that alone he didn't stand a chance of taking on the Soviet Union – his ultimate goal. Hitler was ruthless and power hungry, but he wasn't stupid. He knew he couldn't achieve his goals with German forces alone. He needed help. He needed allies.

NAZI HIGH COMMAND

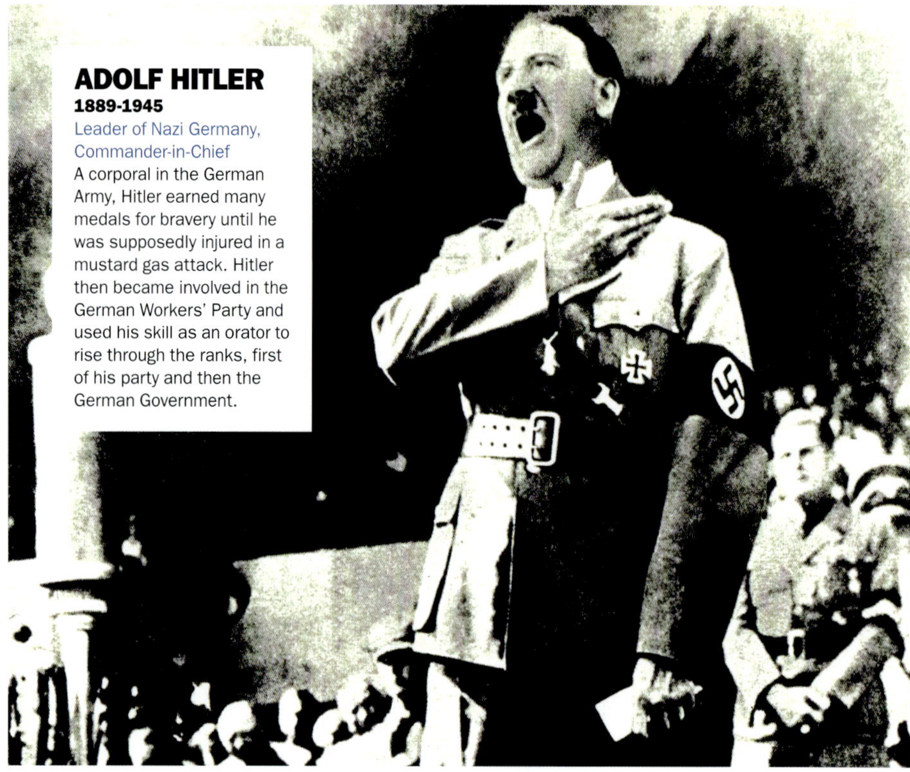

ADOLF HITLER

1889-1945

Leader of Nazi Germany, Commander-in-Chief

A corporal in the German Army, Hitler earned many medals for bravery until he was supposedly injured in a mustard gas attack. Hitler then became involved in the German Workers' Party and used his skill as an orator to rise through the ranks, first of his party and then the German Government.

HERMANN GÖRING

1893-1946

Commander-in-Chief of the Luftwaffe

A veteran ace fighter pilot of WWI, Göring was a close confidant of Hitler and quickly rose through the Nazi ranks. Although he enjoyed success after the attack on Poland, Göring later became consumed in fighting with his rivals within the party.

JOSEPH GOEBBELS

1897-1945

Minister of Propaganda

Rejected by the army due to his clubbed foot, Goebbels' embittered feelings drove him into the arms of the Nazi Party. He soon became one of the most powerful people in Nazi Germany, but his devious tactics earned him the fitting nickname 'Poison Dwarf'.

MACHINES OF WAR

MESSERSCHMITT BF 109

A trailblazer of modern fighter planes of the era, the Bf 109 formed the backbone of the German air force. Originally used in the Spanish Civil War, this fighter plane was constantly developed and improved upon throughout the war. The Bf 109 became the most-produced fighter aircraft in history and was supplied to many Axis countries, not just Germany.

Strengths Small, fast, powerful and cheap to produce.
Weaknesses Narrow wheel track making it unstable on ground; hard to control in high winds.

TIGER I

When German forces encountered the impressive Soviet tanks during their invasion of the Soviet Union, they realized they would need to produce a machine to rival them. The Tiger I was their answer. With a focus on firepower and armor, the Tiger I was employed on all German battlefronts. Five British Sherman tanks were generally needed to take down a Tiger I.

Strengths Powerful 88mm (3.5in) gun; tough armor.
Weaknesses Limited mobility; frequent breakdowns; difficult to transport.

BISMARCK

One of the famous ships of the 20th century, Bismarck was one of the largest ships ever built by a European country and served as a symbol of Hitler's supremacy and power. In design Bismarck was a throwback to the ships of WWI, and at a massive 50,000 tons it defied the restrictions placed on the German Navy following the war.

Strengths Supremely strong armor; speed; mobility.
Weaknesses Lack of turret protection; steering issues made it difficult to keep on course.

ITALY

The would-be Caesar desperate to carve out an empire to rule

Benito Mussolini had big plans for Italy. He was the father of the Fascist Party and had built it from the ground up, swelling its ranks with embittered war veterans. By 1922, Italy had descended into political chaos and the king had no option but to appoint Mussolini prime minister. Mussolini was intelligent, shrewd and ambitious, and when his leadership brought new jobs to the unemployed, he became popular too. Mussolini was a war hero – he had fought on the front lines in WWI until he was injured – and the pride he wished to instil in his country drove his ruthless actions.

Mussolini believed it was his destiny to re-forge the Roman Empire with himself ruling as a modern-day Caesar. In 1935, he invaded Ethiopia with the full might of his army. The ill-equipped Ethiopians easily fell and the Italian Empire grew. When civil war broke out in Spain, Mussolini leapt on the opportunity to spread his influence and sent support to the fascists.

Mussolini was making enemies – and fast. But there was one nation that offered support – Nazi Germany. The ruthless actions of the Italian dictator caught Hitler's attention and he invited him to Germany with aims to impress the brash Italian leader.

Mussolini, too, had been paying close attention to Hitler. With the return of the Roman Empire as his aim, Mussolini was keen to hold a prime spot at the table if the world was to be carved apart. If it went well, the meeting of these two power-hungry dictators could be the beginning of a strong and dangerous partnership, one fit to bring Europe to heel.

FATHERS OF FASCISM

BENITO MUSSOLINI

1883-1945

Prime Minister, Duce (leader) of Fascists

When Italy entered WWI, Mussolini broke his socialist ties and became a fascist. He organized supporters into armed squads and used terror and intimidation to become dictator.

ITALO GARIBOLDI

1879-1970

Commander at the Battle of Stalingrad

Gariboldi's military skill saw him rise through the ranks of the Italian Army, receiving several medals, including one for service in the Battle of Stalingrad. By 1941, he was supreme commander of the Italian forces in Africa, and in 1942 he became head of the army in Russia.

UGO CAVALLERO

1880-1943

Chief of Italian Supreme Command, Marshal of Italy

A talented tactician, Cavallero achieved success during WWI and became Mussolini's Undersecretary of War in 1925. When Italy entered WWII, he was made commander-in-chief of the Italian Supreme Command and was involved in many major battles.

MACHINES OF WAR

MACCHI C.202 FOLGORE

This aircraft served as proof that the Italian Air Force was capable of producing a world-class fighter plane. The Folgore saw service on all the fronts where Italy fought during the war, proving itself a deadly foe.

Strengths Speed and maneuverability.
Weaknesses Under-gunned; inefficient oxygen system; unreliable radio.

ZARA-CLASS CRUISER

The Zara cruisers were developed to combat the latest French-designed cruisers. By using the French designs as a base, the Zara cruisers were heavily armored and powerful. The British Navy struggled to match them when they faced each other in conflicts in the Mediterranean Sea.

Strengths Heavy firepower and well armored.
Weaknesses Not able to carry radar.

L3 TANKETTE

This two-man tankette saw action before, during and after WWII. It was the most common Italian armored fighting vehicle throughout the war, with between 2,000 and 2,500 L3 tankettes built in various models and also sold to a variety of countries.

Strengths Cheap to produce; speed.
Weaknesses Thin armor and weak firepower.

JAPAN

The developing power striving for continental domination

Japan needed help. The country had undergone a dramatic industrialization in the mid-19th century and now considered itself a major power. The rest of the world, however, disagreed. Japan had played a part in the Allied victory in WWI, but the Western powers were wary of Japan's growing imperialist tendencies. Instead of forging powerful new alliances, Japan found its military limited, and America even prohibited Japanese immigration into the country. To the Japanese nationalists these were racist actions, and those who could have been allies became enemies.

This was bad news for Japan. It was struggling under a domestic crisis due to economic collapse. Control slipped away from the government and the military began to act alone. Eventually, even the role of prime minister was filled by an admiral. Desperately in need of natural resources and hungry for the power it felt unfairly deprived of, Japan undertook plans for a unification of Asia under Japanese leadership. This meant one thing – an invasion of their long-time rivals, China.

Japan began an offensive against China that erupted into a full-blown war. The League of Nations criticized Japan, so the country simply left the League and continued its conquest. Although Japan occupied almost the entire coast of China, the Chinese refused to surrender and the war continued. Japan, with its limited resources, was pushed to breaking point. It was too late for Japan to make friends, but partnering with the enemies of its enemies was now a very appealing prospect.

LEADERS OF IMPERIALISM

HIROHITO

1901-1989

Emperor of Japan, commander of the Imperial General Headquarters

Hirohito became emperor in 1926. Although in theory he had extreme authority, he gave much of his power to ministers. As a result his personal involvement in Japan's expansionist policies remains a subject of debate.

FUMIMARO KONOE

1891-1945

Prime Minister of Japan 1937-1941

Born to a noble family, Konoe was made premier in 1937. When Japanese troops clashed with the Chinese he was keen to avoid an all-out war, and as the conflict escalated he resigned from his post.

HIDEKI TOJO

1884-1948

Prime Minister of Japan 1941-1944, Minister of War

A decorated general, Tojo became prime minister after Konoe's resignation. He supported expansionist policies, was responsible for the attack on Pearl Harbor and pumped nationalist indoctrination into the education system.

MACHINES OF WAR

MITSUBISHI ZERO

A symbol of Japan's aerial power, the Zeroes served throughout the war from the attack on Pearl Harbor to the very last kamikaze missions. There were 11,283 produced between 1939 and 1945, and the planes were regarded as being near-invincible.

Strengths Long range; maneuverability.
Weaknesses Limited firepower, armor and engine power.

MITSUBISHI G4M BETTY

Nicknamed the 'Flying Cigar' due to its shape, this Japanese bomber operated from the start of the war through to the end, with a total of 2,435 built.

Strengths Incredible range and high speed.
Weaknesses No armor plating or protection for crew; unprotected fuel tanks that easily ignited.

YAMATO

This gigantic battleship was the heaviest and most powerful armed battleship ever constructed. It was specifically designed to counter the United States' battleship fleet.

Strengths Massive firepower; speed.
Weaknesses Structural weaknesses in the armor made it susceptible to air-dropped torpedoes.

A DEADLY ALLIANCE

Hitler spared no expense to ensure he impressed Mussolini. When the Italian leader met the German dictator, Hitler put on an elaborate show of his nation's power with a long parade of German troops and impressive demonstration of military equipment. It sent a strong message – this is the nation you want to fight with, not against. Italy agreed and Mussolini was impressed. Two months later, in November 1936, Italy joined Germany and Japan in signing the Anti-Comintern Pact.

Although appearing to aim at the communist international organization Comintern, in reality the pact was directed toward the Soviet Union. By signing, the countries agreed if any of them should become involved in war with the Soviet Union they would consult on measures "to safeguard their common interests". On the outside it painted Hitler and Mussolini as crusaders defending Western values against communism, but in reality the pact fueled their expansionist goals. It was the first sign of what would become known as the Axis powers.

By May 1939, Germany and Italy knew war was inevitable, and the countries again demonstrated their allegiance by signing the Pact of Friendship. The agreement committed the two nations to supply aid to the other if they found themselves at war. However, it also contained secretive protocols preparing Italy and Germany for a future European war they would wage together. Japan originally intended to sign, but as the focus was aimed at Britain and France, not the Soviet Union, they declined.

A German general in an armored car accompanying tanks in the invasion of Poland in 1939

The wartime alliance was now a very real, tangible thing. But when Germany invaded Poland in September 1939, Italy was not ready. It needed years to train its army for war, so there was no way it could join the German invasion. In fact, Italy was not ready to declare war until June 1940, by which point Hitler had conquered most of Western Europe. However, this was irrelevant to Japan and Italy, as, conveniently, all the Axis powers wished to obtain territory in different areas of the world.

Although they fought for domination in different arenas, the three leaders knew the power of presenting a united front, so on September 27, 1940, the Tripartite Pact was signed. The main aim of the pact was to keep the huge power of the US out of the war.

The powers agreed to unite against anyone who dared to oppose them. It also established two spheres of influence, with Japan acknowledging Germany and Italy as the leaders of a new European order, and vice versa for Japan in East Asia. What had begun as three separate states with grand ambitions had transformed into a united and dangerous force prepared to take on all comers. The Axis was born.

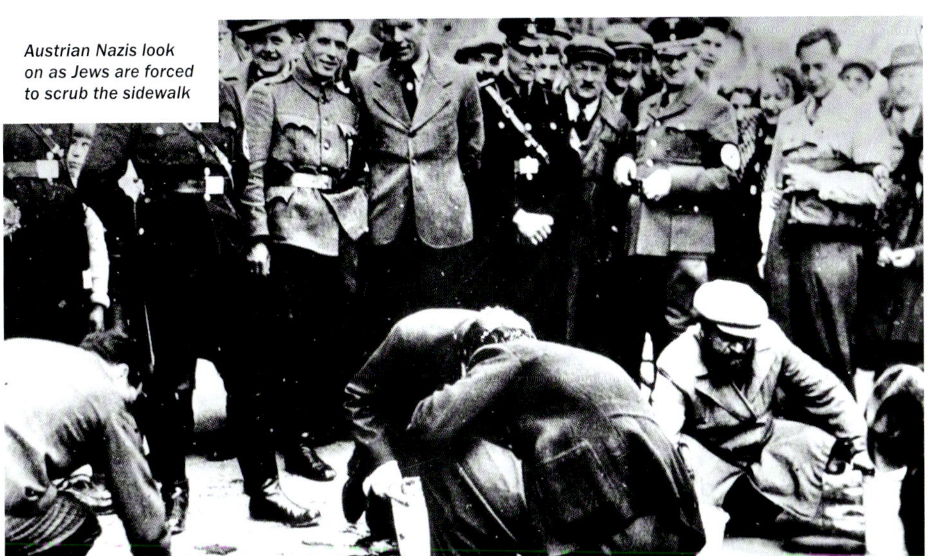

Austrian Nazis look on as Jews are forced to scrub the sidewalk

AXIS STRENGTHS & WEAKNESSES

TECHNOLOGY

German scientists and engineers were, at the beginning of the war, miles ahead of their Allied counterparts, for they were already equipped with new technological advances like jets, synthetic oil and the latest rockets and bombs. In fact these German scientists were so impressive that after the war they were employed by the Allies as part of Operation Paperclip.

NUMBERS

The German Army was already 3 million strong by 1936. Hitler had been preparing his forces for war years in advance, and it showed. For his 100 infantry and six armored divisions in 1939, Britain had 24 and two respectively. Italy too had one of the largest bomber forces in the world, while Japan boasted one of the largest navies.

INITIATIVE

At the beginning of the war, the Axis felt the benefits of having the strategic initiative. While the Allies were still waiting to see how far Hitler would push his luck, the Führer had already made plans to invade Poland and eventually the USSR. Initially the Allies had no choice but to wait and react to what their enemies did, putting the Axis in a very powerful position indeed.

LACK OF RESOURCES

The problem that drove the Axis powers to war also plagued them throughout it. The three powers were going bankrupt, and as the war dragged on they struggled to obtain enough resources for their forces. By the time the conflict had ended, Germany didn't even have enough oil left to fuel its airplanes.

SOLE COMMAND

Although this was initially an advantage, as Hitler was free to take whatever actions he saw fit, this came to be a major weakness as the war progressed. Hitler attempted to micro-manage all his battles, when in reality this job should have been handled by his skilled and talented generals – as in the Allied countries.

FRACTURED ALLIANCE

The Axis aligned with each other, essentially, because their enemies were the same, and cracks gradually began to form. Italy was hesitant throughout the war due to its own lack of military strength. Hitler's early victories had inflated his ego and he was unwilling to compromise his goals. Japan was generally distrustful of any European power, allies or not. A true alliance was, ultimately, impossible.

THE TRIPARTITE PACT

September 27, 1940

Japanese Ambassador Saburo Kurusu, Italian Foreign Minister Galeazzo Ciano and Adolf Hitler sign a mutual defense treaty in Berlin. With this, the three nations agreed to unite against any aggressor who violated their sovereignty, officially making them allies in war. After this, Germany, Italy and Japan formally took the name 'Axis powers'.

AXIS DIPLOMACY

On the surface the Axis Powers were brothers united by a common cause, but just how close were these alliances behind closed doors?

MUSSOLINI + HITLER

On paper the Führer and the Duce should have gotten on well: Italian fascism and Nazism were very similar ideologies, and Hitler was a great admirer of Mussolini. In reality, their relationship was a tense one. Mussolini immediately disliked Hitler. He described *Mein Kampf* as boring and refused to use a translator when they first met. Mussolini spoke little German and could barely understand Hitler's accent and after the meeting described the dictator as "a silly little monkey". This scorn was not helped by the fact that Mussolini did not agree with Hitler's extreme racial views. Despite their differences, they both realized that personal clashes were subservient to their political aims. Propaganda that displayed the two as friends was pumped out, and their alliance was one that was to alter the course of European history.

HITLER + HIROHITO

There is no record of Hitler and the emperor meeting in person, and this fact is symbolic of their entire relationship. It was a friendship of convenience and, had it continued, might have ended disastrously.

Despite dubbing the Japanese as 'honorary Aryans' to legitimize them as allies, in private he was recorded as saying "let us think of ourselves as masters and consider these people at best as lacquered half-monkeys who need to feel the knout."

The Japanese high command was no better, as they considered themselves racially superior to Europeans. However, both saw the advantages of having the other as an ally, and despite their differing racial views, the two leaders were almost mirror images of the other. Had the Axis won, the outcome of this relationship would have been very grim indeed.

MUSSOLINI + HIROHITO

If there was little interaction between Hitler and Hirohito, there was even less between the Italian dictator and Japanese emperor. It's unlikely the two had much, if any, communication. However, Mussolini was convinced of Japanese support, even when Hitler was dubious. Mussolini was especially delighted by the attack on Pearl Harbor as he viewed the US as cowards for not joining the war and approved of Japan forcing their hand.

TIMELINE

September 19, 1931
The Kwantung Army of Japan invades Manchuria. They will later create a puppet state named Manchukuo. Mussolini and Hitler watch closely as the League of Nations is powerless to stop the invasion.

October 3, 1935
Under Mussolini's instructions, Italy invades Abyssinia (modern-day Ethiopia). The League of Nations condemns the invasion and votes to impose sanctions, however these are largely ineffective.

October 25, 1936
The Italian and German leaders sign a treaty that informally links the fascist countries, which will serve as the basis for the Rome-Berlin Axis.

November 1937
The Anti-Comintern pact is signed. This extends the Rome-Berlin Axis to Tokyo, and the three nations unite against the colossal Soviet Union.

March 12, 1938
The German Army marches into Austria amid cheers and celebration. The country is then annexed into the Third Reich. The Allies do nothing to stop it, despite verbally condemning German expansion.

September 1938
The Munich Agreement is signed. It allows Germany to annex parts of Czechoslovakia. Churchill warns "England has been offered a choice between war and shame. She has chosen shame, and will get war."

September 1, 1939
Germany and the Soviet Union invade Poland. By October 6, the country will be divided between the two occupiers.

April 9, 1940
Germany invades Denmark and Norway in the early hours of the morning, steamrolling any opposition.

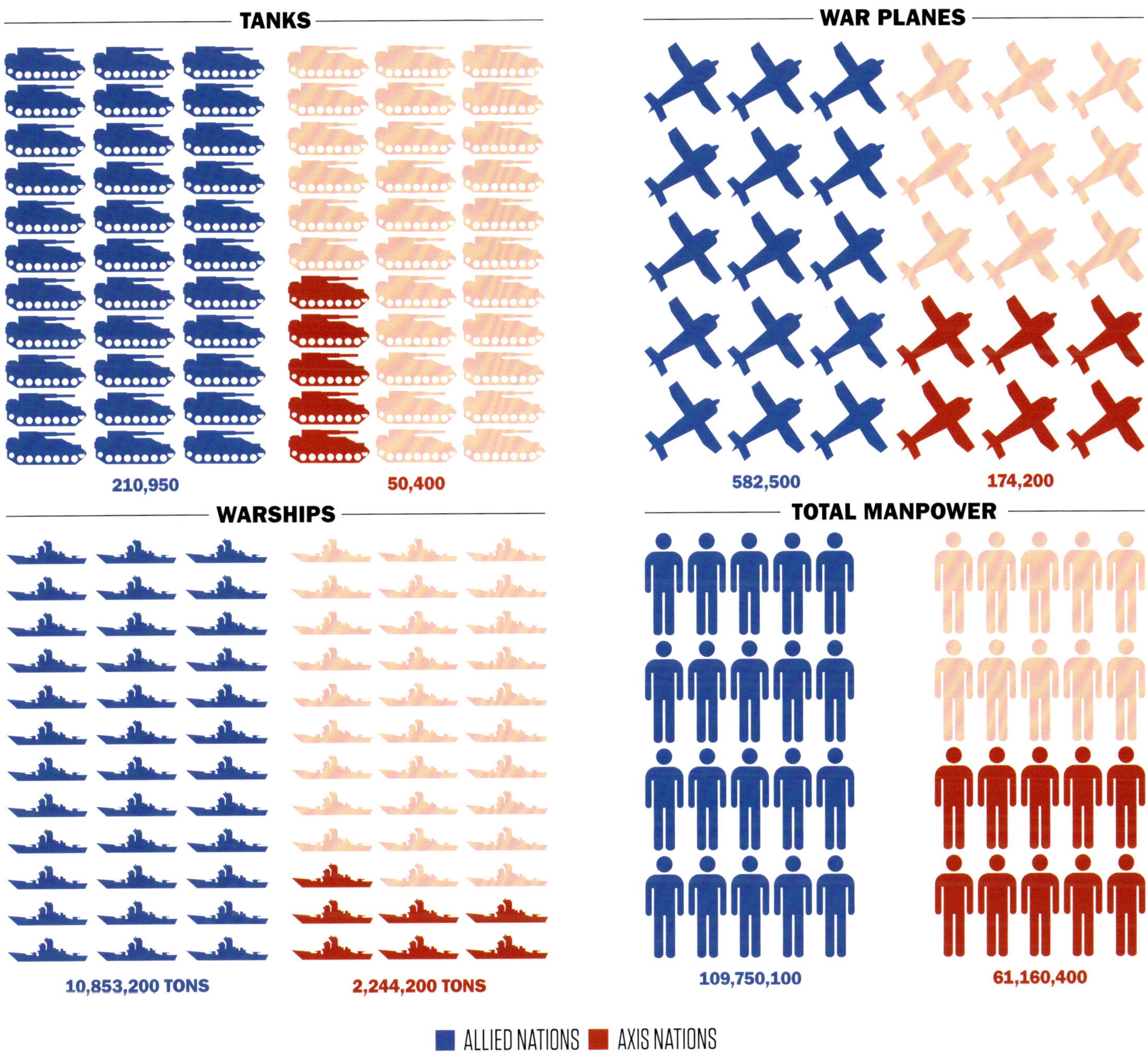

May 10, 1940
Germany invades the Netherlands, Belgium and Luxembourg. On the same day, British Prime Minister Neville Chamberlain resigns and is replaced by Winston Churchill.

June 14, 1940
French and Allied forces retreat as German forces march into Paris to little resistance.

April 6, 1941
The Battle of Greece begins as Germany invades Greece. Greek troops find themselves outnumbered and the Axis occupies the country.

June 22, 1941
Under the codename Operation Barbarossa, Germany invades the USSR. The invasion represents Hitler's ultimate goal – the elimination of the communist threat and acquisition of land for German expansion.

December 8 1941 (local time)
Malaya is invaded by Japan. The battle is fought between the British Indian Army and the Empire of Japan. It is the first major conflict of the Pacific War.

December 7, 1941 (local time)
Japan unleashes a surprise attack against the United States by bombing Pearl Harbor. The attack is planned to keep the US fleet from interfering in Japan's plans for expansion in Southeast Asia.

December 8, 1941
Japan invades the Philippines just ten hours after the attack on Pearl Harbor. The province of Bataan is captured by April, and Japan will occupy the country for three years.

June 28, 1942
Germany begins a summer offensive toward the Russian city of Stalingrad. The offensive will eventually be defeated at the Battle of Stalingrad on February 2, 1943, turning the tides in the European Theater.

King Victor Emmanuel III of Italy hosts Prince Hirohito, future emperor of Japan, in 1921. The pair would both reign throughout the chaos of WWII

Japanese Foreign Minister Yosuke Matsuoka is all smiles while riding beside his German counterpart, Joachim von Ribbentrop, in an open car during a visit to Berlin in 1941

Japanese, German and Italian ministers raise a toast to their new alliance, September 1940

A beaming Hitler shares a joke with Mussolini while journeying through Munich in 1940. Due to its importance to the rise of Nazism, Hitler called the city the "Capital of the Movement"

Flanked by senior Nazis, Mussolini and Hitler emerge from the Führerbau (a key Nazi building in Munich) during the former's visit to Germany in 1938

THE DESTRUCTION OF POLAND

Germany's swift and devastating invasion of Poland ignited a global war that led to over 60 million deaths

Hitler's decision to invade Poland set the world on a course toward a global war of unprecedented savagery that would take six years and millions of deaths to end. The conquest of the Polish state was to be a rapid victory for the Wehrmacht, the first of many stunning triumphs in the first years of WWII. But it was by no means an inevitable step in Germany's efforts to wage the war that Hitler deemed vital to the country's very survival.

Prior to the invasion, Hitler had in fact viewed Poland as a potential ally in a future invasion of the USSR, a war that he had stated was his ultimate desire in his infamous book *Mein Kampf*. Germany's Führer believed that offering Poland both territorial gains in Ukraine and aid in its own efforts to relocate its persecuted Jewish population in return for supporting a war on Stalin's people would prove to be a very attractive offer. The two nations had even signed a non-aggression pact on January

26, 1934, as Hitler moved quickly to secure the cooperation of Poland. But in fact Hitler had grossly miscalculated.

Following a series of approaches from the Third Reich, Poland's foreign minister, Jozef Beck, rejected Hitler's personal advances on January 5, 1939. Germany's own foreign minister, Joachim von Ribbentrop, made another effort to persuade the Poles to back Germany on January 25 but was also rebuffed.

Poland's refusal to acquiesce sealed its fate. Hitler resolved to wipe the entire Polish state off the map. In his eyes, Poland had forfeited the right to even exist. Plans to invade Poland (codenamed Case White) had first been drawn up in 1928 by the commander-in-chief of the German Army, Werner von Fritsch. These plans were adapted by generals Gunther Blumentritt and Erich von Manstein and finalized (following Poland's rebuttal) on June 15, 1939.

Germany was to invade Poland from three sides. On September 1, 1939, it did just that, but not before Hitler's outrageous claims on the radio that Germany was responding to a Polish assault in what was a flagrant effort to portray the doomed state as the aggressor. This was accompanied by an SS commando unit attacking a German radio station clad in Polish uniforms and a foiled plan to blow up schools, theaters and monuments as 'evidence' of Polish violence.

Hostilities began with the Luftwaffe bombing the town of Wielun, destroying three quarters of it and killing around 1,200 people. Shortly afterwards, a German battleship opened fire on a Polish military depot in a harbor in Danzig. The main land assault soon followed, with German forces penetrating the borders from the north and west, and a combined German-Slovak army invading from the south. The target of this three-pronged attack was Warsaw.

The speed of the German onslaught was astounding, catching the Polish Army mid-mobilization. By September 3, Hitler's forces had reached the Vistula River, six miles from the German border. Four days later the 30th Infantry Division crossed the river Warthe via German-engineered bridges, and on the same day the 8th Army took the textile city of Lodz. The Wehrmacht looked unstoppable.

A German gunner looks down upon Poland from a Heinkel bomber

Retreat

The Polish forces were reeling, desperately scrambling to forge a cohesive defense. As they did so, the 4th Panzer Division approached the outskirts of Warsaw on September 8, with General Heinz Guderian leading his 3rd Army tanks across the Narew to assault the Bug River line on September 9. Warsaw itself was attacked on the same day. It was all Poland could do to engage in a general retreat, abandoning the Polish Corridor and Upper Silesia as it fell back.

A faint ray of hope finally appeared for the Polish forces in the guise of General Tadeusz Kutrzeba's plan to lead a counter-attack. Hemmed in by German forces to the north on the Vistula and the south on the Bzura River, Kutrzeba recognized that his Poznan Army had one advantage: the Germans didn't quite know where his forces were. On the night of September 9, Kutrzeba's army began its assault from the south of the Bzura, starting the single largest battle of the entire campaign and one that would adopt the river's name.

Realizing that the 8th Army was inadequately secured by the overstretched 30th Infantry, the wily Polish general had opted to target them. The counter-attack (which also included cavalry) was launched with such ferocity that the Germans were pushed back around 12 miles and approximately 1,500 of their soldiers were killed or wounded, as were around 3,000 prisoners. The 4th Panzer Division was forced to halt its assault on Warsaw in order to come to the aid of the shocked 8th Army. Fortunately for them, the Polish attack rapidly faded, despite them retaking numerous towns.

With the German 10th and 4th armies now converging on the Bzura, along with Army Group South and aircraft from the 4th Air Fleet, the Poles' situation quickly became a precarious one, forcing them to adopt defensive positions. They were soon encircled by the Germans, who began an attack from all sides on September 16, supported by 800 tanks and the Luftwaffe. While the bulk of the Polish forces were

TIMELINE

The invasion begins
Germany begins a brutal invasion of Poland in the early hours, beginning with an aerial assault.
September 1, 1939

Battle of Westerplatte
In the first hours of the invasion the German battleship Schleswig-Holstein fires on a Polish military depot.
September 1, 1939

The Vistula
Within two days of launching their attack the Germans reach the Vistula River, six miles from the German border.
September 3, 1939

Britain and France
Britain declares war on Germany in response to its invasion of Poland. France follows suit at 5pm on the same day.
September 3, 1939

Fall of Lodz
The city of Lodz falls to the German 8th Army after the Lodz Army initially repels their advances.
September 7, 1939

Outskirts of Warsaw
The following day the German 4th Panzer Division reaches the perimeters of Warsaw.
September 8, 1939

Battle of Bzura
General Tadeusz Kutrzeba launches a valiant Polish counter-attack, inflicting heavy losses on the shocked German troops.
September 9, 1939

Polish cavalry ride through the rubble-strewn streets of Sochaczew during the Battle of Bzura

annihilated (an estimated 20,000 died) or surrendered, some did manage to spring the trap and fight their way toward Warsaw. Among their number was Kutrzeba, who managed to reach the capital.

The vanishingly small chance of Poland holding out for any length of time evaporated on the 17th when the USSR invaded from the east, fulfilling their secret agreement with Nazi Germany. Signed just eight days before Germany had begun its invasion, the Molotov-Ribbentrop pact (named after the Soviet and German foreign ministers) outlined how Poland would be divided between the two superpowers. Caught between these two military juggernauts, Poland didn't stand a chance.

The Polish Government now realized that fleeing the country was their only option. Its members crossed the Romanian border on the same day as the Soviet assault and established themselves in exile in Paris. The soldiers who had managed to survive the Battle of Bzura surrendered two days later. But their efforts had not been in vain, buying time for the defenses of Warsaw to be bolstered.

Surrender

Upon reaching the capital on September 22, General Kutrzeba set about fighting to defend it for as long as possible, briefly becoming deputy commander of the Warsaw Army. However, his valiant efforts proved futile. The commander of the Warsaw Army, Juliusz Rommel, could see the writing was on the wall and implored his colleague to begin surrender talks with the rampant Germans.

On September 28, Kutrzeba signed the official surrender documents: the conquest of Poland was complete. The Polish state was swiftly dismantled by its German and Soviet occupiers, and vast swathes of its elite classes were massacred almost immediately in an effort to extinguish any threat of rebellion. The wrath of these ruthless invaders would soon be directed at the rest of Poland's population.

The conquest of Poland had required 62 German divisions and taken a month to complete, resulting in the deaths of around 66,000 Poles and 16,000 Germans. The courage and tenacity displayed by its armies simply could not prevail in the face of the German blitzkrieg (lightning war), an attack that resulted in Britain and France declaring war on Hitler's Germany on September 3, setting the wheels in motion for a bloody global struggle that would claim the lives of millions.

TADEUSZ KUTRZEBA – POLAND'S DEFIANT GENERAL

The man who led the Polish fightback against the German invasion had already experienced the horrors of WWI. The son of a captain of the Imperial Austrian Army, Tadeusz Kutrzeba commanded forces in Sarajevo, as well as seeing action on the Serbian and Russian fronts.

Following the siege of Warsaw in WWII, Kutrzeba was captured by the Germans and spent the rest of the war in various POW camps. Liberated by American forces in April 1945, he was summoned to London and offered the post of defense minister in the exiled Polish Government. He declined, instead heading up a commission that evaluated the Polish Army's campaign of 1939 and the contributions of Polish fighters in the west throughout the war. He would die in London in 1947 at the age of 61.

Digging in
As two German armies approach, the Poles dig in to defensive positions and await the onslaught.
September 15, 1939

Trapped
The Germans quickly encircle the Polish defenders and begin to bomb their positions.
September 15-16, 1939

Soviet invasion
The Red Army sweeps across the border of eastern Poland, fulfilling the Soviet Union's part of the pact with Germany.
September 17, 1939

White flag at Bzura
With thousands of soldiers killed in the fighting, the Polish surrender at Bzura.
September 19, 1939

Government-in-exile
With all hope lost, the Polish government escapes the country, setting up in Paris.
September 17, 1939

Victory parade
In one of many examples of German-Soviet cooperation, forces from both sides hold a victory parade in the town of Brest-Litovsk.
September 22, 1939

Surrender
With German ground troops closing in and the Soviets occupying the east of Poland, Warsaw is finally forced to surrender.
September 22, 1939

Annexation
With the conquest of Poland complete, Germany formally annexes the western half of Poland.
October 8, 1939

KEY MOMENTS

— THE MIRACLE OF —
DUNKIRK

In May 1940, 340,000 Allied soldiers were saved from the full fury of the German blitzkrieg in an evacuation that kept Britain in the war

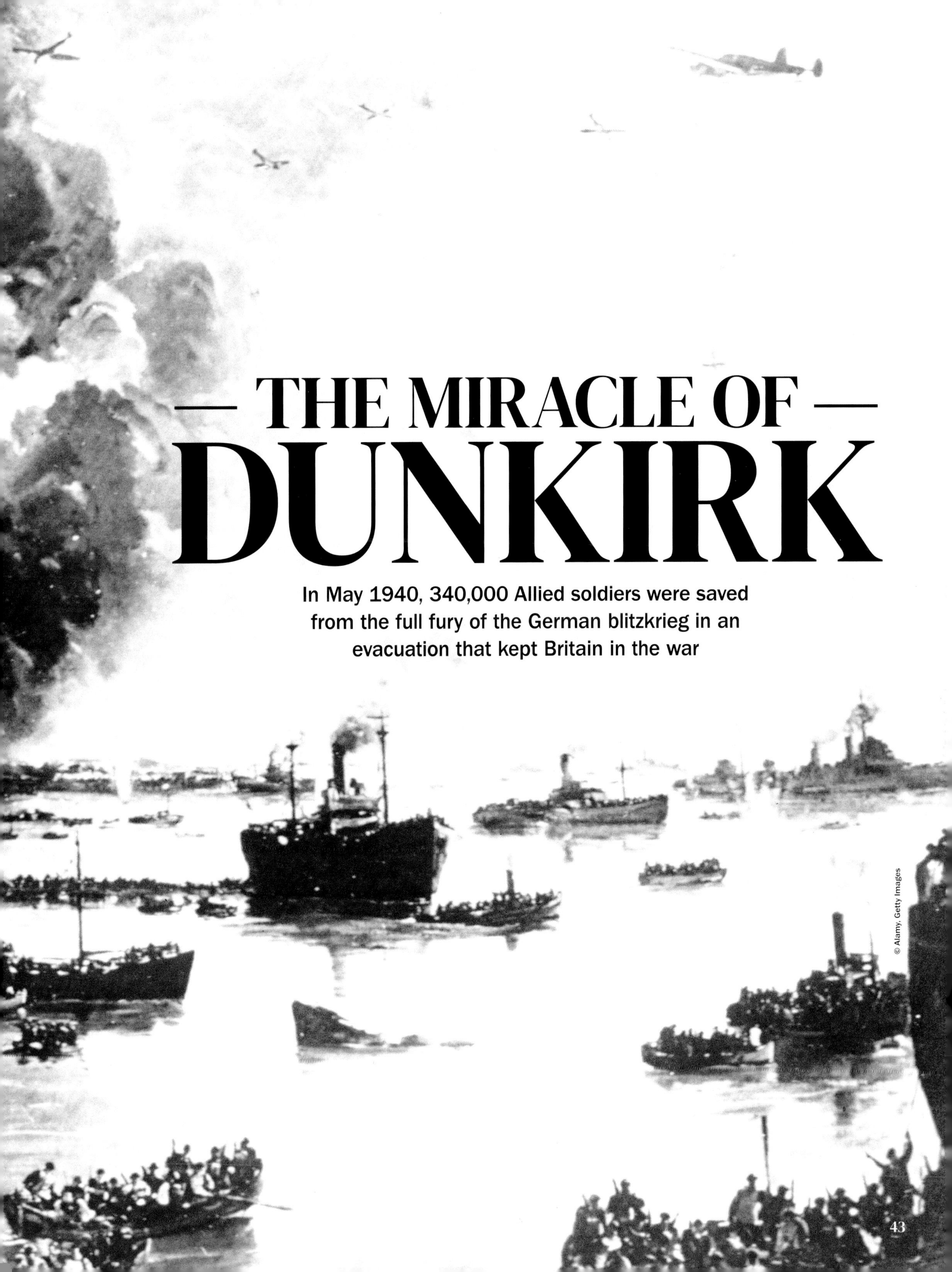

© Alamy, Getty Images

The Dunkirk spirit helped stiffen British resolve as the country now stood alone against Nazi Germany, who turned her attention to the planned invasion of the British Isles

After the French surrender on June 22, 1940, Britain stood alone against Nazi Germany. A scintillating blitzkrieg had knocked France out of the war in a matter of months and the British Expeditionary Force (BEF) had only just escaped from continental Europe thanks to a hurried withdrawal across the English Channel. The miracle of Dunkirk was an incredible feat that gave Britain both the morale and the manpower required to continue the fight against the Third Reich. Without it, Britain would have stared down the barrel of defeat.

The eight-month Phoney War came to an abrupt end in May 1940 as the German panzer divisions rolled into the Ardennes. Britain and France had agreed on a defensive strategy that would keep the Wehrmacht and the Luftwaffe at bay. Both countries were well aware of the threat that Hitler posed and had done all the appeasement they possibly could to avoid another war. The invasion of Poland finally brought them both into conflict, and now Hitler turned his attention to Western Europe.

The French Army had a reputation as one of the best in the world, and what they believed to be a near-impenetrable defensive fortification called the Maginot Line stretched across its eastern border, while the BEF would protect the Low Countries from invasion.

Nine months after the German invasion of Poland, three German Army groups made their advance on May 10, 1940, the same day Winston Churchill replaced Neville Chamberlain as prime minister. The German plan was for Army Group A to hurtle through the Ardennes, a hilly, wooded area of France, while B would take care of the Netherlands and Belgium, and C would keep tabs on the Maginot Line. The attack was a masterstroke by Hitler and caught the Allies completely by surprise. Both the British and French had severely underestimated the strength of the German war machine, especially the armored divisions, and were shocked at the speed and ferocity of the German advance through an area believed to be too densely forested for tanks.

The trap closes

The neutral Netherlands surrendered within a week, the white flag being waved after the intense bombing of Rotterdam had claimed the lives of 1,000 civilians. The Allied armies soon withdrew from Belgium, too, under Plan D, a strategy to let Belgium be invaded before beginning the fight back.

The French and British were under the command of generals Pierre Billotte, Alphonse Georges and Maurice Gamelin, who constantly clashed. The French, in particular, were poorly organized, the result of too much money and attention being spent on the Maginot Line, which was simply outflanked by the Germans. This coupled with poor communication lines, obsolete tactics and a poorly trained and equipped BEF left the Allies exposed.

BEF commander Lord Gort takes his leave of Dunkirk, one of 68,000 men now evacuated

"THE HURRIED WITHDRAWAL MEANT TROOPS HAD TO WADE INTO THE COLD WATER OF THE CHANNEL – SOMETIMES UP TO AS DEEP AS THEIR NECKS"

On May 16, Brussels had fallen. The British and French forces were being pushed further west, and there was real concern that the dual Wehrmacht attack through the Low Countries and the Ardennes would split the Allied forces in two. Between May 16-21, German panzer divisions sped rapidly through France, making up 50 miles of ground as the British and the French carried out a fighting retreat. Army Group A now held three vital bridgeheads over the River Meuse as the Germans poured further and further west.

With the Battle of France seemingly lost already, plans for the evacuation of the BEF got underway, a massive shock to Churchill, who, with little communication on the events, had expected the BEF to hold its ground.

Despite their overwhelming success, the German panzers were in need of repair. On May 23, Commander Gerd von Rundstedt requested permission for a halt from Hitler, who agreed with fears that the front, which was now as far west as the Somme, could become overextended. This gave the BEF valuable time to begin the evacuation. They were given a three-day respite before the port of Boulogne fell on May 25. The Allied armies were getting squeezed to the coast and the next day Operation Dynamo was ordered.

Devised by Vice-Admiral Bertram Ramsay and directed from his headquarters in Dover, the withdrawal had been mooted since May 20 and was expected to save, at most, 45,000 men. It began at 7pm that evening. On the continent, the BEF were led by Lord Gort, who had withdrawn to Dunkirk without informing his French or Belgian allies. Initially, the operation was only intended to be a partial evacuation as there was still hope that the majority of the BEF would be able to join with the remainder of the French armies in a counterattack. This belief was a vain hope, as aside from an attack on Arras on May 21, which did little except buy a bit of time, the British and French were still engaging in a fighting retreat.

For the evacuation the British mustered a flotilla of 1,000 vessels. Beside the Royal Navy destroyers were an assortment of civilian vessels. Manned by a mixture of civilian and navy crews, cross-channel ferries, pleasure steamers and cabin cruisers were all readied for the journey across the Channel. These 'little ships' (the smallest of all was the tiny 14-foot-long Tamzine) comprised a volunteer force that demonstrated the British fighting spirit. Nine hundred in all made the journey in a story that has since become historical legend.

Overnight on the May 26, 8,000 BEF troops were safely evacuated. The hurried withdrawal meant troops had to wade into the cold water of the Channel – sometimes up to as deep as their necks – for them to reach the smaller boats that would then ferry them to the larger vessels in the flotilla. As more and more companies made it to the coast, lines of men began to litter the beaches, awaiting the next vessel out of Dunkirk. The next day, Calais fell to the Germans as the pressure started to increase on the evacuation to get as many of the BEF as possible back to Britain before the blitzkrieg made it to the coast. Around 25,000 soldiers departed overnight on May 27-28 as the withdrawal picked up more momentum. The port of Dunkirk had been reduced to ruin by the Luftwaffe so the extraction had to be done from

Evacuations weren't just limited to Dunkirk; Allied soldiers were taken back to Britain from many French towns

HITLER'S HALT ORDER

The infamous order to halt the advance of the German panzers at 11.42am on May 24 was controversial. The command was given due to concern about the German lines becoming overextended and the belief that tank tracks may struggle in boggy coastal terrain. It gave the BEF a window in which to form a defense around Dunkirk and then up the scale of the evacuation. The order only lasted for three days, but this was crucial in allowing the Allies to recover and the Germans to lose momentum.

Hitler's order had a mixed response from his generals, and whether such precaution was merited remains a subject of debate. Either way, as the German panzers were only less than 19 miles away from Dunkirk, a further push could have altered the outcome of Operation Dynamo.

the beaches, although British destroyers were at points able to utilize a long causeway called the Eastern Mole at the entrance of Dunkirk harbor. This had deeper water that they could sail into without fear of running aground.

Sitting ducks

The defensive perimeter around Dunkirk was getting smaller by the day, but in an incredible turn of events, the German land attack stopped. Wary of the prospect of losing more men to the French garrison protecting the beaches, Hitler instructed Göring's Luftwaffe to finish the job. The coast was bombed heavily as Stukas and Dorniers strafed the beaches with machine-gun fire. Although the BEF were sitting ducks, poor coordination, adverse weather conditions and the sand deadening the impact of bombs prevented the Germans from landing a potential death blow on the BEF. The RAF also helped matters. Often criticized for their lack of input during the events of Dunkirk, they managed to down around 100 Luftwaffe aircraft, four German planes for every British plane, but could not stop the majority of the bombing. Not for the last time, Göring failed to complete the task assigned to him.

On the final day of May, it was Gort's turn to leave France. By now 68,000 men had been safely evacuated. Many of the troops had spent days huddled on the beaches, but slowly and surely the withdrawal was succeeding. Both the destroyers and the little ships were unable to take any heavy equipment on board, so the majority of BEF vehicles and heavy weaponry was left strewn across the shoreline. This loss of vehicles actually caused a shortage in Britain that lasted until 1941.

By June, the evacuation started to become more strained. The German air assault was becoming more devastating by the day as the port became blocked by the wrecks of sunken ships. The evacuation was now restricted to just hours of darkness. It wasn't just the BEF fleeing across the Channel anymore either: the British Tommies were now joined by French and Belgian soldiers eager to reach the safety of Britain to regroup. Previously, only BEF soldiers had been allowed to leave on the boats, but it was now a full Allied operation.

On June 3, the final men stepped onto the boats and slipped away into the darkness of the Channel. The evacuation was complete. On June 4, Churchill addressed the House of Commons at 3.40pm. He praised the achievements of Dunkirk but warned that "wars are not won by evacuations". The address culminated in one his most famous speeches: "We shall fight on the beaches, we shall fight in the landing grounds, we shall fight in the fields and in the streets, we shall fight in the hills; we shall never surrender."

The German 6th Army entered Dunkirk the same day as Churchill's resolute words rang around parliament. The beaches were strewn with the corpses of the soldiers who hadn't made it, victims of Luftwaffe machine guns. The Führer's gaze had already turned to Paris and the remainder of France, confident that Britain, even with this successful evacuation completed, would soon capitulate after the loss of its major ally. The following day the Wehrmacht marched south toward Paris as 5 million French refugees fled south in search of safety. Wary of what had already happened to Rotterdam and Warsaw, the French capital was declared an open city and taken with little resistance. On June 22 the Battle of France was over, a peace treaty hastily signed at Versailles, where just 22 years earlier France had sat at the table of victors of the Great War.

Dunkirk was a huge feat, but it wasn't without loss. The Luftwaffe sunk six British and three French destroyers, and 161 of the brave little ships were now at the bottom of the Channel. In total 217 Allied vessels were sunk and 177 Allied aircraft were downed. The little ships had done their bit, but it was ultimately the 39 British and French destroyers who ferried two-thirds of the men off the beaches. In total,

TIMELINE

The Western Front re-opens
The Phoney War ends nine months after the invasion of Poland as the Wehrmacht cross the border into Belgium. Neville Chamberlain resigns as prime minister.
May 10, 1940

Bombing of Rotterdam
The Dutch city of Rotterdam is heavily bombed, with the Netherlands surrendering to the Germans the next day.
May 14, 1940

Belgian withdrawal
Allied armies retreat from Belgium after the fall of Brussels, fearing that they will be caught in a pincer by the dual German advance from the north and the south.
May 16, 1940

Operation Dynamo
Plans for the evacuation get underway as the Wehrmacht armored divisions make up 50 miles of ground in under a week. A French counterattack on Arras holds the Germans off.
May 20, 1940

Halt Order called
Hitler's calls a stop to the panzer advance with the front now only 19 miles from Dunkirk. This gives the BEF vital time to begin the evacuation.
May 23, 1940

The evacuation begins
The day after Boulogne falls, 8,000 troops are taken back across the Channel overnight. The next day Calais falls as the race to leave France becomes a priority.
May 26, 1940

19,000 more
As the perimeter around Dunkirk is held, 19,000 more BEF soldiers make their escape, but the majority of heavy equipment is left scattered across the beaches.
May 28, 1940

The Dutch city of Rotterdam was heavily bombed. The Netherlands surrendered to the Germans the next day

340,000 British, French, Belgian and Canadian troops had been evacuated to safety from Dunkirk and a total of 558,000 from ports all across France.

Living to fight another day

Britain was down but not out. The failure of the BEF to stem the Wehrmacht advance was testament to the strength of Germany's blitzkrieg tactics but also advertised how ill-prepared the British and French were for this lightning war. Dunkirk could have been a catastrophe, but this successful withdrawal of troops gave hope to what was left of the Western Allies to fight on. It may not have been a victory, but critically for Churchill, it hadn't been a rout. Newspapers across Britain were hailing it as a miracle, but there were negatives.

Soldiers returned with low morale, disheartened that they simply could not cope with the strength of the German panzers and convinced that the invasion of Britain was not far off. There were even reports of desertion and infighting at Dunkirk with British soldiers forcing their French counterparts off the boats. This is known as the myth of Dunkirk, that the evacuation was deemed much more of a success than it actually was. The facts are that if the evacuation was not made, Britain would have lost huge numbers of POWs and likely been forced to seek peace terms with Hitler.

As Hitler had his photo taken in front of the Eiffel Tower, the plans for the invasion of mainland Britain (codenamed Operation Sea Lion) were underway. The French General Weygand remarked that "in three weeks, England will have her neck wrung like a chicken". The battle for France was over. The battle for Britain was about to begin.

Gort leaves
BEF commander Lord Gort takes his leave of Dunkirk, one of 68,000 men now evacuated.
May 31, 1940

Overnight withdrawal
As the Luftwaffe bombardment escalates, evacuations are limited to just night-time hours under the cover of darkness.
June 1, 1940

The final night
This is the last night of the evacuations, completing the rescue of 340,000 British, Belgian and French troops.
June 3, 1940

German Dunkirk
Just one day after the final Allied troops have made their escape, German soldiers enter Dunkirk and claim the port for their own. Churchill makes a rousing speech to the House of Commons.
June 4, 1940

The Battle of France resumes
Turning south, Hitler orders the Wehrmacht to invade the remainder of northern France and to take any remaining soldiers prisoner.
June 5, 1940

French government moved to Tours
With Paris now threatened, the French Government leave Paris to set up a new base in Tours.
June 10, 1940

French surrender
Hitler orders peace terms and the French agree, signing the documents at Versailles. The Battle of France is over.
June 22, 1940

OPERATION BARBAROSSA

Germany's invasion of the Soviet Union was Hitler's greatest gamble of WWII and the bloody realization of his most ambitious dreams

In the summer of 1940, with much of Europe crushed beneath the boot of a rampant Wehrmacht, Hitler had every reason to be euphoric. His pact with the Soviet Union, signed in August 1939, had held, enabling his forces to sweep through Poland before surging into Western Europe. By late June of 1940, only the British remained to stand against them, the narrow escape of over 300,000 troops from Dunkirk scarred into the national consciousness. And yet despite a torrent of victories that led Field Marshal Wilhelm Keitel to label Hitler as "the greatest warlord in history", the Führer was not satisfied.

Britain's refusal to acknowledge Germany's triumph and submit to peace talks puzzled Hitler. After all, he had always been open about his desire for peace, going so far as to "appeal to reason" during his annual speech in the Reichstag on July 19, 1940. To Hitler's chagrin, Churchill and the British people remained resolute, leading Hitler to surmise that Britain was pinning its hopes on the Soviet Union. Hitler's delusions led him to reason that only the complete annihilation of the Soviets would force Britain to recognize her cause was lost.

During a conference with his military commanders at his lair in Berchtesgaden, Bavaria, on July 31, 1940, Hitler outlined his most ambitious plans yet: Germany would invade the Soviet Union the following year. "The sooner Russia is crushed, the better," he explained. "If we were to start in May 1941, we would have five months to finish the job."

However, while there were strategic motives behind Hitler's determination to destroy the USSR, arguably the more pressing desires behind Hitler's greatest gamble were of an ideological nature. While the summer of 1940 may have witnessed the germination of an idea that would become Operation Barbarossa, a cataclysmic showdown with 'Judeo-Bolshevism' was something that Hitler had first mentioned while writing his book, *Mein Kampf*, in 1924/25.

The storm clouds gather

When discussing the apparently pressing need for Germany to secure *Lebensraum* (living space) in order to ensure a future in which the nation would have ample space and resources, Hitler was characteristically blunt when outlining his intended targets. "If we speak of soil in Europe today, we can primarily have in mind only Russia and her border states." Describing the Slavs of Russia as "an inferior race", Hitler warned that "the end of Jewish rule in Russia will also be the end of Russia as a state."

Hitler viewed the fate of the human race as an endless struggle for resources in a finite space, one that would end, in his twisted view, in the eventual triumph of "inferior" races (namely the Jews) unless a "pure" race was willing to fight to prevent them. In his primal opinion, "Nature knows no boundaries. She places lifeforms on this globe and then sets them free in a play for power."

Believing that every evil on Earth could be placed at the feet of Jews, Hitler sought to tear down anything that he perceived as being a Jewish entity or system. Communism, he claimed, was one such policy, and it was this distorted belief that led him to state that it was

A Wehrmacht soldier takes cover during the winter of 1941. Barbarossa cost Germany around 775,000 casualties

THE SHADOW OF EVIL

The Einsatzgruppen (SS death squads) tasked with following the Wehrmacht into the Soviet Union were ruthless in the execution of their primary task: murdering civilians. From Soviet commissars to Jews and Romani, millions of innocent people were shot, hanged or otherwise killed by the SS commandos scouring the lands already scorched by the advancing German armies.

The predominant method of execution involved lining victims (including women, children and the elderly) along the edge of pits they had been forced to dig themselves, then shooting them in the back of the head or neck.

One of the most famous examples of such a mass execution was the Babi Yar massacre of September 1941. Over two days German soldiers and Ukrainian police officers shot 33,771 people in a ravine north of Kiev, many of whom were forced to lie down on the corpses of those who had gone before them.

Aside from Poland, it was the Soviet nations (notably the Baltics) that witnessed the worst atrocities of the war. Estonia, just one of a group of countries that suffered the horrors of Hitler's genocidal war, lost almost 99 per cent of its Jewish population.

Within five months of the invasion of the Baltics, Einsatzgruppe A alone had slaughtered nearly 140,000 people. Yet such figures failed to satisfy Reichsführer-SS Heinrich Himmler, who in time decided that gassing "undesirables" would be a quicker and cleaner method. By the war's end, Himmler's charges had murdered approximately 1.5 million Jews along the Eastern Front and thousands of Romani.

Germany's duty to defeat the nation that had given communism a home: the Soviet Union.

Unswerving in his confidence that Britain was already beaten and thereby would not present a second front, Hitler directed the German high command to begin planning the invasion. The operation was to be codenamed Barbarossa (it was originally slated as Fritz) in honor of the Holy Roman Emperor Frederick Barbarossa, a talented military commander.

Scheduled for May 15, 1941, the operation would see three army groups (North, Centre and South) pouring across the Polish-Soviet border under the respective leadership of Wilhelm Ritter von Leeb, Feodor von Bock and Gerd von Runstedt. Von Leeb's forces were tasked with taking the Baltics and Leningrad; Bock's men were to head first to Smolensk and then onto Moscow; and Runstedt was to race to secure the "breadbasket" of Ukraine and the oil-rich Caucasus.

Certain of victory, Hitler boasted "we only have to kick the door in and the whole rotten structure will come crashing down."

Unleash hell

While Germany began to make the necessary preparations for Barbarossa, the target of its impending assault sat paralysed. In the wake of Stalin's ruthless purges in the late 1930s, which saw three quarters of the Red Army's leadership executed or imprisoned, the forces of the USSR were woefully short on both morale and efficiency. To compound its already significant problems, Stalin insisted on controlling the placement of his divisions, further hamstringing the Red Army.

Laboring under the false belief that Hitler could only attack the USSR once he had dealt with Britain, Stalin was sure that any invasion was at least a year away. His obstinate refusal to accept the threat massing on his borders was further emboldened in April 1941 when Stalin received a letter from Winston Churchill warning of the Germans' intentions. Instead of heeding the British Prime Minister, Stalin discarded Churchill's correspondence as an Allied attempt to provoke the Soviets into launching a pre-emptive strike against their German allies, thereby opening a new theater and reducing the pressure on the Allied troops.

Although Stalin's suspicions about Churchill's true motives may be understandable, his dismissal of the warnings of another, closer source were nothing short of catastrophic. In May of 1941, Richard Sorge, a Soviet spy working in Japan, informed Moscow that Germany was indeed planning to attack, information that he had received from none other than Colonel Eugen Ott, the military attaché at the German embassy in Tokyo.

Amazingly, even when Sorge provided a date of June 20, 1941, (just two days off the actual launch date of June 22), Stalin remained implacable, the Soviet ruler insisting that Hitler was not "such an idiot" as to risk a war on two fronts. Less than a month after receiving Sorge's detailed report, Stalin would be proven disastrously wrong.

A five-week delay due to Hitler's decision to invade Yugoslavia in May 1941 after its pro-Nazi government had been toppled meant Germany was not ready to unleash its eastern campaign until June. A delay in massing sufficient fuel and vehicles for the operation was also a telling factor in the hold up.

Barbarossa was to be a campaign of extermination, with the ruthless removal of the elites and mass starvation employed as a method of subjugating Soviet cities. In fact, the German high command went so far as to devise a 'Hunger Plan' that would see food taken from

Soviet bombers soar over Moscow. Following horrendous losses in the early stages of the war, the Red Army Air Force gradually recovered and played a key role in offensive operations

the Soviet Union and given to German soldiers and citizens. (According to historian Timothy Snyder, approximately 4.2 million Soviet civilians were starved to death between 1941 and 1944.) No quarter was to be given.

At 3.15am on June 22, thousands of Luftwaffe engines burst into life to signal the beginning of Barbarossa, the fleet sailing high over the German assault boats bobbing on the River Bug. As the planes zeroed in on their targets (airfields lined with neat rows of stationary Soviet planes), thousands of German artillery pieces began to belch flame into the sky. Hitler was finally attacking the entity he loathed the most, and he'd gathered 3.8 million soldiers (including Romanians, Italians and Slovaks) for the job, well-trained men supported by 600,000 vehicles, 3,350 armored vehicles, 3,000 aircraft and 500,000 horses.

As millions of troops raced into the USSR, their counterparts radioed their superiors demanding to know what to do. Such was the shock of the assault that many border guards were gunned down in their nightwear, their homes and families engulfed in the flames of the bombardment. Despite this, Stalin was still – inexplicably – wary of some Allied trick and ordered that nothing be done to provoke the Germans, clinging as he was to the idea that Hitler would not have dared to double-cross him and start a war on two fronts.

In all their wildest dreams, the German commanders could never have dared to hope to find their adversaries so woefully off guard. Many of the Soviets' defensive positions lacked the weaponry needed to counter a concentrated panzer attack, and they could not hope to rely on any aid from above; on the first day of the operation the Soviets lost approximately 1,800 planes to the Luftwaffe's 35.

Scything through the USSR

Within two days of the start of the attack, many of the 49 German panzer battalions selected for the invasion were 50 miles inside the USSR. By June 28, over 400,000 Soviet troops were encircled outside of Minsk as the Second Panzer Group, under the command of General Heinz Guderian, linked up with Hermann Hoth's Third Panzer Group.

To the north, General von Leeb was faring just as well, his troops hailed as emancipators by the violently suppressed peoples of the Baltics, many of them actively helping the Germans by attacking a number of Red Army positions. However, the invaders certainly didn't have it all their way.

Army Group South, charged with taking Kiev and then hurrying on to the priceless oilfields of the Caucasus, was finding the going difficult in the face of determined resistance. Rundstedt was doubly unfortunate as he was not only marching on the most heavily defended region of the front lines, but his men were doing so as KV and T-34 tanks (the latter the best all-round tank of the entire war) rolled toward them. While the central and northern thrusts of the German assault continued to slice into Soviet territory, Rundstedt found himself increasingly bogged down. His failure to keep up with the rest would ultimately prove fatal for Hitler's hopes of a rapid victory. Yet as July approached, the overall picture from a German perspective seemed unexpectedly rosy.

Upon finally realizing that Hitler had betrayed him, Stalin had fallen into a stupor of despair that lasted for over a week. Now, with machinery being evacuated from Ukraine, Stalin finally began to emerge from his trance, and on July 3 he addressed the Soviet people as his "comrades" as he called on them to "selflessly join our patriotic war of liberation against the fascist enslavers".

While the idea the Soviet people were fighting to defend a communist utopia that upheld their rights and shunned the violence so freely used by the Wehrmacht (especially the SS divisions attached to it) is laughable, Stalin was not exaggerating when he referred to the threat of enslavement. From the outset of the war, Hitler had expressed his desire to carve Germany's new eastern territories into a series of states filled with Soviet slaves. A cruel tyrant he may have been, but in his speech at the start of July, Stalin was, for once, telling his people at least some of the truth.

On the same day that Stalin addressed the nation, German General Franz Halder, chief

German soldiers attack a Soviet bunker with a Flammenwerfer, which was capable of spitting flames up to 82 feet

of staff of Army High Command, confided in his diary that it was "no overstatement to say that the Russian campaign has been won in the space of two weeks". In hindsight this statement reeks of hubris, but at the time German confidence was more than justified.

By July 13, the German armies had advanced between 186 and 372 miles, incapacitated (either by killing, injuring or capturing) over 589,000 enemy soldiers and obliterated over 6,850 aircraft. The Wehrmacht was edging ever closer to Moscow, and the First Battle of Smolensk was about to finish with the entrapment of almost 760,000 Soviet troops. A glorious triumph loomed, a historic martial achievement that would echo for eternity. Then came an Army High Command directive that would change the course of the entire war.

On Saturday, July 19, 1941, Hitler issued an order that the Soviet armies trapped around Smolensk (the 16th, 19th and 20th) were to be utterly destroyed before Army Group Centre advanced, not toward Moscow but south to the outskirts of Kiev to aid Army Group South, which was still 50 miles outside of the Ukrainian capital.

Longing to continue the drive for Moscow, both Halder and von Bock were adamant that the city had to remain their priority, but Hitler was unmoved. And so, on August 23, Army Group Centre swung south. Three weeks later its southern counterpart started to drive north, and on September 16 two more Soviet armies were annihilated as the pincer closed east of Kiev. Stalin's order that the city be held at all costs had condemned over 700,000 Soviet troops to encirclement.

"A GLORIOUS TRIUMPH LOOMED... THEN CAME A HIGH COMMAND DIRECTIVE THAT WOULD CHANGE THE WAR"

Moscow or bust

Still progressing steadily in the north, the forces under the command of von Leeb had sealed off the city of Leningrad eight days prior to the encirclement of Kiev. Hitler had selected the city as a primary target during the planning of Barbarossa, and now his armies (with the support of Finnish troops sent to retake lands lost to the Soviets during the Winter War of 1939-1940) had provided him with the chance to put his Hunger Plan into action once more. Instead of bombarding the city, its people were to be starved into submission in a siege that would last until January 1944 and claim over 800,000 lives.

Now that the resistance shielding Kiev had been removed, Army Group Centre could once again turn its gaze on Moscow. Despite the panic that had spread throughout the city, Stalin had chosen to stay and invigorate its people with his presence. He had placed the defense of the city in the hands of General Georgy Zhukov, a formidable figure who had overseen the desperate efforts to counter the Siege of Leningrad.

Zhukov wasted little time in putting the men and women of Moscow to work excavating defensive trenches and anti-tank ditches (nearly 10.6 million cubic feet of earth was moved by hand). The factories that continued to function (much of the Soviets' industry had been evacuated east) were also turned to military tasks (a clock maker was asked to begin building mine detonators). If the Germans were to take Moscow, Zhukov was determined they would pay dearly for every street.

Codenamed Operation Typhoon, the assault on Moscow began on October 2, 1941. At the outset of the attack the Germans enjoyed a two-to-one superiority in tanks and troops and a three-to-one advantage in aircraft. It seemed that it would only be a matter of time before the Soviet capital fell. But there was one enemy that the German high command had failed to account for: Mother Nature.

Known as the *rasputitsa* (the time without roads), on October 8 a yearly deluge began, churning the roads into sucking quagmires that dramatically slowed the German advance. By the end of the month the Wehrmacht was still 50 miles from its target. Yet while the rain was a frustration, the freezing temperatures that followed in December were a death sentence.

By December 5, the Germans were forced to halt 19 miles short of Moscow as the conditions froze both men and machines, the lack of proper winter clothing (a result of Hitler's assurances the campaign would be over in a few weeks) condemning thousands to death.

On the same day as the Germans stopped their advance the Soviet armies behind Moscow (carefully husbanded by Zhukov and reinforced by soldiers transferred from Siberia once it had become clear that Japan was not planning to attack the region) were readying to unleash a merciless counteroffensive. Certain that the Red Army was all but beaten, the unfortunate German troops dug in around Moscow did not know what hit them when the Soviets began their attack with a massive bombardment. The moment the guns settled waves of T-34s poured across the frozen earth toward the German positions accompanied by a total force of over 1 million men and a resurgent Red Army Air Force.

Stunned by the sudden change in fortunes, Hitler demanded that every patch of ground be fought for, and in time the retreating German forces steadied themselves and consolidated their lines, but the threat to Moscow, built over months of fighting, had been eradicated in a matter of days.

Now it was the Red Army's turn to advance. It would do so relentlessly, forcing a doomed enemy closer and closer back toward its homeland, the men and women among its ranks hungry to enact a bloody revenge on the invaders of the motherland for the atrocities they'd committed. Germany's day of reckoning was now an inevitability.

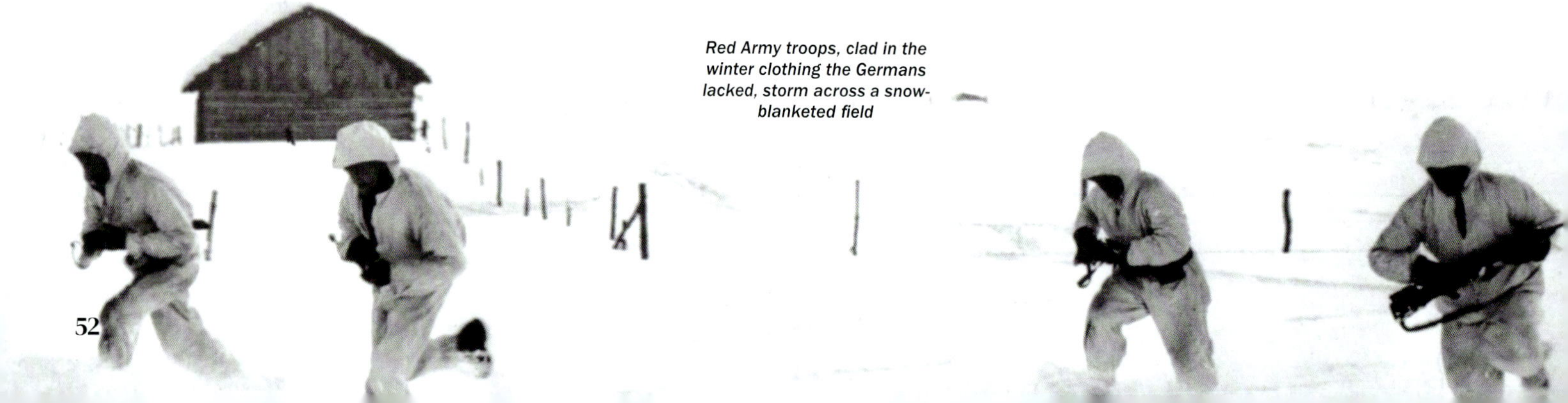

Red Army troops, clad in the winter clothing the Germans lacked, storm across a snow-blanketed field

THE BLOODY PURSUIT OF LEBENSRAUM

How the Wehrmacht blazed a trail through the plains and cities of Eastern Europe

1. THE DISTANT RUMBLE OF PANZERS
June 22
Barbarossa gets under way as German armored divisions race east to deliver what they hope will be a knock-out blow to their unprepared Soviet enemy.

2. ROMANIAN ALLIES
June 22
It isn't just the Wehrmacht plowing east, as two allied Romanian armies press into Ukraine heading for the city of Odessa.

3. MORE CITIES FALL
July 3
The onslaught continues as Volkovysk and then Minsk are both taken as German forces encircle the Red Army and take 324,000 prisoners.

4. FINNISH ASSISTANCE
July 10
While the Romanians plug away in the south, the Finnish army moves toward the Karelian Isthmus. In total, 300,000 Finnish soldiers join in the fight against the USSR.

5. SMOLENSK
July 16
Another important city on the road to Moscow is taken by the Germans. Resistance lasts in the city until August 5. By September 1, the front line has extended as far as Leningrad in the north and the Crimea in the south.

6. THE TAKING OF KIEV
September 16
The capital of the Ukrainian Socialist Soviet Republic is the next settlement to fall as Soviet troops are trapped inside a pocket east of the city. A month later, the Wehrmacht has advanced even further, reaching both Bryansk and Belgorod.

7. OPERATION TYPHOON
October 2
An all-out assault on Moscow begins after much deliberation in the Nazi hierarchy. The Germans manage to fight their way to the capital's suburbs but ultimately fail to take the city as winter sets in.

8. SIEGE OF SEVASTOPOL
November 16
Crimea falls into the hands of the Germans after a lengthy siege that eventually results in an Axis victory. The area will be used as a launchpad for the drive toward the oilfields of the Caucasus in Operation Blue.

9. WINTER TAKES HOLD
December 5
Horrendous weather conditions and fresh Soviet recruits take their toll on the exhausted Wehrmacht, which has no alternative but to turn back. Operation Barbarossa has failed in its objectives, however, Eastern Europe has fallen under the shadow of the Greater German Reich.

JAPAN'S FIRST STRIKE

Imperial planning and preparation for the surprise attack on Pearl Harbor began months before the Sunday morning aerial assault

© Piotr Forkasiewicz

Just before sunrise on Sunday, December 7, 1941, six aircraft carriers of the Imperial Japanese Navy's 1st Air Fleet under the command of Vice-Admiral Chuichi Nagumo, turned into the wind, ready to launch a striking force of 353 aircraft.

Nagumo's flagship, Akagi, and her consorts, Kaga, Soryu, Hiryu, Shokaku and Zuikaku, set in motion the marauding strike force that would plunge the Pacific into WWII. Its target was the US Navy's Pacific Fleet, which was anchored at Pearl Harbor on the island of Oahu in the territory of Hawaii. Other US Navy and Army installations on the island – Hickam Field, Wheeler Field, Bellows Field, Ewa Marine Corps Air Station – and the naval air stations at Kaneohe and on Ford Island in the heart of Pearl Harbor were to be hit as well.

The opening blow was intended to cripple the American military presence in the Pacific; allow the Japanese armed forces to seize and consolidate strategic gains throughout the region; and bring the US Government to the negotiating table where Japan would dictate favorable terms of an armistice. To that end the Pearl Harbor raid was co-ordinated with attacks on the Philippines, Wake Island, Midway Atoll and Malaya. The gambit was all or nothing for Imperial Japan.

Although senior Japanese commanders were confident of a swift victory, at least some of them acknowledged that a prolonged war with the United States was a daunting prospect, considering the industrial might and resources at the disposal of their adversary. Years of rising militarism and imperialism in Japan had placed the island nation on a collision course with the United States, a preeminent power in the Pacific since the Spanish-American War. Japan's provocative military moves on the Asian mainland, particularly the occupation of the Chinese region of Manchuria and later of French Indochina, had brought the two nations to loggerheads. While negotiations were continuing, most observers on either side of the Pacific believed war was inevitable.

Vice-Admiral Chuichi Nagumo led the 1st Air Fleet during the Pearl Harbor operation, but later lost his command

The British influence

At 9pm on the evening prior to the Pearl Harbor attack, Nagumo ordered all hands aboard the Akagi to attention. He solemnly read a message from Admiral Isoroku Yamamoto, commander-in-chief of the Combined Fleet. "The rise or fall of the empire depends on this battle. Everyone will do his duty to the utmost."

Yamamoto meant the communication not only as an encouragement to the Japanese sailors and airmen, but also as homage to naval esprit de corps. During the decades preceding WWII, the Imperial Japanese Navy had embarked on a lengthy program of expansion, modernizing and modeling itself on the finest naval tradition in the world – the British Royal Navy. The message from Yamamoto echoed Admiral Horatio Nelson's rousing words prior to the epic Battle of

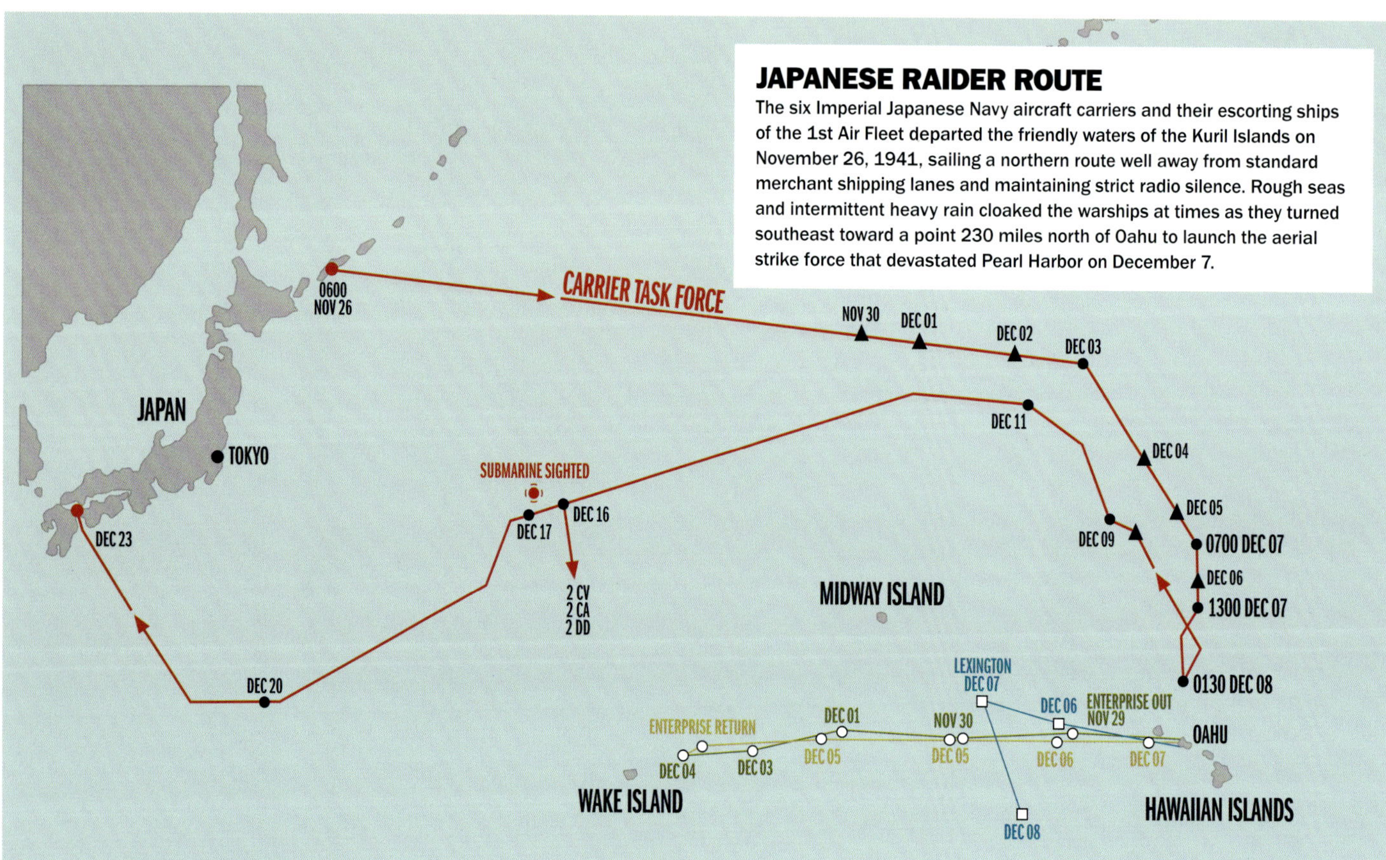

JAPANESE RAIDER ROUTE

The six Imperial Japanese Navy aircraft carriers and their escorting ships of the 1st Air Fleet departed the friendly waters of the Kuril Islands on November 26, 1941, sailing a northern route well away from standard merchant shipping lanes and maintaining strict radio silence. Rough seas and intermittent heavy rain cloaked the warships at times as they turned southeast toward a point 230 miles north of Oahu to launch the aerial strike force that devastated Pearl Harbor on December 7.

IMPERIAL WAR MACHINES

The Japanese armed forces employed the latest technology available during the opening phase of WWII in the Pacific

MITSUBISHI A6M ZERO FIGHTER

For a time, the Mitsubishi Zero reigned supreme as the finest carrier-based fighter aircraft in the Pacific. Developed in the 1930s, it was already reputed as a highly maneuverable, heavily armed and deadly opponent by the time of the Pearl Harbor attack. However, the Zero was also vulnerable. Its design sacrificed armor and self-sealing gasoline tanks to achieve remarkable performance.

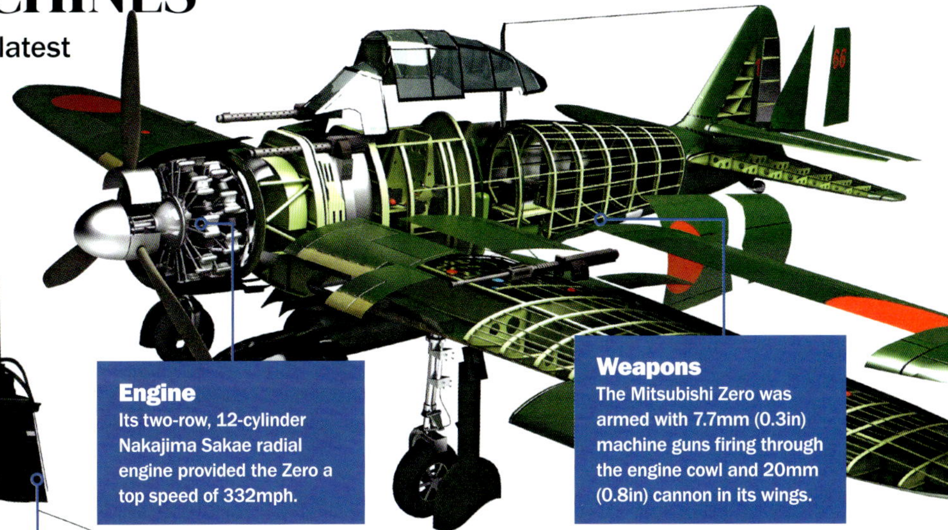

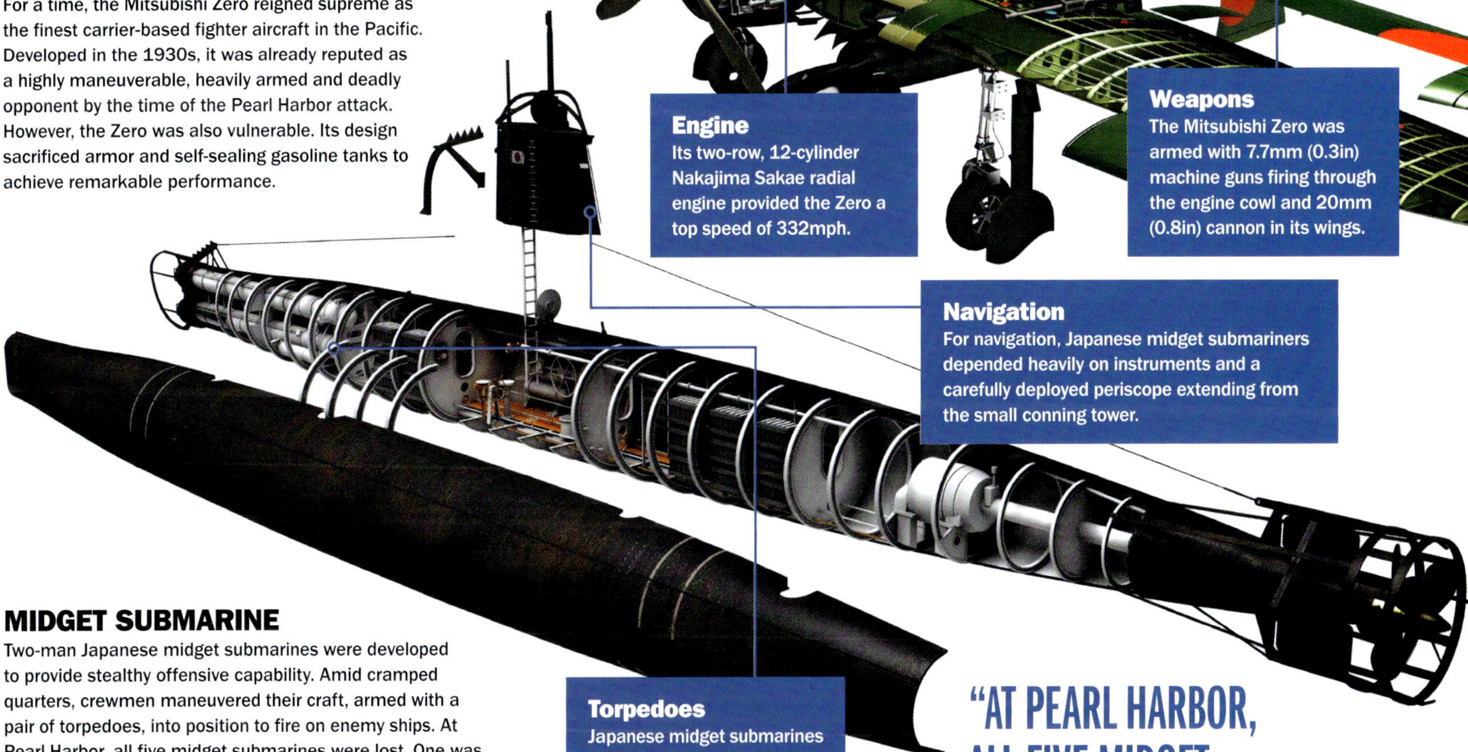

MIDGET SUBMARINE

Two-man Japanese midget submarines were developed to provide stealthy offensive capability. Amid cramped quarters, crewmen maneuvered their craft, armed with a pair of torpedoes, into position to fire on enemy ships. At Pearl Harbor, all five midget submarines were lost. One was captured intact after it beached and its commander became the first prisoner of the Americans during WWII.

> "AT PEARL HARBOR, ALL FIVE MIDGET SUBMARINES WERE LOST"

AIRCRAFT CARRIERS

At the time of Pearl Harbor, the modern aircraft carriers of the Imperial Japanese Navy included converted battlecruisers Akagi and Kaga, along with those built from the keel up, such as the smaller Soryu and Hiryu. The newest fleet carriers were the Shokaku and Zuikaku, both displacing more than 26,000 tons and carrying more than 80 combat aircraft.

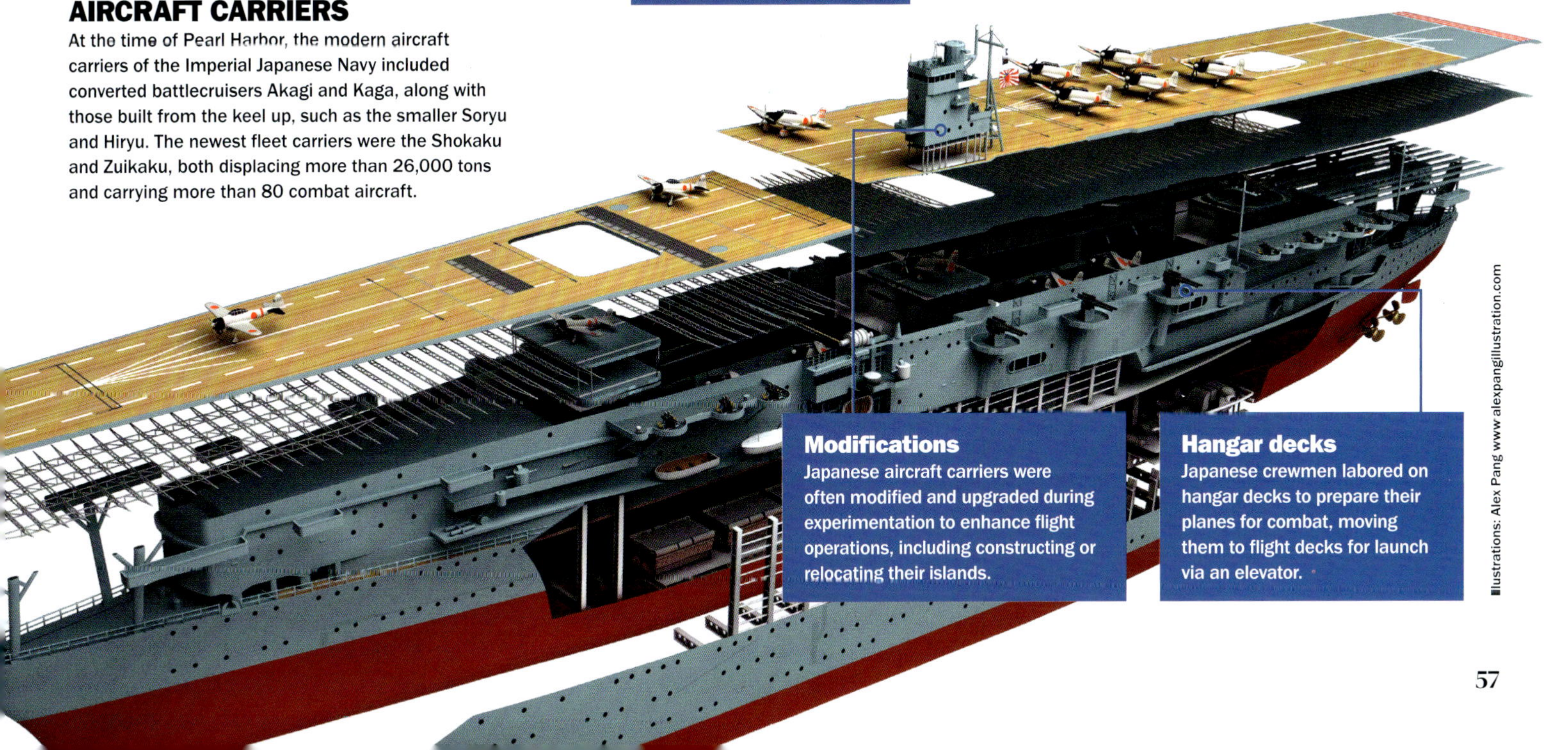

Illustrations: Alex Pang www.alexpangillustration.com

NAVAL AIR JUGGERNAUT

The British Royal Navy pioneered many aspects of the development of naval aviation in the early 20th century, and Japanese naval observers also recognized its potential.

Intent on emulating the Royal Navy's successes, the Japanese received a British mission headed by Captain William Sempill in the fall of 1921. Sempill led 29 air operations instructors charged with assisting the development of the Japanese naval aviation program. By 1922, the Japanese had also constructed the Hosho, the world's first aircraft carrier that had been purpose-built, rather than converted from another ship type as others before it had been.

Sempill, who was later exposed as a spy for the Japanese, hoped to secure substantial sales of British arms to Japan in exchange for valuable expertise and advice. His team brought the blueprints of the most advanced British carrier designs, protocols involving elements such as pilot training; the launch and recovery of aircraft; refueling and maintenance; and airborne operations. The British trained the young Japanese pilots in the latest Royal Navy aircraft, such as the Gloster Sparrowhawk fighter, along with torpedo bombers and dive bombers, and introduced torpedo tactics to the Imperial Navy.

Japanese engineers and designers experimented with their own ordnance and aircraft, several of which were patterned after British types, and perfected carrier operations and doctrine during the 1920s and 1930s.

Prior to Pearl Harbor, Lieutenant Commander Takeshi Naito, a naval attaché in Berlin, traveled to the port of Taranto, Italy, where the British had executed a successful attack against the Italian fleet at anchor in November 1940. With the assistance of the Italian Navy, Naito assessed the dynamics of the Taranto raid and advised the Pearl Harbor planners on modifications to existing tactics. Wooden stabilizing fins were attached to Japanese aerial torpedoes, allowing them to run true in Pearl Harbor's shallow waters.

The battleship USS Pennsylvania lies behind the battered destroyers Cassin and Downes in dry dock at Pearl Harbor

Dive bombers crowd a flight deck prior to Pearl Harbor

Type 91 Kai 2 torpedoes on the flight deck of the Imperial Japanese Navy aircraft carrier Akagi. The carrier is at Hitokappu Bay in the Kurils just prior to departing for the attack on Pearl Harbor

Trafalgar in 1805, in which he reminded his men that "England expects that every man will do his duty."

Japanese respect for the Royal Navy ran deep. Since the turn of the 20th century, some vessels of the Imperial fleet had been constructed in British and French shipyards, while Japanese training, operational standards, uniforms and rank insignia were similar to those of the British.

Following the outbreak of war in Europe, the Royal Navy again served as a role model for the Japanese. On the night of November 11, 1940, Fairey Swordfish torpedo bombers of the Fleet Air Arm flew from the deck of the aircraft carrier HMS Illustrious in the Mediterranean Sea and attacked the Italian naval anchorage at Taranto. The 21 obsolescent British biplanes sank one Italian battleship and damaged two others.

For the Japanese, the idea of a preemptive raid on Pearl Harbor had been discussed, war gamed and shelved several times between the world wars. However, bolstered by the British success, the staff of the Combined Fleet began, with renewed purpose in January 1941, to plan for just such a bold stroke.

Lieutenant Commander Minoru Genda, one of the best-known and most respected aviators in the Japanese armed forces, had observed American carriers operating in a unified, single strike force and attended war games in 1936, during which an offensive scenario against Pearl Harbor had ended in simulated disaster for the attacker. Still, Genda remained one of a relative few Japanese officers who believed it was possible for a carrier task force to successfully deliver a stunning blow against an enemy fleet at anchor.

As Japanese aircraft carrier strength reached sufficient levels to support a Pearl Harbor attack, Yamamoto instructed Admiral Takajiro Onishi, chief of staff of the 11th Air Fleet, to order Genda to evaluate the potential for success with "...special attention to the feasibility of the operation, method of execution and the forces to be used". Yamamoto was reluctant to go to war with the US, however, he strongly believed that a substantial and successful first strike at the Pacific Fleet was the only option to bring such a conflict to a fast, favorable conclusion for Japan.

Yamamoto's assertion that Pearl Harbor should be Japan's target actually reversed traditional thinking at the highest command levels within the Imperial Navy. Although the army had been active on the Asian continent, naval doctrine had previously assumed a defensive posture. In the fall of 1940, Yamamoto's assertion became an ultimatum. He eventually threatened to resign if senior commanders within the Combined Fleet refused to support the proposal.

The blueprints for war

By the following August, the basic plan for the Pearl Harbor attack had been approved. The six aircraft carriers of the 1st Air Fleet were to be accompanied by an armada of two battleships, two heavy cruisers, a light cruiser,

The battleship USS Arizona belches black smoke as its superstructure buckles after a devastating explosion during the Pearl Harbor attack

A DAY OF INFAMY

As soon as Lieutenant Commander Mitsuo Fuchida was back aboard the Akagi, the leader of the Pearl Harbor strike reported to Vice-Admiral Chuichi Nagumo on the carrier's bridge. Fuchida is said to have begged his commander to let the troops launch another attack. Nagumo declined. The risk was too great, and so he ordered the 1st Air Fleet to retire. When news of the successful attack reached Tokyo, citizens took to the streets in celebration. The highest echelons of the military exuded optimism.

However, Admiral Isoroku Yamamoto, architect of the raid, brooded. The American carriers had not been destroyed. Retribution would soon come. He had once warned fellow officers, "If I am told to fight regardless of the consequences, I shall run wild for the first six months or a year, but I have utterly no confidence for the second or third year."

Pearl Harbor had been a tremendous tactical victory. The US Pacific Fleet was crippled, but Yamamoto's words proved prophetic. Machine stores, repair facilities and stockpiles of fuel and oil were untouched. The submarine base was operational. The Americans recovered rapidly, and just six months after Pearl Harbor, four of the Japanese carriers that had executed the raid were sunk by American planes at the seismic Battle of Midway.

Admiral Isoroku Yamamoto envisioned a bleak future for the Japanese nation in the wake of the Pearl Harbor attack

nine destroyers, three submarines and eight tankers – a total of 31 vessels – sailing from their rendezvous point at Hitokappu Bay in the Kuril Islands. The fleet was to sail on November 26; take a northerly course, in order to avoid the busy Pacific trade routes and merchant shipping that plied the ocean; maintain strict radio silence; and launch its aircraft in two waves from a position 230 miles north of Oahu.

The tentative date for the attack was designated as December 7, 1941. A cordon of fleet submarines was positioned around Oahu to provide early warning of American ship movements and attack any US Navy vessels that might be at sea near the harbor. Five midget submarines were to be launched from their mother submarines hours before the aerial attack, with the hope that they might infiltrate Pearl Harbor and launch torpedoes at anchored vessels of the Pacific Fleet.

Early in September, senior Japanese officers convened at the Naval War College in Tokyo and finalized the plans for the attack. One month later, senior pilots were informed of their target. They already had some idea of its nature, since the torpedo groups had worked to perfect their runs against capital ships anchored in shallow waters: they knew it would be an enemy port.

Combined Fleet Top Secret Operational Order No 1 was issued on November 5, followed 48 hours later by Order No 2, authorizing the fleet to weigh anchor at the end of the month and to execute the attack on Pearl Harbor.

When the fleet set sail, Admiral Kichisaburo Nomura and Special Envoy Saburo Kurusu were in Washington, DC, conducting last-ditch negotiations with Secretary of State Cordell Hull and President Franklin D Roosevelt. These negotiations were expected to fail, and when the impasse was reached, specific orders to launch the attack would be issued to Nagumo at sea. At the same time, the envoys, oblivious to the details of the Pearl Harbor attack, were instructed to deliver a message to the US Government, officially terminating the negotiations. The government in Tokyo considered this diplomatic step essentially a declaration of war, timed for a half hour before the Japanese aircraft appeared in the sky above Pearl Harbor.

Lieutenant Commander Mitsuo Fuchida, leader of the air groups of the 1st Air Fleet, was assigned the task of allocating aircraft to specific targets, organizing the two waves of planes to co-ordinate their attacks and allotting fighter protection against any defending American planes.

Fuchida assigned 185 aircraft to the first wave. It consisted of 49 Nakajima B5N 'Kate' bombers carrying armor-piercing bombs, 40 Kates with aerial torpedoes, 51 Aichi D3A 'Val' dive bombers with general-purpose bombs, and 45 superb Mitsubishi A6M Zero fighters to provide escort and strafe targets of opportunity.

While the Kates hit the warships anchored in Pearl Harbor, 25 Vals were designated to blast the primary American fighter base at Wheeler Field. Seventeen Vals were assigned to destroy Ford Island's patrol plane and fighter base and nine were to strike American bombers based at Hickam Field. The second wave included 54 Kates armed with 550- and 125-pound bombs to demolish installations and crater runways at the airfields, 80 Vals with 550-pound bombs to renew the attacks on the warships in the harbor and 36 marauding Zeroes.

Fuchida received an intelligence message from a Japanese spy operating on Oahu the day before the attack was launched. It was tinged both with optimism that the element of surprise would be achieved and disappointment that the three American aircraft carriers, Enterprise, Lexington and Saratoga, were not present at the anchorage:

"No balloons, no torpedo defense nets deployed around battleships in Pearl Harbor. All battleships are in. No indications from enemy radio activity that ocean patrol flights being made in Hawaiian area. Lexington left harbor yesterday. Enterprise also thought to be operating at sea."

Engulfed in thick smoke, a US vessel burns on the waves off Oahu

"THE AMERICANS WERE CAUGHT COMPLETELY BY SURPRISE, AND FOR SEVERAL HOURS THE JAPANESE WROUGHT DEVASTATION ON THEIR TARGETS BELOW"

The Saratoga was steaming into the harbor at San Diego, California, when the Japanese attackers arrived above Pearl Harbor on December 7. Although the aircraft carriers were absent, there was no turning back; the attack had to proceed as ordered, and the Japanese rationalized that the remaining targets, particularly the US battleships, were high-value enough to justify the risk being undertaken.

"Tora! Tora! Tora!"

As the sky was still dark over the deck of the Akagi, pitched in rough seas, a green lamp was waved in a circle and the first Zero fighter roared down the flight deck into the air. Within 15 minutes the entire first wave was airborne.

At 7.40am, the north shore of Oahu came into view. Fuchida was exultant. He radioed "Tora! Tora! Tora!" to the anxious Nagumo, signifying that complete surprise had been achieved. The Americans anchored in Pearl Harbor were indeed caught completely by surprise, and for several hours the Japanese planes wrought devastation on their desperate targets below.

Elsewhere in the Pacific, Japanese forces moved aggressively in concert with the Pearl Harbor attack, lunging for objectives that would minimize US interference with coming operations to seize the Dutch East Indies, secure vital resources such as oil and rubber for the Japanese war machine, and extend their defensive perimeter further into the expanse of the world's greatest ocean.

As the attack got underway in Hawaii, word was flashed to Midway Atoll at 6.30am local time on December 7. The Marine garrison went on high alert, and by dusk the Japanese had arrived. Two Imperial Navy destroyers, the Akebono and Ushio, were sighted as they prepared to shell the installations on Midway.

War came to the atoll at 9.35pm as Japanese five-inch shells crashed down on Sand and Eastern islands, the two spits of land that, within months, would become the epicenter of WWII in the Pacific.

As the destroyers cruised back and forth, the Marine guns responded with three- and five-inch rounds. Japanese shells set the large seaplane hangar ablaze. One enemy round scored a direct hit on the concrete structure that housed the Sand Island powerplant, smashing through an air intake and mortally wounding a young Marine officer, 1st Lieutenant George H Cannon, who refused to leave his post for medical treatment and later received a posthumous Medal of Honor.

The Midway battle lasted for about half an hour, and Marine gunners claimed to have scored hits on at least one enemy destroyer, which was seen belching smoke and flame. When the Japanese finally withdrew, four Americans were dead and ten wounded.

Thirty-six Japanese bombers hit Wake Island on the morning of December 8 (across the International Date Line), destroying a dozen Grumman F4F Wildcat fighters on the ground. Meanwhile, Japanese troops landed at Kota Bharu on the coast of Malaya while the Pearl Harbor attack force was in the air. Within hours of the strike against Pearl, Japanese bombers hit Clark Field and other installations in the Philippines, catching American planes on the ground again.

Shocked and bloodied, the United States was suddenly at war. For a time, Japanese domination of the Pacific was virtually uncontested, but just as Yamamoto feared, a protracted conflict soon developed.

Even as Allied forces turned the tide and fought their way inexorably to Tokyo Bay and victory in 1945, the specter of Pearl Harbor still continued to haunt the Americans in the same way as Stalingrad haunted the Russians.

While conspiracy theories have surfaced in the three quarters of a century since the 'Day of Infamy', these remain the topic of heated debate. Some revisionist historians have reviewed all the proof they need to conclude that President Roosevelt and other high-ranking Allied civilian leaders and military officers – even British Prime Minister Winston Churchill – were aware that the attacks on Pearl Harbor and other locations were coming. However, the 'case' will probably never be closed.

On the tactical level, the Americans received several warnings of the Japanese air armada approaching Pearl Harbor on December 7, 1941, including an encounter with a midget submarine and a radar sighting at Opana above Kahuku Point on the north shore.

The question remains whether US commanders should have taken action to improve preparedness and should have been more responsive to the signs of imminent attack on that fateful Sunday morning.

ENIGMA

HOW BRITAIN'S CODEBREAKERS TURNED THE TIDE IN WWII

Discover how the men and women of Bletchley Park cracked the 'unbreakable' German Enigma and helped defeat Hitler's Nazis

It's February 1942, and the carnage of WWII shows no signs of stopping. The balance of world power is precariously poised. Night is about to fall on the Atlantic Ocean, and as darkness comes the water is inky-black and icy. In the depths of seas around the world, German U-boats cruise like predators stalking their prey, patiently waiting their turn to pounce. Brazenly, some even encircle convoys, sailing invisibly around them. On this night one U-boat fires off its torpedoes and an American convoy ship is engulfed in bright flames that light up the sky. The crew on this convoy know they will perish in this freezing sea and that the vital supplies and provisions they are carrying across the Atlantic to Britain will also be lost. As screams and shouts finally give way to an eerie silence, its neighbors can only watch helplessly, fearing their turn may soon come. The lethal wolfpack has claimed another victim. The Allies are virtually defenseless against these menacing groups, knowing only that these deadly ships will strike again, but not where or when.

As the year draws to a close a German U-boat, the U-559, is spotted off the coast of Palestine by HMS Petard and subsequently depth-charged. This time it is the U-boat crew who know that all is lost: their vessel is sinking and they must abandon ship. Lieutenant Anthony Fasson, Able Seaman Colin Grazier, and Tommy Brown swim out to it, even though the boat is rapidly sinking below the waves. Seeing some lights remaining on inside the boat, they are astounded to find a four-rotor Enigma (the machine the Germans use for communications) and a book of current Enigma keys. In a remarkable act of bravery, they wrap the machine, the keys and the bigram tables in waterproof material and rescue them for the Allies, not realizing how vital their discovery will prove to be. With supreme effort they manage to reach 15-year-old Naafi boy Tommy Brown, who has waited outside the boat, and hand him the machine and the books. It is the last act of Fasson and Grazier, for they go down with U-559 as it sinks. They are both posthumously awarded the George Cross.

This treasure – for that is what it was to the British codebreakers – made its way to Bletchley Park, a country house in rural Buckinghamshire that had been set up as Intelligence Headquarters at the start of the war. Those based there knew they now had a good chance to get back into breaking the German naval codes, codenamed 'Shark', and affect the outcome of WWII. An eccentric young mathematician named Alan Turing would have a key role to play in breaking the Nazi code.

The eccentric genius

Born in 1912, Turing came to Bletchley from Cambridge at the age of 27, the day after Britain declared war on Germany. His clothes were dishevelled at best; others thought he often dressed like a tramp. When excited over some problem or idea, he would stutter with his eagerness to express his legion of ideas. He would often be seen riding his bicycle around the Bletchley countryside, wearing a gas mask to avoid the pollen that set off his hay fever. In his office, he would chain his coffee mug to the radiator so no one else would take it. With little faith in banking and

German forces disguised their communications through the Enigma machine

GLOSSARY

Enigma: Resembling an expanded typewriter, the Germans used this machine for communication. It is a portable machine that enciphers and deciphers messages using a keyboard, rotors and electrical impulses in order to generate millions of possible letter combinations.

Typex machine: Standard British cipher machine with special modifications so that it operated like Enigma, with rotors, keyboard and a paper feed with a printer. It was used to turn encrypted text back into German.

Bombe: Not a computer but an electronic machine that could check off, at speed, hundreds of possible letter combinations to reduce the potential number of that day's possible Enigma settings.

Crib: An intelligent guess by looking for patterns in the coded text, usually found in common phrases or words used by the German operators, or sometimes by spotting their mistakes, such as lazy, repeated word use, use of their girlfriend's name, or a rude word.

Cillis: Procedural errors by German Enigma operators, where they used recognizable message settings instead of random, or had failed to alter the rotor wheel position before sending their text.

Menu: A set of diagrams based on that day's 'cribs' to feed into the Bombes to help reduce the length of time needed to confirm that day's Enigma settings.

Wrens: Name given to members of the Women's Royal Naval Service.

Colossus: The world's first semi-programmable computer. A practical, digital processing machine, it used 1,500 valves and could do mathematical calculations in hours that had taken weeks by hand.

THE 'UNBREAKABLE' ENIGMA

Discover the main devices on the complicated and portable German communications machine

Lampboard
Each typed key sent an electrical impulse through the machine and a letter would light up on the adjacent lampboard. This would be repeated until the whole message had been enciphered, when it would then be radioed in Morse to its recipient. The lampboard would light up with the real letters as the cipher was typed in.

Rotors
The standard Enigma had three rotors, while the advanced machine had four. These scrambled messages into unintelligible cipher text. Each rotor had numbered ring scales for each of the German armed forces and the rotors could be changed daily. The settings were changed at midnight and each rotor could be set to any one of 26 different ring settings.

Plugboard
This made the machine's wiring much more complicated, increasing the possible encoding combinations by millions. The plugboard settings could also be changed daily. The A-socket of the plugboard connected to the first terminal inside the entry plate, the B-socket to the second, and so on.

Keyboard
As the operator pressed one of the 'typewriter' keys, an electric current was sent through the rotating code-letter wheels. No Enigma letter could ever be enciphered as itself. The recipient operator would type into his machine the received Morse message in the same order.

currency during wartime, he put his money into silver bars that he then buried, intending to dig them up after the war – not realizing that by the time he had followed his own elaborate set of instructions for finding them, a new town called Milton Keynes was being built over the countryside. To the onlooker, Alan Turing totally fitted the bill of a typical, eccentric, academic boffin; to his colleagues, themselves some of the brightest minds in the country, he was a true genius of his time.

Bombes away

The Allies knew the Germans were using a machine named Enigma, and teams of codebreakers at Bletchley were trying to crack the code this machine used. The teams worked in newly constructed prefabricated huts, each given a number instead of a name for secrecy.

In Hut 8 they were concentrating on cracking the German Naval ciphers. They already knew that Naval Enigma operators were more careful than Army operators, thus making it harder to use educated guesses, or 'cribs', to spot German mistakes. But now they realized the number of possible settings were hugely expanded due to the increase in code wheels on the four-rotor Enigma.

Turing, who was already working on updating the Polish Bombe machines, realized the vital importance of having machines that could speed up the process by mechanically checking off these millions of settings combinations. While at Cambridge before the war, Turing had developed an original idea: a 'Universal Turing Machine', a sort of 'super-typewriter' that could identify symbols, write, erase and carry out other tasks, all automatically and without human intervention. However, having studied previous Polish encryption machines and a replica Enigma, Turing knew he needed more than even his hypothetical machine. So he studied the mechanics of Enigma, the rotors, wiring and boards, and sought to devise an electrical system with circuits that could decrypt that same text.

Human intervention, Turing knew, was still essential: 'cribs' and mathematical work would

TIMELINE

Invention
A Dutch invention, the first cipher motor machine is patented by Dr Arthur Scherbius, who markets it at the 1923 International Postal Union Congress for use in banking, but it proves unsuccessful. Enigma is marketed for use in Germany's armed forces instead for its potential for military use.
1923

The Poles
Three Polish mathematicians – Marian Rejewski, Henryk Zygalski and Jerzy Rozycki – make the first break into military Enigma using mathematical methods. This includes the invention of Zygalski sheets, a slow and time-consuming method that was used in the days before advances were made to the Enigma machine.
1932

Sharing secrets
In July, a secret meeting takes place in Poland between representatives of Bletchley Park (Peter Twinn, Dilly Knox, Alan Turing and Tony Kendrick) and Gustav Bertrand of French Intelligence to share discoveries made since 1932 by Polish cryptanalysts. By September, the Poles have passed models of Enigma to British intelligence.
1939

Breaks, Bombes and tips
In January, the 'Green' (Army) and 'Red' (Luftwaffe) Enigma keys are cracked, and in February the sinking of U-33 brings Bletchley its first 'pinch': an Enigma machine. By March, the first Bombe machine, 'Victory', is installed into Hut 1, and later that year a new Enigma key is introduced.
1940

STEP-BY-STEP GUIDE TO CODEBREAKING

Follow our five-point guide to crack codes like they did in Bletchley Park

01 Listen to the enemy to gather the intelligence

At Station X, Bletchley originally used a radio-transmitting room at the top of the Mansion House's turreted tower to intercept Morse, teleprinter and radio codes. However, Bletchley's secret location needed protection, so a series of 'Y' stations were set up across the country. Intercepts were sent to Bletchley either by motorcycle courier or by direct teleprinter line and were logged into the Registration Room.

02 Break the cipher using mathematics and cribs

Using brainpower and ingenuity, the codebreakers first worked by hand by looking for features that corresponded to the original plain text. Using cribs and contact analysis, the codebreakers could often spot a possible pattern in the text. Human error on the part of the operators and psychology (imagining how the operators might undertake their work) also came into play when looking for cribs.

03 Make sense of the nonsense

Process and check that day's 'cribs', then set up the Typex machines to the same settings as the Enigma machine and type in the enciphered message. Once deciphered it would come out on long strips of paper. Cut and glued onto the back of the original message, these were sent back to Hut 6 to finish any decryption left over via a specially built chute, and then ultimately to Hut 3 for final translation and strategic analysis by a special team.

04 Translate and understand the German plain text

Hut 3 would use linguists to translate German, Italian and Japanese codes, using the decrypted text sent from Hut 6. At this stage, the Index room would check and cross-reference to see if anything could be spotted that had been seen before using Hollerith machines and thousands of index cards in Block C. Once analysed the information was ready to send on as usable intelligence to Churchill in his daily update.

05 Send intelligence to Churchill and commanders in the field

Only a few commanders knew about Bletchley, and they were forbidden to act on its findings, codenamed 'Ultra', until the Germans had been deceived into thinking it had come from another source altogether. 'Special Communication Units' were set up to feed information to the field, first in France in May 1940, then in North Africa and elsewhere from March 1941. All 'Ultra' messages were destroyed once they had been received.

Cracking Dolphin
Using the 'rodding' technique, the Italian Naval cipher is broken after the Battle of Matapan by Dilly Knox and his 'girls.' With the recovery of Enigma coding documents and notebooks from German submarines, notably U-110, along with repetitive weather transmissions, Bletchley is finally able to read German Naval Enigma.
1941

Cracking Shark
In February, the Germans introduce a more complex four-rotor Enigma for U-boats: 'Shark', leading to a blackout. In October, two German short-signal codebooks arrive at Bletchley, rescued from U-559 by Fasson and Grazier on HMS Petard. Shaun Wylie and the Hut 8 codebreakers can now break Shark and read U-boat traffic.
1942

Colossus
The Germans introduce a new short weather code, but Hut 8 avoid another blackout with the help of the faster Bombes. Shark is re-broken within ten days – a deciding factor in the Second Battle of the Atlantic. Max Newman and Tommy Flowers design and build Colossus, the world's first semi-programmable computer.
1943

D-Day success
Hut 8 and Hut 4's crucial decryption and translation of German Naval Enigma plays a key role in the Double Cross deception, codenamed Operation Fortitude South, fooling Hitler into believing the Allied landings were planned for Pas de Calais and not Normandy, thus having a huge impact on the outcome of D-Day.
1944

EYEWITNESS JEAN VALENTINE

How did you come to be at Bletchley?
I grew up in Perth, Scotland, and when I was 18 I decided to join up. I took an intelligence test at a local Navy recruiting center. When I got my summons, I was given a railway warrant to go to a training center for Wrens in Dumbartonshire. After two weeks I was told I was going to be sent to London, but was not told what my work would be. I was then sent on to a Y Station in Eastcote, Middlesex, where I first saw a Bombe machine. Later I was sent to work at Bletchley Park.

Were you aware of the other work going on at the Park?
No, everything was compartmentalized. When I was working on the Bombes, if we got a possible result we would phone it through to an extension number: it wasn't until after the war that I realized I had been phoning Hut 6 just across the path! If the menu had worked and German text came out on the tape, it went to the pink hut just opposite Hut 11, where it was translated. Apart from that small section of the Park, I had nothing to do with any other work carried out elsewhere.

What did you do in your free time?
We used to go to the village on a free Saturday night. There were lots of clubs and societies at the Park, which men and women could attend if their shifts allowed and if they could get to and from their billets to attend: music, theater, sports; [it featured] a huge variety.

What was the work like?
The shifts were quite arduous: 8am to 4pm, 4pm to midnight or midnight to 8am. Once you had learnt how to work the Bombe it wasn't complicated, just repetitive. The Bombe would search for answers and would stop if it thought it had found one. It was noisy, but like a tickety-click noise; it didn't really bother me, although it did others. We were young and disciplined and knew we were part of the war effort so we just got on with it. I found the work a rather fascinating experience; I enjoyed it! There were all sorts of people working at the Park; everyone was treated the same, whether military or civilian. The night shifts were a bit disruptive - especially on our eating patterns. There were some cases of burnout: I was once sent to the sick bay and slept for nearly three days! Then I had two weeks leave and came back refreshed.

What did you do after Bletchley?
In 1944, when I was 19 years old, I was sent to Ceylon to work on Japanese meteorological codes; I stayed there for 15 months. I never told a soul I was working at Bletchley. It was a great surprise when the first book came out in 1974 and the big secret was out. However, many people were uncomfortable with talking about Bletchley after all that time, and some are still.

still be needed to help the Bombe machine, the device that would work to decipher encrypted German messages.

The thought of a machine capable of checking millions of combinations at speed was revolutionary. However, Turing was a theoretician rather than a practical codebreaker, so Gordon Welchman, a codebreaker and brilliant administrator working in Hut 6, recruited Oliver Lawn, a mathematician from Cambridge, to help with the making of the machine. 'Victory', the first Bombe, was built and installed in Hut 1 on March 18, 1940. Welchman later improved the design of the Bombe with an electronic diagonal board, which increased the machine's powers and capabilities.

Although the German Air Force Enigma was by now being read daily, the Naval Enigma proved a tougher nut to crack. In 1941, two significant sea battles – one inside the Arctic Circle, one in the Atlantic – led to the recovery of Enigma coding documents. It was with this information that Turing calculated a new method he called 'Banburismus', because it involved holes punched on long pieces of paper made at Banbury.

For the rest of the summer of 1941, Bletchley was able to read the majority of German Naval Enigma, thus providing vital protection to British shipping and a real success story for Bletchley. A significant breakthrough had been achieved, but the team would face tougher battles as the war rumbled on.

Calculating conflict

The genesis of Bletchley occurs in August 1938 when, at a small rural railway station half way between the university cities of Oxford and Cambridge, a group of ordinary-looking people arrive for a social gathering at Bletchley's Victorian country house. Led by Captain Ridley, the entourage are here to enjoy that simple but favored pursuit of the upper classes: a shooting party weekend. Or are they? In fact, the group of men assembling at this isolated location in the depths of the Buckinghamshire countryside are all either members of MI6 and the Government Code & Cipher School (GC&CS) or esteemed scholars and academics turned codebreakers. For now, they will assess the mansion house and its surrounding area as a possible location to site intelligence operations in the event of a war that seems likelier with every inflamed speech Hitler gives.

When the inevitable happens, they and others return to begin the work that some later believed shortened the war by two years. Men and women from all walks of life will descend onto the railway platform and begin the walk up to Bletchley Park: mathematicians, classicists, engineers, Wrens, WAAFs, linguists, typists, administrators and even debutantes. Each will become a small cog in a large wheel, working independently in extreme secrecy, unaware of the work being carried out in any hut outside their own. Having signed the Official Secrets Act, they are aware only of the vital importance their work could have to the war effort and that they can never speak of it to anyone.

Despite their undoubted brilliance, it wasn't the British at Bletchley who first made a break into Enigma: that distinction belongs to another nation entirely. In 1932, the Polish had first cracked Enigma; at the time, the cipher changed only once every few months, but by the outbreak of the war it was daily. With the invasion of Poland imminent, they turned to the British for help in breaking the Enigma settings, now running at an intimidating 15 trillion possible combinations – that's a staggering 15 billion billion.

Teams of top codebreakers were installed at Bletchley Park in the prefabricated numbered

MAP OF BLETCHLEY PARK

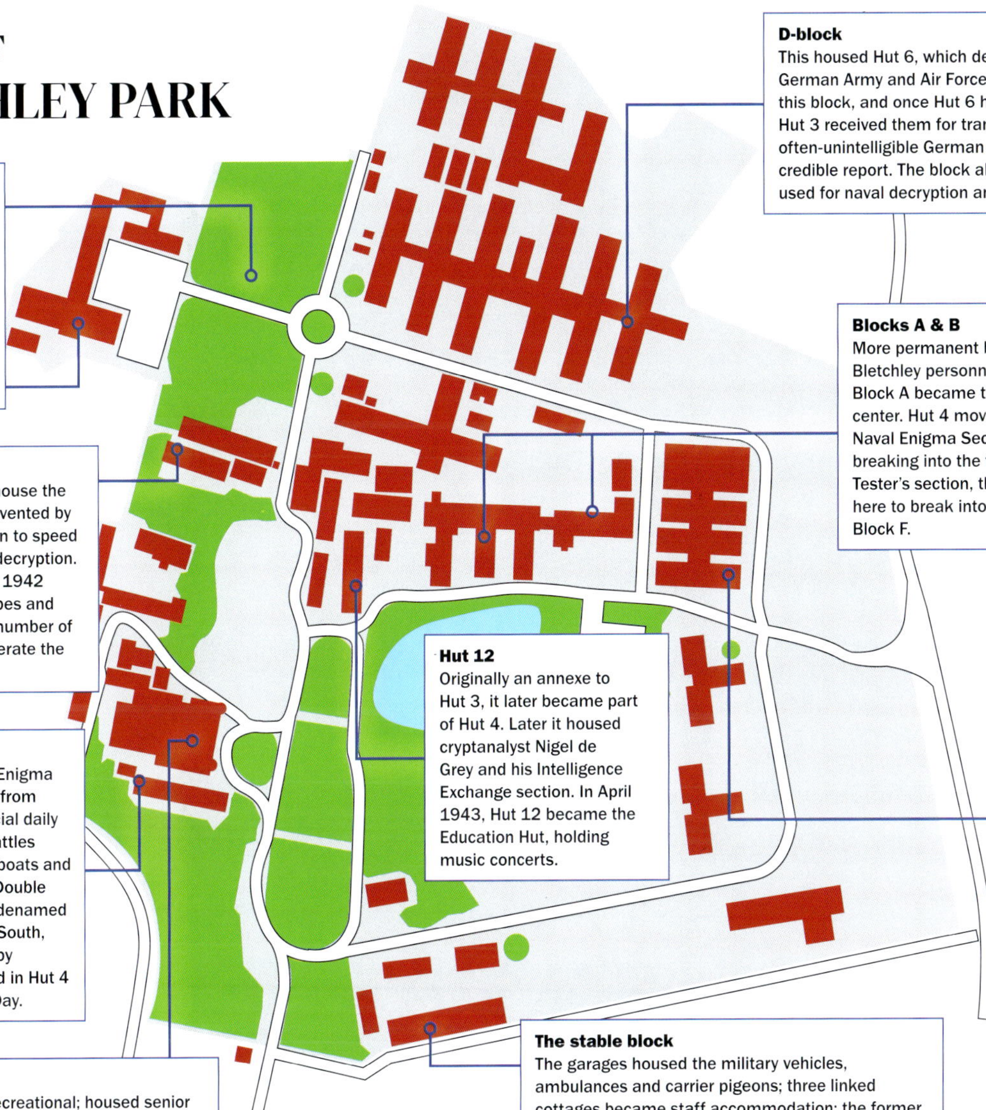

Blocks F & H
These housed the Testery, Newmanry and the Heath Robinson and Colossus machines. Block F also housed Japanese codebreaking.

Huts 11 and 11A
Hut 11 was built to house the Bombe machines, invented by Turing and Welchman to speed up Enigma settings decryption. Hut 11A was built in 1942 to house more Bombes and train the increasing number of Wrens needed to operate the complex machines.

Hut 4
Used for decrypting Enigma messages sent over from Hut 8, providing crucial daily intelligence in the battles between German U-boats and Allied convoys. The Double Cross Deception, codenamed Operation Fortitude South, was made possible by messages processed in Hut 4 in the lead-up to D-Day.

The mansion
Headquarters and recreational; housed senior staff's offices. Originally held the telephone exchange and teleprinter rooms, later moved to a blast-proof hut. This Victorian country house also had a dining room, library, billiard room and ballroom.

D-block
This housed Hut 6, which decrypted daily settings of the German Army and Air Force Enigma. Hut 3 was also in this block, and once Hut 6 had decrypted the messages, Hut 3 received them for translation and analysis, making often-unintelligible German military language read like a credible report. The block also housed Hut 8, which was used for naval decryption and was first headed by Turing.

Blocks A & B
More permanent buildings were needed as Bletchley personnel outgrew the wooden huts. Block A became the Naval Section's decoding center. Hut 4 moved to Block B in 1942. The Naval Enigma Section now concentrated on breaking into the four-rotor Enigma. Ralph Tester's section, the Testery, was also housed here to break into Lorenz, before moving into Block F.

Hut 12
Originally an annexe to Hut 3, it later became part of Hut 4. Later it housed cryptanalyst Nigel de Grey and his Intelligence Exchange section. In April 1943, Hut 12 became the Education Hut, holding music concerts.

Block C
A huge clerical index was created by punching onto cards using Hollerith machines. Clerical staff built up a cross-referencing system to help the codebreakers, detailing names of personnel, locations and units. Each week, up to 2 million cards were used; they were stored in thousands of brown cardboard boxes. Each card was photographed and sent to the Bodleian Library in Oxford as a back up.

The stable block
The garages housed the military vehicles, ambulances and carrier pigeons; three linked cottages became staff accommodation; the former fruit store became Turing and Knox's 'think-tank' room, known as 'the bungalow'.

What the senior staff's offices are believed to have looked like

The British used Typex cipher machines from 1937

huts. These teams were led by Dilly Knox, John Jeffreys, Peter Twinn and Alan Turing. The first breakthrough came with the unravelling of the administrative key used by the German Army, simply known as 'The Green.' This was followed by breaking the 'Red' key, which was used by the Luftwaffe. Of course, it was of paramount importance that the secret that Enigma's code was being broken was kept secure, so a cover MI6 'spy' nicknamed Boniface was invented; throughout the war, Germany believed any breaks in intelligence came as a result of double agents working in the field instead of a remote codebreaking team.

One step ahead

The codebreaking mechanism was industrialized by the Bombe machine, invented by Alan Turing and Gordon Welchman in response to the need to speed up the process of running through all the possible Enigma wheel configurations. Operated by Wrens, the work was hot, smelly and noisy, but it was invaluable. By 1942, Bletchley's success had reached North Africa, where intelligence enabled the Royal Navy to cut Rommel's supply lines and keep General Montgomery informed of his every move. Early that year, however, the Germans introduced a more complex Enigma machine with an extra rotor. This caused a major information blackout and proved to be one of the greatest challenges to the codebreakers at Bletchley. However, by the end of 1942, the codebreakers had cracked that one too thanks to the bravery of the seamen Fasson and Grazier ,who captured vital Enigma keys and books from the sinking U-559. From now on Bletchley was able to read 'Shark'.

However, it was the breaking of the German's strategic ciphers that gave Bletchley arguably its greatest success. Initially, manual efforts enabled the cracking of these ciphers, used by Hitler to communicate with Berlin and his commanders in the field. Professor Max Newman realized a new type of machine was needed to keep up with the increasing volume of intercepts being received.

With the help of a brilliant young General Post Office (GPO) engineer, Tommy Flowers, such a machine was designed and constructed. This became known as Colossus: the world's first semi-programmable electronic computer, and it became essential to the planning by Allied forces for the looming invasion of Europe – codenamed Operation Overlord.

Such successes were hoped for at that first 'shooting party' at the mansion in 1938, but, certainly in the beginning, there were many – even within the government itself – who doubted the impact codebreakers could make to the strategic planning of the war. Of these codebreakers, perhaps the most famous known today is Alan Turing. He may have looked and even acted like a true eccentric, but he possessed one of the finest brains of his generation, and his unique ideas for a Universal Turing Machine undoubtedly laid the groundwork not only for the development of the electronic machines built inside Bletchley as the war progressed, but also for the concept of the computer age. Even in a setting such as Bletchley that was filled with great minds he stood out, leading the historian and wartime codebreaker Asa Briggs to comment, "You needed exceptional talent, you needed genius at Bletchley and Turing's was that genius."

Of all his colleagues and codebreakers at Bletchley, his work with Tommy Flowers may have excited Turing the most. They first met in 1939, when the talented young GPO engineer was first introduced to the Enigma secret. Both men were enthusiastic, experts in their fields and respected each other from the outset. Turing would sometimes visit Flowers at his laboratory workshop in Dollis Hill, where they first discussed the idea of building a machine that could decrypt Enigma by using electromagnets. While this would prove to be beyond the scope of the technology then available, Turing's blueprints and vision for such a machine stayed with Flowers and later resulted in Colossus.

Behind this genius was a troubled man, though. The former Cambridge student could be awkward socially and was a homosexual in an age when this was not only frowned upon but actually illegal. He proposed to a colleague at Bletchley, Joan Clarke, who accepted, but he then recanted and told her of his sexuality.

CHURCHILL'S GOLDEN GEESE

Daily boxes of high-level decrypts were sent to Churchill's office in locked boxes, the key to which he carried on his personal key ring. Only a select few in the Foreign Office and the military knew where they had come from, and not all of those shared Churchill's faith in Bletchley Park. During his visit in September 1941 he inspected the machines and huts, meeting senior codebreakers. Afterward, he gathered them outside Hut 6 for a short speech, in which he famously described them as his "geese that lay the golden egg – and never cackled". Recognizing Churchill's support and respect, Bletchley sent him a letter asking for more staff. The prime minister's response was swift and decisive: "Make sure they have all they want on extreme priority and report to me that this has been done. Action this day."

A reconstruction of the Phoenix Bombe at Bletchley Park

Turing became something of an all-purpose consultant for the growing operation and crossed the Atlantic in November 1942, for highest-level liaison not only on the desperate U-boat Enigma crisis, but on the electronic enciphering of speech signals between Roosevelt and Churchill. His genius and contribution to the war effort was never properly acknowledged in his lifetime, though, and in 1952 he faced criminal charges after he struck up a relationship with another man, and was placed on hormonal treatment designed to reduce libido. In 1954, at the age of 42, Turing was found dead in his home in Manchester, having apparently committed suicide by cyanide poisoning.

Alan Turing devised a number of ways for breaking ciphers

Enduring legacy

Today, Turing is rightly celebrated for his many and varied achievements, and a bust of his head sits beside an exhibition of some of his personal effects. In 2009, Prime Minister Gordon Brown apologized on behalf of the government and the nation for Turing's prosecution and publicly acknowledged the debt of gratitude owed to him by the Allies.

The nation and the world's gratitude should be directed at Turing and those he worked with, all of whom passed through Bletchley's nondescript railway station. That station saw so much: the girl who joined the Wrens for the dashing uniform and a chance to serve at sea, who then found herself posted to a place just about as far from the sea as it was possible to get in England. The young man in the middle of his mathematics degree and a renowned chess champion, invited to put aside his studies for the duration, and the secretary, eager to 'do her bit', who applied for a clerical position in London but was found to be fluent in German and instead surprisingly given a train ticket to a small town called Bletchley.

They were ordinary men and women, some barely out of school, whose unique talents and skills were put to use in an extraordinary way. They all came willingly, if a little unknowingly – often via a small, anonymous house in Baker Street, where they signed the Official Secrets Act – to this seemingly insignificant Buckinghamshire town. As they stepped off those trains, they would have had no idea what amazing achievements they would become part of, even if they would never see recognition for it in their lifetime; nor could they have known the legacy they would help bestow on the nation. But come they did: first slowly, in their hundreds, then more and more as Britain faced the horrors of the Blitz, and then battles at Dunkirk and D-Day, until by 1945 there were about 10,000 people working at the Park. Bletchley is where their story begins, a story that can now be told in full and rightfully celebrated by a grateful world.

BLETCHLEY'S THREE GREATEST SUCCESSES

01 Cracking Lorenz

Although the 'Y' Stations were intercepting the German cipher machine Lorenz messages in early 1940, they had no idea how the machine was encrypting them. John Tiltman spotted an operator's repetition with abbreviations in August 1941 and used these small inconsistencies to crack the code. Bill Tutte used mathematical analysis to work out how the Lorenz machine worked without even seeing one, and by 1942 Lorenz messages were being deciphered. Complications to the Lorenz design in 1943 led Max Newman and his team to need to design an entirely new electronic machine that would break Lorenz: the Colossus.

02 The invention of Colossus

Tommy Flowers, a brilliant GPO engineer, built Newman's design and created the world's first electronic semi-programmable computer in December 1943. By the end of the war, the ten Colossus machines in use were ordered to be dismantled, along with all records, but only six were. It had taken weeks to break Lorenz with mathematical calculations: Colossus could do this in hours, reading the paper tape at 5,000 characters a second and sending the tape traveling in the wheels at 30 miles per hour.

03 D-Day

Without Bletchley, D-Day may well have had a different outcome. In June 1944, Colossus helped to fool German high command of Allied plans. As well as providing information on German positions, the breaking of ciphers sent by the German Secret Intelligence Service allowed the Allies to confuse Hitler over where they would land; Hitler decided to divert his troops away from the very beaches the Allies had chosen in Normandy. Bletchley was able to read messages between Garbo (a network of 27 fictitious spies) and the Abwehr, showing Hitler had fallen for the deception.

N1535
A PS
L7026
V

BATTLES

L7026

THEIR FINEST HOUR

As Britain stood alone against Nazi Germany, young fighter pilots of the Royal Air Force defeated the vaunted Luftwaffe in the pivotal Battle of Britain

The Nazi conquest of France and the Low Countries was swift and decisive. In a matter of weeks, the British Expeditionary Force had been ejected from the European continent at Dunkirk and Hitler stood on the brink of total victory.

One significant challenge remained in the West, however. As German troops paraded down the Champs Elysées in Paris, Hitler and his generals contemplated the invasion of Great Britain, the island nation that now stood alone against the Nazi juggernaut in the summer of 1940. For Britain, the situation was grave.

On June 18, Prime Minister Winston Churchill addressed the House of Commons with a warning that the Battle of France was over and the Battle of Britain was about to begin. "Let us therefore brace ourselves to our duties," he intoned, "and so bear ourselves that if the British Empire and its Commonwealth last for a thousand years, men will still say, 'This was their finest hour.'"

German troops and tanks were poised along the coastline of France. Officers gazed across the English Channel at the white cliffs of Dover, a scant 20 miles distant. Hitler and his senior commanders knew that the invasion and conquest of Britain would be their sternest challenge to date. However, they were brimming with confidence as they planned Operation Sea Lion, marshalling barges from Germany and across occupied Europe to ferry combat troops to Britain's shores and considering the prospects for holding the might of the Royal Navy and the Royal Air Force at bay.

Dogfight

One fact was plain: Soldiers could not cross the Channel without the threat of air attack, and Britain's naval might could not be restrained until the Luftwaffe owned the skies over land and sea. Control of the air was a prerequisite to any successful invasion, and Reich Marshal Hermann Göring, chief of the Luftwaffe, assured Hitler that his fighters and bombers would sweep the RAF aside within a few weeks.

Göring gathered more than 1,200 Messerschmitt Me-109 and twin-engine Me-110 fighters and 1,300 bombers for the air assault. The nimble Me-109 was heavily armed and fast; however, fuel consumption as German squadrons flew from bases located from Norway to the Cotentin Peninsula restricted actual time over Britain and the Channel to only about 20 minutes during a typical sortie. The Luftwaffe bombers included a mixed bag of Heinkel He-111, Dornier Do-17, and Junkers Ju-88 aircraft capable of carrying only relatively light bomb loads. The Junkers Ju-87 Stuka dive bomber, a terror weapon that had been effective as flying artillery during the German Army's blitzkrieg across Europe, was quickly proven unsuited for a sustained bombing campaign. So many of the lumbering Stukas were lost to Royal Air Force fighters that the planes were quickly withdrawn from combat.

Opposing the vaunted Luftwaffe, the RAF mustered roughly 700 frontline Hawker Hurricane and Supermarine Spitfire fighters along with other somewhat obsolescent types under the control of RAF Fighter Command led by Air Chief Marshal Hugh Dowding. The Hurricane was slower than the Spitfire, so a cooperative tactic effectively emerged. While the Hurricanes primarily targeted the bomber formations, the sleek, powerful Spitfires matched up with the Me-109s in epic dogfights that have come to symbolize the desperation, heroism, and sacrifice of the RAF during the Battle of Britain.

Air Chief Marshal Trafford Leigh-Mallory led the Big Wing faction of the RAF and later commanded Allied air forces during the 1944 Normandy invasion

As the threat of invasion loomed, Britain's air defense preparations began to pay off. Fighter Command was divided into four defensive sectors, and group headquarters were established to dispense real-time intelligence as Luftwaffe air raids materialized. Headquartered at Uxbridge, Middlesex, No. 11 Group defended London and southeastern England and bore the brunt of the Nazi air onslaught. Number 12 Group at Watnall, Nottinghamshire, defended Wales and the Midlands, while No. 10 Group covered southwestern England and No. 13 Group was charged with the defense of Scotland and northern England.

As the Battle of Britain developed, the RAF came to fully appreciate the value of a new early warning device called radar. A system of radar posts called Chain Home effectively eliminated any hope the Germans had in the element of surprise. Even while under direct Luftwaffe attack, the most sophisticated radar network in the world continued to function.

Hitler shared Reich Marshal Göring's optimism for an easy aerial victory and issued Directive No. 16 tentatively scheduling Operation Sea Lion for August 15, 1940, just over a month after the effort to eradicate the RAF was undertaken. The Germans referred to the opening phase of the Battle of Britain as Kanalkampf, or the Channel Battle. The earliest targets of the Luftwaffe air offensive were shipping and barge traffic in the English Channel, port facilities at Dover and other harbors on the southeastern coast of England, and aircraft manufacturing facilities.

Marauding German bombers sank numerous British merchant ships during more than a

TIMELINE

Miracle at Dunkirk
The evacuation of the British Expeditionary Force, the bulk of British troops on the continent of Europe, and other Allied soldiers is completed at the port of Dunkirk.
June 4, 1940

The Battle begins
The first engagements of the Battle of Britain occur as Luftwaffe planes attack shipping in the English Channel and draw RAF fighters into the air.
July 10,1940

The Greatest Day
RAF fighters claim 75 German planes and lose 30 to enemy fighters while defending against heavy bombing raids on their precious airfields.
August 15, 1940

Bringing bomber pilots
RAF Fighter Command calls for Bomber Command pilots to transfer in order to make good the losses sustained thus far in heavy air combat.
August 17, 1940

The Hardest Day
Called Black Thursday by the Germans, both sides lose heavily during continuous air battles. Losses among Stuka dive bombers are so severe that the planes are withdrawn from combat.
August 18, 1940

Errant bombing
Apparently off course, Luftwaffe bombers drop their deadly cargoes on London, hitting the center of the city, residential areas, factories, and the docks of the East End.
August 24,1940

Defining moment
Der Adlertag
August 13, 1940
On Eagle Day, the Luftwaffe stages large-scale raids against targets in England, including radar stations and airfields. RAF fighters shoot down 46 German planes.

RIVALRY IN THE SKIES

Air Chief Marshal Hugh Dowding is rightly given the lion's share of credit for the RAF victory in the Battle of Britain. However, for Dowding it came at personal cost. In the midst of the fighting, a difference in tactical perspective emerged within the highest echelons of the RAF. Dowding pursued a Fabian strategy, avoiding major air battles that might cripple Fighter Command beyond repair. Meanwhile, another RAF faction, the Big Wing advocates, championed large, set-piece encounters with the Luftwaffe. While Dowding was supported by Air Vice Marshal Keith Park of No. 11 Group, their opponents were powerful, including Air Chief Marshal Trafford Leigh-Mallory of No. 12 Group. The debate rages, but on November 24, leadership of Fighter Command passed to Marshal of the Royal Air Force Sholto Douglas, a Big Wing supporter.

Air Chief Marshal Hugh Dowding, who won the battle but lost the command due to tactical disagreements

month of Kanalkampf raids, and the Royal Navy relocated most of its ships and personnel westward from Dover to Portsmouth. On July 25, Stukas ravaged a convoy transporting coal. When RAF fighters intervened, the Germans lost 16 aircraft and the British seven. Two weeks later, German bombers sank four ships and damaged six others in a 20-ship convoy. RAF fighters shot down 31 German planes but lost 19 of their own.

Death in the skies

At first, the Admiralty directed that all convoys embark only at night, but subsequently the decision was made to discontinue Channel convoys and transport cargo by rail where. Still, despite pitched dogfights and daily encounters, the Luftwaffe failed to sufficiently erode the defensive strength of the RAF.

Round two of the preparation for the invasion of England was postponed several times due to poor flying weather. Finally, August 13, 1940, was designated as Der Adlertag, or Eagle Day. The objective of the renewed Luftwaffe offensive was the destruction of RAF Fighter Command during days of unrelenting air combat. Still confident of victory, Luftwaffe pilots often sang a jaunty tune with the lyric, "Wir fliegen gegen England," or "We are flying against England."

Although the Germans were aware that Chain Home radar stations provided the RAF – particularly Air Vice Marshal Keith Park's No. 11 Group – with some measure of early warning, they never fully grasped the significance of the network in RAF fighter deployment and readiness. Hitting the radar stations was, however, an initial component of Adlertag and the following two weeks.

The continuing effort to bring the RAF to its knees included the systematic bombing of its airfields scattered across southern and central England, the destruction of the 300-foot towers and installations of the Chain Home radar network, and the elimination of the planes and pilots of Fighter Command once and for all.

During Adlertag three radar stations were hit by Luftwaffe bombers, knocking them off the air for only six hours as a lack of planned

Defining moment
"To so few"
August 20, 1940
Prime Minister Winston Churchill tells the House of Commons, "Never in the field of human conflict has so much been owed by so many to so few."

follow-up attacks allowed Chain Home to recover. Airfields in the south were attacked. On Adlertag the Germans lost 46 planes and the RAF just 13. However, days of intense aerial combat followed.

By August 15-16, the air battles above England had reached fever pitch as the number of combined combatant sorties neared 2,700. Scores of RAF and Luftwaffe planes were seen tangled in the skies. On the 15th, later known as "The Greatest Day," RAF pilots destroyed 75 German planes and lost 30 of their own.

August 18, known to the British as "The Hardest Day" and to the Germans as "Black Thursday," left RAF commanders deeply concerned with the staying power of their planes and pilots while Hitler's confidence in his aerial might was shaken. The Luftwaffe lost 69 planes, the RAF 68. Raids on British airfields continued with telling effect. At RAF Kenley in Surrey, all 10 hangars were demolished. A dozen planes, including 10 precious Hurricanes, were destroyed, and bombs cratered runways.

Scuppering Sea Lion

In ten days of aerial combat from August 8-18, the RAF lost 175 planes, while Luftwaffe losses reached a staggering 332 aircraft. Although its losses were only about half those of the

RAF retaliates
In response to the Luftwaffe bombing of London, 40 RAF bombers attack Berlin, the Nazi capital, causing Hitler to change tactics during the Battle of Britain.
August 25, 1940

Debden Airfield hit
Hit by at least 100 German bombs, RAF Debden, located in Essex northeast of London, endures its third Luftwaffe air raid.
August 31, 1940

The Blitz begins
The Luftwaffe sends 400 bombers escorted by 600 fighters to attack the docks of London's East End. Raids occur around the clock, and later the Luftwaffe switches to nocturnal attacks.
September 7, 1940

Sea Lion denied
Aware that the Luftwaffe cannot achieve air superiority over Britain, the RAF, and the English Channel, Hitler postpones and eventually cancels Operation Sea Lion, the proposed invasion of the British Isles.
September 17, 1940

Last great gasp
Three coordinated Luftwaffe air raids hit London, Portsmouth, and other targets in the last large-scale attacks of the Battle of Britain, although the Blitz continues against British cities.
October 29, 1940

Final victory
Generally accepted as the end of the Battle of Britain, air operations are hampered by bad weather, and Luftwaffe attacks are no longer daily events.
October 31, 1940

Luftwaffe, the RAF was strained to breaking point. Some replacement pilots were procured from Bomber Command, and the pace of new fighter production peaked.

On August 20, at the height of the great air battle, Churchill rose once again in the House of Commons. He offered, "The gratitude of every home in our Island, in our Empire, and indeed throughout the world, except in the abodes of the guilty, goes out to the British airmen who, undaunted by odds, unwearied in their constant challenge and mortal danger, are turning the tide of the World War by their prowess and by their devotion. Never in the field of human conflict was so much owed by so many to so few."

The prime minister's stirring words touched the people of Britain, the fighting pilots of the RAF who came to be known as "The Few," and the free world. Still, the issue remained in doubt. By the end of the month, six out of seven main RAF bases in southeastern England had been severely damaged. Nevertheless, the RAF had given Hitler pause. On September 3, Operation Sea Lion, already postponed once, was delayed another three weeks.

While Luftwaffe daylight raids against RAF installations and manufacturing facilities continued, Göring also directed nocturnal attacks against military targets across Britain. However, major cities were not targeted due to the certainty of RAF retaliation against German population centers. On the night of August 24, a few Luftwaffe bombers drifted off course, dropping their bombs on London. The following night, RAF bombers hit Berlin.

Hitler flew into a rage and directed a new strategy, demaning a campaign of terror bombing to break the fighting spirit of the British people. On September 7, German bombers appeared over London in strength. More than 2,000 civilians were killed or wounded in the ensuing raid, which marked the start of 57 consecutive nights on which the city was mercilessly ravaged.

The Luftwaffe's refocus on British cities did not fully suspend daylight operations. However, Fighter Command was given the opportunity to rest and refit. Then the turning point in

Defining moment
Battle of Britain Day
September 15, 1940
Heavy Luftwaffe raids target London, but RAF fighters shoot down 80 enemy aircraft, wresting the initiative from the Germans during the Battle of Britain

the struggle for air superiority occurred. Two massive raids were launched against targets in Britain on September 15. The RAF put 300 fighters into the air and shot down 80 enemy planes. The Luftwaffe could not sustain such losses; the number and size of further raids were curtailed. The date is still commemorated annually as "Battle of Britain Day."

The catastrophe prompted Hitler to cancel Operation Sea Lion indefinitely two days later. He then ordered the barges and other naval craft assembled for the cross-Channel invasion to disperse. By mid-October, it was clear that the Royal Air Force had won the Battle of Britain and saved the nation from a Nazi invasion.

Casualties during four months of aerial combat included nearly 1,600 RAF airmen killed and over 400 wounded with 1,744 planes lost. The Luftwaffe suffered 2,600 dead, 735 wounded, and more than 900 taken prisoner. Nearly 2,000 German planes were destroyed.

Although the Nazi war machine had been slowed in the skies over England, the Luftwaffe continued its terror bombing campaign for months. However, London was not the only city to suffer the wrath of Hitler and the Luftwaffe.

On November 14, 1940, Coventry was assailed by 400 bombers, whose deadly payloads killed 568 people and injured another 1,200. Liverpool, Manchester, Birmingham, and others were subjected to intense air raids. The Blitz, as it came to be known, lasted for months, until May 1941.

By then Hitler had already concluded that Britain would never buckle under an aerial assault. British cities had burned and crumbled, thousands had perished, and yet the RAF remained resolute. The Führer turned away from the stubborn island and its courageous people, for he had other targets in mind. Operation Barbarossa, the Nazi invasion of the Soviet Union, was only weeks away. The Battle of Britain was won, but others were just beginning.

THE BLOODIEST BATTLE IN HISTORY

The outcome of WWII and the fate of the Third Reich was decided in the bloodied ruins of Stalingrad

The pivotal battle of WWII was fought in the Soviet city of Stalingrad. While not the most strategically vital location for either side, its very name made it a point of obsession for both Hitler and Stalin. When the guns finally fell silent among the ruins in February 1943, over 1 million Wehrmacht and Soviet soldiers, not to mention innocent Soviet civilians, lay dead.

The idea of Stalingrad's capture began to germinate in Hitler's mind in April 1942, following the petering out of the Soviet counter-offensive that prevented the Wehrmacht taking Moscow. The objective was to take the city before racing on to secure the oilfields in the Caucasus beyond, simultaneously securing a vital supply for the German armies while cutting off the Soviet's access to it. With the Soviet offensive at Kharkov defeated in May, the path to Stalingrad lay open.

As General Timoschenko's battered forces retreated in the face of two German panzer armies (the 17th under Ewald von Kleist and the 6th under Friedrich Paulus) a Stalingrad Front was declared by the Soviets, which they frantically raced to fill with reserve forces from Moscow. The race was on to adequately prepare the city for the German onslaught. But it would not just be the soldiers who would be required to defend Stalingrad.

Almost 200,000 civilians were mobilized and organized into workers columns to dig anti-tank ditches up to six feet deep while army sappers laid mines. Even schoolchildren were deployed to construct earth walls around the precious petrol tanks along the Volga River. Anti-aircraft batteries were formed by young women, with guns situated on both banks of the Volga in order to defend vital positions such as the Beketavka power station and the infamous Tractor Factory, which had been converted to build the much-feared T-34 tanks. Every single pair of hands would be needed if total annihilation was to be averted.

Overall command of the operation to save Stalingrad fell to the ruthless General Vasiliy Chuikov. Notorious for his incredibly explosive temper, Chuikov worked tirelessly to raise the morale of his beleaguered troops while instilling terror into any commanders that dared to imagine retreat. Any deserters would be shot without hesitation.

Chuikov's approach to the perilous situation was simple: "Time is blood." The longer the

coming battle raged, the more it would cost the Germans. Every obstacle was to be placed in their way. Even immobile tanks were dug into positions to provide fire. If Stalingrad was to be taken, it would be inch by blood-soaked inch.

Firestorm

Having battled across the Don River on August 21, the Germans began their assault on Stalingrad on the August 23 even before they'd reached the Volga. Under the command of General von Ricthofen, the entire 4th Air Fleet, comprising 1,200 aircraft (both Junkers 88 and Heinkel 111 bombers) headed for Stalingrad to ignite a biblical inferno. In a total of 1,600 sorties, Richthofen's pilots dropped approximately 1,000 tons of explosives, losing only three planes in the process. Thousands of civilians died in the carnage, still in the city due to Stalin's refusal to evacuate them for fear of spreading mass panic. Wooden houses were reduced to ash as apartment blocks were either gutted or collapsed entirely. By indiscriminately carpet-bombing the entire city, the Luftwaffe hit the hospital, waterworks and telephone lines, as well as bombing the petrol tanks lining the river, sending flames 1,500 feet into the blackened sky above Stalingrad.

With what was to become a lengthy bombardment now underway, the 16th Panzer Division surged across the steppe toward the city. Despite the efforts of the anti-aircraft batteries, who rained 37mm (1.5in) shells down upon the invaders, the panzer crews pressed on, aided by Stuka aircraft. By the afternoon of the 23rd they reached the Volga.

Sergeant Yakov Fedotovich Pavlov became a hero after his platoon recaptured and aggressively defended a building that came to be known as 'Pavlov's House'

Confident that such a pulverizing would have broken the Soviet's will and ability to resist, the Germans anticipated a relatively swift victory. But in a dark twist of irony, they had actually helped to sow the seeds of their own downfall. The churned up remains of Stalingrad would prove to be a cramped killing field in which snipers and close-quarters fighting ruled. This was no place for the rapid, sweeping maneuvers favored by the Germans.

In the days that followed the terror bombing, General Hoth's forces slowly trudged forward, pushing the Russian 64th Army back. Emboldened by the relatively weak Soviet resistance in the lead up to the assault, Paulus decided to send his men straight into the fray upon their arrival instead of allowing them to rest. As Germans fed into the streets, so did Soviet reinforcements.

The situation facing the Soviets was utterly dire, so desperate in fact, that as their men ran toward the enemy, machine gun posts were set up behind them. Their choice was clear: die fighting or die retreating. The fact that they had to rely on supplies shipped across the Volga under heavy German fire didn't help either.

Working in tandem with their pilot colleagues, the panzers continued to fight their way through the city, all the while conscious of the vulnerability of their tanks in the narrow streets. By August 31, the Germans were at the Stalingrad-Morozask railway. Paulus now firmly believed that the Russian 62nd and 64th armies could be divided and finished off.

The arrival of Marshal Georgy Zhukov two days earlier had again revealed the scale of the task facing the Soviets. Morale was

The four-storey Pavlov's House became a symbol of Stalingrad's resistance to the bloody German assault

DEFENDING PAVLOV'S HOUSE

The siege of Pavlov's House (named after Sergeant Yakov Pavlov, who contributed to its defense) cost the Germans dearly and became a symbol of the Red Army's will to resist.

Having retaken the four-storey building from the Germans, the soldiers of the 13th Guards Division positioned machine guns in every window and ringed the building with barbed wire and mines. They also discovered that an anti-tank gun on the roof of the building was too high up for the German tanks to fire on.

Overlooking the Volga (from which supplies were brought to the house via a trench), the defenders had a clear view to the north, south and west for a mile. From September 27 until November 25, they managed to repel waves of German assaults until they were relieved by Soviet reinforcements.

The air attacks on Stalingrad began on the third anniversary of the pact that should have prevented them

collapsing under the strain of the German aerial bombardment, with one divisional commander resorting to lining up his men and shooting every tenth one until his gun ran out. Just as the Soviets were preparing to unleash a counter-attack in an attempt to stem the panzer advance, Zhukov began imploring Stalin to delay it.

The marshal discovered the troops assigned to the job were poorly equipped, low on ammunition and predominantly made up of old reservists. Yet despite the obvious flaws in the Red Army, Stalin became increasingly nervous, citing the encroachment of German tanks as the reason that any delay could prove fatal. Zhukov did eventually succeed in gaining an extra two days, but they made little difference, for the advance that proceeded was short-lived.

Fight back

The 1st Guards Army only managed to push on a few miles into the Russian steppe, while the 24th Army literally found itself back at square one, having totally failed to gain any ground. However, the attack had not been completely in vain. It had forced Paulus to divert his reserve forces just as the shattered remains of the 62nd and 64th armies were pushed back to the perimeters of the city. The Germans had paid heavily, losing six battalion commanders in a single day and seeing many companies decimated, some left with as few as 40 men.

From grenades to Molotov cocktails, the Soviets used all available means. Many rushed into the fray without weapons, forced to wait until a comrade fell before taking their rifle. It's no surprise that the life expectancy for a soldier arriving in the city was less than 24 hours.

With fewer than 40,000 fighters left to confront the 6th Army and 4th Panzer Army, the Germans believed that it was simply a matter of time before Stalingrad would fall.

Following a summit with Hitler in his Vinnitsa headquarters, Paulus unleashed the next major assault on September 12. With yet another artillery bombardment and bombing attack having pounded the city beforehand, the Wehrmacht began to make progress, fighting toward the Mamayev Kurgan, a mound overlooking the Volga, also known as Hill 102 on account of its height in metres. Soldiers pressed on to the railway station as Hoth's panzers aimed for the grain elevator.

Stalin ordered that men be sent across the Volga to secure the west bank. The 13th Guards Division lined up to await the journey under German fire. Those that reached the bank leapt from the boats to rush the enemy, knowing that the slightest delay meant death. Close-quarter combat ensued as reinforcements poured in from both sides. The hill was strategically vital; its loss would allow the Germans to control the entire river, across which all of the Soviet supplies had to travel.

Factories of death

The further the Germans advanced the stiffer the resistance they encountered. Every single building had to be fought for, with numerous tales of grossly outnumbered men holding out against wave upon wave of attacks. One of the most well-known examples is Pavlov's House, which is said to have cost the Germans more men than the entire thrust into France. In such

The hill overlooking the city had been of strategic importance as a line of defense for centuries

Defining moment

Battle for the Mamayev Kurgan

September 12 onwards

Aware that the loss of this strategically vital hill would hand the Germans total control of the Volga, Stalin orders troops be sent over to retake it. A bloody struggle for Hill 102 begins.

TIMELINE

● Bombing raid
On the third anniversary of the Molotov-Ribbentrop Pact, the Germans pulverize Stalingrad from the air, killing thousands of people.
August 23, 1942

● Wehrmacht on the Volga
Such is the ferocity of the German assault, Hitler's forces gaze out over the Volga (not the buildings that used to block the view of it) by sunset.
August 23, 1942

● Stalingrad-Morozast railway
The Germans press on, fighting bitterly to reach the key railway line, forcing the desperate Soviets back.
August 31, 1942

● Soviet counter-attack
The Soviets launch a doomed counter-attack in early September, gaining little ground but sparing the remnants of their 62nd and 64th Armies from the German advance.
September 1942

● Fresh German offensive
Paulus begins a new offensive by pounding the city with artillery and aerial bombardments. His men then reach the Mamayev Kurgan.
September 12

● Fighting in the factories
As the Germans continue their march further into the city they reach the industrial district. Fighting erupts as the Soviets struggle to hold key buildings, including the Tractor Factory.
October 4

encounters flamethrowers proved very effective, but it was the snipers, such as the famed Vasily Zaitsev, that reigned supreme among the rubble. Appropriately, the German name for this merciless fighting was Rattenkrieg (Rat War).

By early October the Germans began their assault on the factory district to the north of the city. Many of these installations, including the Red October Complex and the Tractor Factory, had been turned into fortresses, and these changed hands many times as the battle ebbed and flowed. In some instances, the panzers resorted to ramming the buildings to gain entry.

The key positions were finally in German hands come the end of October, but the price paid for them was nothing short of catastrophic. The last heave of the attack has been curtailed by a rain of Katyusha and mortar fire. Just as winter approached the Wehrmacht found itself running out of steam, bled almost dry.

A final attempt at a decisive breakthrough came on November 11. As the Luftwaffe obliterated the factory chimneys, infantry seized buildings from the enemy, only to relinquish them shortly after. Burning tanks littered the streets as the Soviets dug in, some down to their last rounds. Such was their determination, a band of 15 men held off a thrust toward the petrol tanks on the Volga. The tenacity of these courageous men led the Germans to believe that they were fighting "creatures". And it would be these seemingly superhuman warriors that would soon wreak an almighty revenge.

Thanks to the movement of industry back beyond the Volga, Soviet factories were continuing to produce an immense amount of weaponry. Some estimates place monthly tank production, including the much-feared T-34, at 2,200. Hitler not only underestimated his enemy's industrial capacity: he also genuinely believed them to be exhausted and at the very end of their strength.

This hubris made the thunderclap of Operation Uranus all the more stunning. The supposedly spent Soviets had in fact been secretly amassing a gargantuan force with which to launch a staggeringly ambitious flanking attack of brutal simplicity. A main assault force would set off over 100 miles west of Stalingrad, while another horde of troops struck out from south of the Don River as an armored thrust launched from the south of the charred city. On the morning of November 19, a huge Soviet bombardment opened fire as the snow fell. The Germans, supported by Italian and Romanian troops, didn't know what hit them. The encirclement of the 6th Army had begun, and would culminate in its destruction. Hitler's refusal to allow Paulus' men to retreat, combined with Göring's insistence that the Luftwaffe could keep the entrapped soldiers supplied, cemented their doom. By the first days of February 1943, Stalingrad was silent.

The horrific battle for the city is the bloodiest in human history and bore witness to animalistic fighting. In the words of Winston Churchill: "Stalingrad was the end of the beginning". It proved to be a traumatic reversal from which the Wehrmacht never fully recovered. The Red Army would march for Berlin. With over two years of conflict ahead, the outcome of WWII had already been settled in the ruins of Stalin's city, the fate of Hitler's Third Reich permanently sealed.

Bombing raids and their attendant firestorms left Stalingrad a pulverized ruin, but the city fought on

Defining moment

Germans attempt final breakthrough

November 11

Running out of supplies and shattered by the fighting, Paulus attempts to finally end the battle. The Germans force their way forward, taking many buildings from the Soviets but failing to deliver a knockout blow.

The Sniper Movement
As the anniversary of the October Revolution nears a cult of 'sniperism' begins to emerge, with Vasily Zaitsev at its head. Zaitsev, who killed 225 enemy soldiers during the battle, begins to train young snipers.
Mid-October

The fall of the factories
After almost a month, the Germans finally have overall control of the area. However, Soviet defenders remain in the vicinity, with some of them even left inside the Tractor Factory.
Late October

Operation Uranus
With approximately 1 million men amassed over 100 miles from Stalingrad, the Soviets begin a huge encirclement operation, hoping to trap the Germans in the city and out on the steppe.
November 19

The net begins to close
Paulus is horrified to hear that the approaching Soviet forces now threaten both flanks of his 6th Army.
November 21

A panicked withdrawal
Paulus swiftly abandons his headquarters as Soviet tanks approach. General Walther von Seydlitz orders two infantry divisions to burn their supplies and retreat from Stalingrad.
November 21

Hitler dooms the 6th Army
With hope of a breakout fading fast, Hitler issues an order to the trapped 6th Army that, "Surrender is out of the question. Troops must fight on to the end."
January 22, 1943

The 6th Army surrenders
Paulus' trapped forces begin to surrender. Approximately 91,000 troops are taken into captivity. Only 5,000 ever made it back to Germany.
January 31 - February 2, 1943

MIDWAY

THE BATTLE THAT TURNED THE WAR IN THE PACIFIC

"IN THOSE SEVEN MINUTES EVERYTHING CHANGED IN WHAT WAS REALLY THE AMERICAN TRAFALGAR AND WHICH SAW THE IMPERIAL JAPANESE FLEET ANNIHILATED"

Main image: *A still from the movie Midway, which is available on Digital Download, 4K Ultra HD, Blu-ray and DVD*

At 10.20am on the morning of June 4, 1942, the US was losing the war in the Pacific. By 10.27am, it was winning. In those seven minutes everything changed in what was really the American Trafalgar and which saw the Imperial Japanese Fleet annihilated in a spectacular confrontation that was dramatically unexpected. It's an incredible story, and it's no wonder it became the subject of a movie in 2019.

When the Japanese entered the war with their assault on Pearl Harbor in Hawaii on the morning of December 7, 1941, it's important to understand what it was they were trying to achieve. There was certainly no grand plan to conquer the United States and take over the White House. Rather, it was about creating time; the idea was to cripple the US in a dramatic single strike to buy them perhaps six months or more – time in which they would conquer the resource base they would need to continue their war in China. By the 1930s, Japan was rapidly modernizing, and yet it did not have the resources to support this growth. China, on the other hand, most certainly did, and so its increasingly nationalistic and militaristic leadership invaded in 1937. It did not all go to plan, however, and they soon became bogged down in an attritional conflict that quickly began to cost them a lot more than they were gaining.

All around South East Asia, however, were the resources they needed, but these territories were owned by the British, the Dutch and the Americans. In 1940, following the fall of France to the Germans, the Japanese had moved into French Indochina (now Vietnam), a strike that greatly unsettled the Western powers. Most of Japan's oil and steel was provided by the US, who responded to Japanese aggression by making it far harder for them to continue buying these essential goods. This put Japan in a difficult position. Either they had to back down, pull out of Indochina and even China, with the loss of face and economic catastrophe that would entail, or come up with an alternative plan to get them out of the mire. When Prime Minister Konoe resigned in November 1941 and Hideki Tojo took over, the die was cast.

Tojo was an ultra-nationalist and war hawk who believed that for all America's might and wealth, culturally, the US did not have the stomach for a fight. The Japanese might have been materially weak, but they did have a modern, highly trained navy. Mentally and psychologically, they also believed they were superior. And so the idea of a strike on Pearl Harbor was born – a daring attack that would knock out the US Pacific Fleet in one blow and buy them precious time.

An audacious ambush

The attack on Pearl Harbor was the idea of Admiral Isoroku Yamamoto, a highly cultured man who had studied in the US and who was opposed to Japan going to war. However, he believed this gambler's throw of the dice was the only way in which Japan could solve the conundrum in which it found itself. It was daring, it was bold, but it was also flawed because back on November 27, 1941, Admiral Husband Kimmel, commander-in-chief of the Pacific Fleet on Hawaii, was warned by Washington that war with Japan loomed. Kimmel responded by sending two of his four aircraft carriers out of Pearl Harbor to the Pacific outposts of Midway and Wake, two small atolls turned into military bases. A third carrier was undergoing a refit and the fourth was serving in the Atlantic.

USS Yorktown is hit by a Japanese aerial torpedo during the mid-afternoon attack in the Battle of Midway, June 4, 1942

The Japanese attacking Pearl Harbor caused untold damage: 353 aircraft operating from their own carriers achieved total surprise, their torpedo bombers crippling the US Pacific Fleet while dive-bombers hammered the island's airfield. Within minutes all eight battleships had been hit. A further 171 aircraft in the second wave roared in to attack a short while later, so that where once there had been 'Battleship Row' there was now a mass of twisted metal, angry flames and billowing smoke – and a lot of dead American servicemen. On the airfields, 188 aircraft were destroyed and a further 159 damaged. Also hit were three cruisers, three destroyers and three other vessels.

Witnesses were stunned by how low the Japanese pilots flew. "Hell, I could even see the gold in their teeth," observed one army officer. "It was like being engulfed in a great flood, a tornado or earthquake," said another. "The thing hit so quickly and so powerfully it left you stunned and amazed."

Pearl Harbor was seen as a terrific success in Japan, although not by Yamamoto, who was hugely disappointed. He understood that a shift had taken place in naval warfare – that battleships were no longer the pre-eminent warship but rather that mantle had been passed to aircraft carriers, and for all Pearl Harbor's success, not one American carrier had been hit. Yamamoto understood that his navy simply had to destroy those carriers and so immediately began planning how he might get them, and Midway, he believed, held the key.

He would not target the tiny Midway atoll for invasion but rather use it as bait. By threatening this vital US base, the Americans, he hoped, would be forced to defend it and send their carriers. And when they did, his superior force would pounce and destroy them.

Luring the enemy

First, though, the Japanese Army, supported by the Navy, had to consolidate its own position in the Pacific and South East Asia. Malaya, Singapore, the Dutch East Indies, Burma and the US Philippines were all overrun in an astonishing series of rapid and extremely violent strikes. The ABDA command (American, British, Dutch and Australian) was both under-prepared and caught off guard and had no answer, but while the Japanese might have appeared unstoppable, the threat from the rapidly growing US armed forces, and especially its navy, had in no way gone away.

Meanwhile, the US was also planning how to strike back. American strategy in the Pacific was led by Admiral Ernest King, the head of the US Navy. His approach was clear and based around two fundamental factors: first, Hawaii could not be allowed to fall, and second, nor

The pilots of the US Marine Corps scout bomber squadron VMSB-241

A US Navy Grumman F4F-3 in early 1942

Source: Wiki / PD U.S. Navy

could Australia. He ordered Admiral Chester Nimitz, who had replaced Kimmel, to make his first priority to secure the seaways between Hawaii and the island of Midway, just to the east of the international dateline, and the North American mainland. His second priority was to make safe the routes to Australia. Fiji and the Samoan and Tonga Islands needed to be made secure as crucial strong points along the way, and from these bases a counter-offensive could be then launched up through the Solomons, New Guinea, Borneo and then, in time, the Philippines. It was the correct strategy.

On February 1, the US Navy's fightback had gotten underway with a series of raids on shipping and airfields on the Japanese-held Marshall Islands. Although the material damage was less than had at first been thought, it had taught the Americans vital lessons and got the fightback underway.

In April 1942, they launched the Doolittle Raid, flying sixteen B-25 bombers from the carrier USS Hornet and bombing ten different targets on Japan, including Tokyo. While the physical damage was small, the psychological impact was huge as it made the Japanese realize they were not impervious to attack themselves. It also ensured the Japanese Army, which was a ferocious rival of the Navy, now agreed to support Yamamoto's plan to lure the Americans at Midway.

Further US carrier raids were mounted, but the first major naval clash came in May 1942. The Japanese now wanted to disrupt Allied plans by invading and occupying Port Moresby in New Guinea, to the north of Australia, and also the island of Tulagi in the Solomons. Crucially, American cryptanalysts had broken Japanese codes, and learning of the plan, a joint US-Australian naval force of carriers and cruisers was sent to intercept and frustrate the Japanese assault.

Tulagi was invaded on May 3-4, but the Japanese had been surprised to come under attack by American aircraft from the carrier Yorktown. They now advanced to meet the Allied naval forces, clashing in the Coral Sea on May 7.

Shoot 'em down!

This was the first battle in which aircraft carriers engaged one another, and both the Americans and Japanese lost one each and suffered damage to the others. On May 8, US radar screens picked up enemy aircraft heading toward USS Lexington and Task Force 17, and her Wildcat fighters were scrambled to meet them. Then, at 11.13am, lookouts spotted the black dots of enemy aircraft. As they approached, the attacking torpedo bombers

"WHILE THE PHYSICAL DAMAGE WAS SMALL, THE PSYCHOLOGICAL IMPACT WAS HUGE AS IT MADE THE JAPANESE REALIZE THEY WERE NOT IMPERVIOUS TO ATTACK"

US Navy aircraft carrier USS Yorktown shortly after it was hit by Japanese bombs on June 4, 1942

split into two groups while enemy dive-bombers peeled over and down toward the Lexington, which was now frantically taking swerving evasive action. The enemy planes met a wall of anti-aircraft fire as well as the Wildcats.

"It seemed impossible we could survive our bombing and torpedo runs," said Lieutenant Commander Shigekazu Shimazaki, the Japanese attack commander. "Our Zeroes and enemy Wildcats spun, dove, and climbed in the midst of our formations. Burning and shattered planes of both sides plunged from the skies."

Despite the heroic defense, Lexington was hit by both bombs and torpedoes, but amazingly, fire-damage parties managed to restore her to sea-going order before a series of explosions ensured the mighty carrier would have to be abandoned and scuttled.

With both sides suffering heavy losses of aircraft as well as ships, the battle ended as dusk fell on the second day of battle. Crucially, the Battle of the Coral Sea ensured the Japanese were forced to abandon their plans to invade New Guinea.

Forewarning the fleet

Admiral Yamamoto is rightly feted as an inspirational and enlightened commander, but his plan for Midway was too complicated at a time when it did not need to be. At this stage of the war, the Japanese had both quantitative and qualitative superiority over the Americans: their torpedo bombers were better, their pilots were better trained, and they had more warships than the Americans. But these advantages would not last, as Yamamoto was well aware, which was why Midway presented a golden opportunity to set the US Navy back not just by six months but potentially much longer. In the intervening time, the Japanese could further extend their defensive ring. With luck, Yamamoto hoped the Americans would then sue for peace and the Japanese would be left alone, now resource-rich and able to finish a victorious war with China.

His plan was to entice the US Pacific Fleet into battle by separating his forces, with his carriers and battleships several hundred miles apart. The plan was to attack the enemy carriers and then follow up with his battleships and cruisers, who would then engage whatever American ships remained.

Just as Japanese intelligence was poor, however, US intelligence was excellent. American code-breakers had intercepted and cracked enough Japanese naval signal traffic to give them a picture of what the enemy was up to. It was Admiral Nimitz's responsibility to interpret this intelligence picture and work out what to do about it. He knew the Japanese had four or five carriers and that he had three. On the other hand, he could use the airfield of Midway as an unsinkable carrier, which

US Navy Torpedo Squadron 6 and Douglas TBD-1 Devastator aircraft are prepared for launching aboard the aircraft carrier USS Enterprise

potentially evened it up. Even so, his decision to take on the Japanese was a huge one and massive risk, albeit a carefully calculated one.

It was perhaps more so because his main carrier task force admiral, Bill Halsey, was ill, which left him short of a carrier commander. He filled the post with Admiral Ray Spruance, who was hugely competent but whose experience lay with commanding cruisers, not carriers. Spruance was appointed at the last minute and headed out to take command of Halsey's two carriers in what was unquestionably going to prove a decisive clash against the Japanese. Admiral Jack Fletcher was overall US commander at sea.

War on the waves

The clash began on June 4 with the Japanese sending their carrier air forces to attack Midway. Because they had no idea the Americans had cracked their codes, they had been expecting to catch the US air forces napping on the atoll, but in fact the American bomber force had already taken off to attack the Japanese carriers. Yet the first American air strike on the Japanese carriers was a disaster. US naval air forces – a combination of heavy bombers and torpedo bombers – were arriving from Midway at different times rather than as a concentrated mass. Japanese naval fighters were scrambled, and because of their superior skill and capabilities, picked them off with ease. The American torpedo bombers missed entirely and were largely slaughtered. Then the B-17 heavy bombers from Midway arrived, but they were too high, too inaccurate, and although from 20,000 feet up the carriers below had disappeared behind huge fountains of water, not one had been hit.

At this point the Japanese were unquestionably winning the battle, and with it the war in the Pacific. But it was now time for the US carriers to launch their strike force.

Radio intelligence reaching the carriers suggested a location for two of the Japanese carriers but not the remaining pair. All three US carriers were now ordered to send in their own aircraft to attack the Japanese, but the commander of USS Hornet ordered his men to head in a different direction to look for the missing enemy carriers. It was a hunch, and, as it turned out, an entirely wrong one too. This meant that with the Midway air forces effectively destroyed, and Hornet's force heading in the wrong direction, the US now had only two carriers against four Japanese – and so dramatically slashing the odds of success.

The trouble was, those aircraft could not find the Japanese either, and fuel was starting to get a bit low. Commanding the dive-bombing squadrons from USS Enterprise was Lieutenant Commander Wade McClusky, with a further squadron from Yorktown. McClusky was determined not to turn for home without having spotted the Japanese carrier fleet. His courage paid off, because in the nick of time, he spotted the wake of a Japanese destroyer going at speed and realized it had to be trying to rejoin the main force. Instantly ordering his men to head in the direction the destroyer was steaming, sure enough, at 10.22am they spotted the Japanese carriers. And there weren't two of them but all four.

Japanese prisoners of war on board USS Ballard after being rescued from a lifeboat two weeks after the Battle of Midway

Sea of metal

Ahead of McClusky's bombers, however, was one squadron of torpedo bombers from Hornet, commanded by Lieutenant Commander Jack Waldron, who had disobeyed the orders and flown his men toward where he believed the enemy carriers would be. He had been quite right but was about to pay a terrible price. Once again, Japanese naval fighters and gunners on board the ships made mincemeat of the American torpedo bombers, and all 15 were shot down; Waldron was among those killed.

Yet the sacrifice of the torpedo squadron gave a glimmer of hope to the bombers, because with the Japanese fighters focusing on the torpedo squadron as they attacked at low level, McClusky's 30 dive-bombers, as well as the 15 from Yorktown, were left alone. Despite anti-aircraft fire, the dive-bombers now had a fairly clear run. The two squadrons from Enterprise were ordered by McClusky to split in two and attack two of the Japanese carriers at the same time, but through a miscommunication all 30 began diving toward Kaga. Realizing the mistake, Lieutenant Dick Best and two of his wingmen, swung north to attack Akagi. Meanwhile, Kaga was struck between four and five times, with one bomb hitting near the bridge and killing the carrier's commander and senior officers.

A few minutes later, Best and his wingmen were diving on Akagi. Although only hit once, and by Best, it was a fatal strike as it penetrated the deck into the main hanger causing a massive explosion and fires. Another bomb had damaged the rudder.

Two aircraft carriers had been destroyed in a matter of minutes and now it was the turn of Yorktown's dive-bombers, commanded by Max Leslie, this time targeting Soryu, and hit it three times. Three carriers had been stopped dead in the water, their aircraft destroyed and each one now a floating inferno. The fourth carrier managed to survive the onslaught and soon after launched a counter-attack, hitting and crippling Yorktown. Later that afternoon, however, after a scout plane from Yorktown located the final carrier, Hiryu, the dive-bombers of Enterprise took off again, found the fourth carrier, and hit the ship four or five times, including a second bomb from Dick Best.

The Japanese abandoned ship and then scuttled the Hiryu, although Rear Admiral Tamon Yamaguchi and the ship's captain, Tomeo Kaku, decided to go down with the vessel. This act of seppuku robbed the Japanese of their best carrier commander.

Although the loss of Hiryu was a terrible further blow for the Japanese, in truth the battle, and arguably the entire Pacific War, had been won in those seven minutes between 10.20am and 10.27am. It had been an astonishing victory by the Americans, who, without doubt, had begun the day as the underdogs. On that one June day, however, Japanese hopes of further consolidation in the Pacific were dashed for ever, their one chance to best the Americans gone.

And just two years later, the US Navy attacked the Japanese island of Saipan with a staggering 24 carriers. Its moment of weakness had been in the initial six months of war, but at Midway, good fortune, brilliant intelligence and bare-faced courage had conspired with Japanese hubris to bring about surely the greatest victory at sea in American history. The Japanese failure at Midway was one for which they would pay dearly, a devastating setback from which they would never recover.

A formation of Grumman TBF-1 Avenger anti-submarine torpedo planes in flight over the Pacific

THE ASSAULT ON FORTRESS EUROPE

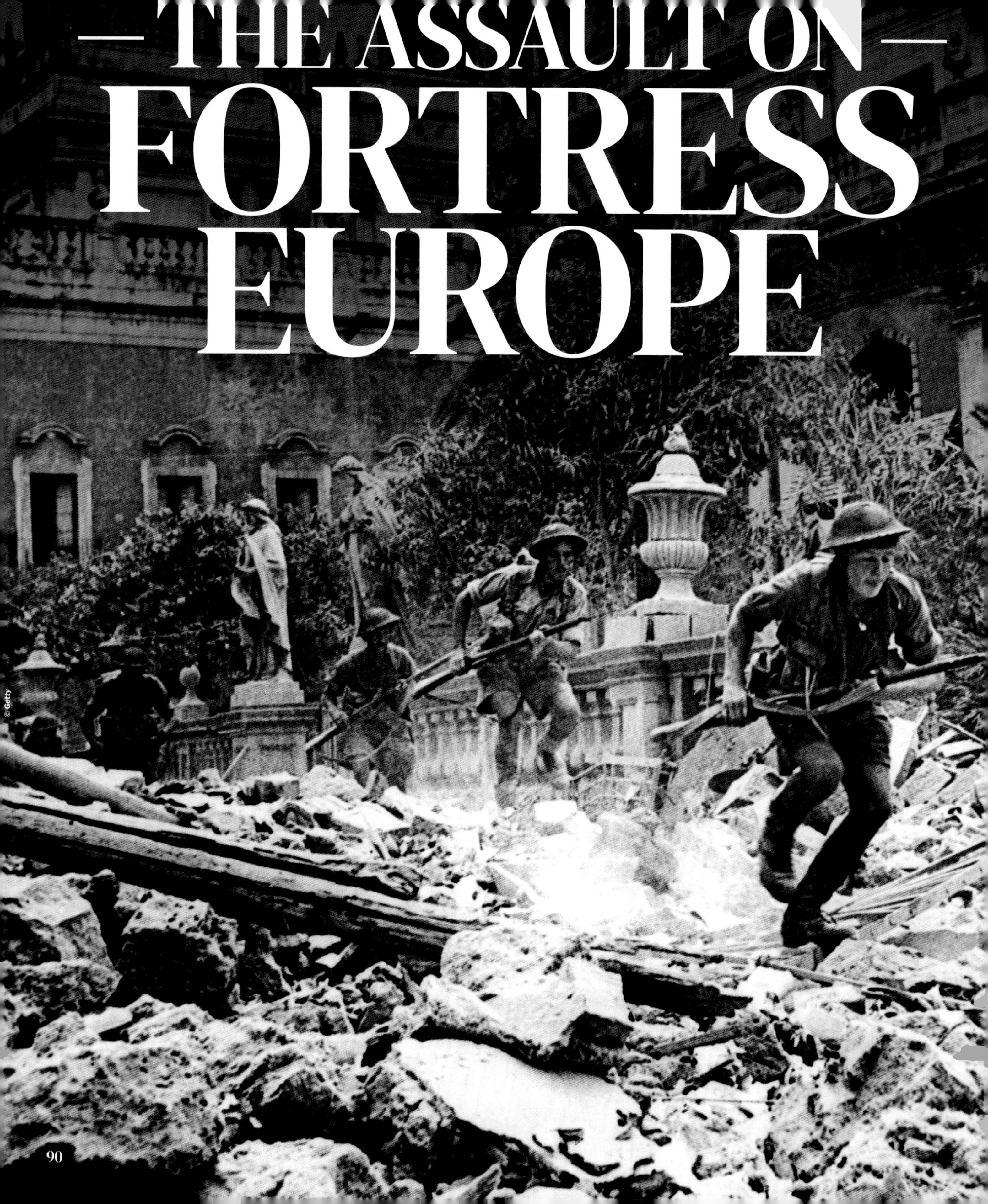

© Getty

A year before the invasion of Normandy, Operation Husky struck the first major blow on Axis soil, with thousands of troops battling against challenging conditions. Here, historian and broadcaster James Holland recounts how the Allies triumphed during this astonishing but often overlooked campaign

In terms of men landed in a single day, Operation Husky, the Allied assault on Sicily on July 10, 1943, remains the largest amphibious invasion ever mounted in the history of the world. More than 160,000 American, British and Canadian troops were dropped from the sky or came ashore that day, more than on D-Day in Normandy just under a year later, or in any of the island battles in the Pacific. It was a remarkable achievement and all the more so since Britain and America had, just three years earlier, almost no armies to speak of and almost no tanks, guns, trucks and other essential equipment.

In many ways, the Battle of Sicily is the moment the Western Allies came of age. It was on Sicily that the British and American coalition began to operate at a war-winning level. Modern warfare by 1943, said General Sir Harold Alexander, commander of all Allied land forces for Sicily, was a correlation of "the three elements we live in: land, air, water. Army, air force and navy must become a brotherhood". At the time, it was only the Western Allies who were bringing these three elements together, and it was to bring about a sea change in how they fought.

Air power, especially, was a vital part of the pre-invasion operations on and around Sicily and continued to play a critical part throughout the entire campaign.

© Getty

US paratroopers being transported to the Allied assault on Sicily

Sand and steel

The 36-day battle for Sicily is an extraordinary story. Its conquest involved the largest airborne operations ever witnessed up to that point, daring raids by special forces, the harnessing of the Mafia, attacks across mosquito-infested plains, assaults up almost sheer faces of rock and scrub, and featured an astonishing array of highly colorful characters, from commanders such as Generals Montgomery and Patton to the German Valentin Hube – nicknamed 'der Mann' – as well as a host of lesser-ranked officers and soldiers, such as Lord Tweedsmuir, the son of John Buchan;

© Getty

Left to right: Field Marshall General Bernard Law Montgomery and General George Smith Patton

Troops from 51st Highland Division unloading stores from landing craft on the opening day of the Allied invasion of Sicily

Philip Mountbatten, later to become the Duke of Edinburgh; and England cricketer Hedley Verity. The legendary Luftwaffe pilot 'Mackay' Steinhoff and the kilt and claymore-wearing Ernst-Günther Baade are two fascinating men who fought on the German side, while hovering in the background was Don Calo Vizzini, the head of the Sicilian Mafia, and Italian-American gangsters Vito Genovese and Lucky Luciano. There were life and death struggles across bridges, plains and mountaintops. It was a period in which fascism was overthrown in Italy, Mussolini was toppled, and in which the pattern for the rest of the war in the West was irrevocably set.

Sicily was, though, a terrible place to fight a battle and especially in the blazing heat of high summer. A Baedeker guide from the 1930s warned that no tourist should consider visiting in the months of July and August, when temperatures were blistering and conditions at their worst – and yet this was precisely when the Sicilian campaign took place. Certainly, it was a brutal campaign in many ways. The violence was extreme, the heat unbearable, the stench of rotting corpses intense and all-pervasive, and the problems of malaria, dysentery and other diseases were a constant plague that affected all trying to fight their way across this island of limited infrastructure, rocky hills, mountains and an all-dominating volcano. Endless dust, dry throats and thirst were constant companions to all those fighting on Sicily.

"THE CAMPAIGN WAS THE BIGGEST BATTLE BEING FOUGHT IN THE WEST AND WAS ON THE FRONT PAGES OF NEWSPAPERS AND HEADLINING NEWS"

At the time, the campaign was the biggest battle being fought in the West and was on the front pages of newspapers and headlining news footage across Europe and the United States. The eyes of the West were on this Italian island, as were those of Nazi Germany. Today it is largely forgotten about, overtaken in the narrative by the battles for Cassino and more especially by D-Day, Normandy and the war in northwest Europe.

The Sicilian campaign also marked a period of dramatic change in the fortunes and tempo of WWII, which marked the end of the Italian participation as an Axis ally, forcing Nazi Germany to considerably extend its active participation on its southern front, as well as witnessing the first major amphibious operation of the war against a defended coastline, and the first coalition operation between the United States and Britain in which both nations fielded entire armies each. A major campaign with far-reaching strategic importance, it was also an important lesson learning exercise before Operation Overlord, the Allied invasion of Normandy in June 1944.

Striking the Axis underbelly

The decision by the Allies to invade Sicily was made at the Casablanca Conference in January 1943, a meeting between British and American war leaders to thrash out a strategy to win the war in the West. By this time, they knew they must surely win in North Africa, and although it had been agreed that they would attempt a cross-Channel invasion of France the following year, in May 1944, there were very good reasons for invading Sicily.

Landing on the island would mean Allied troops would once more be back on European soil; it would help to hustle Italy out of the war for good (if North Africa did not achieve that strategic goal); and it would further tighten the noose around Nazi Germany's neck. In North Africa and the Mediterranean, considerable forces had been built up and they could not sit back and do nothing until the following May.

Complex deception plans were mounted, with a number of sabotage operations in Greece to help point to a landing there, and also Operation Mincemeat (a cunning plan that entailed dropping the corpse of a homeless man dressed in a pilot's uniform into the

English troops take off in a Horsa glider plane for the military offensive in Sicily

A British Universal Carrier Mark I comes ashore during the invasion of Sicily

Crew of M4 Sherman tank 'Eternity' checking the tank after landing at Red Beach 2, Sicily, July 10, 1943

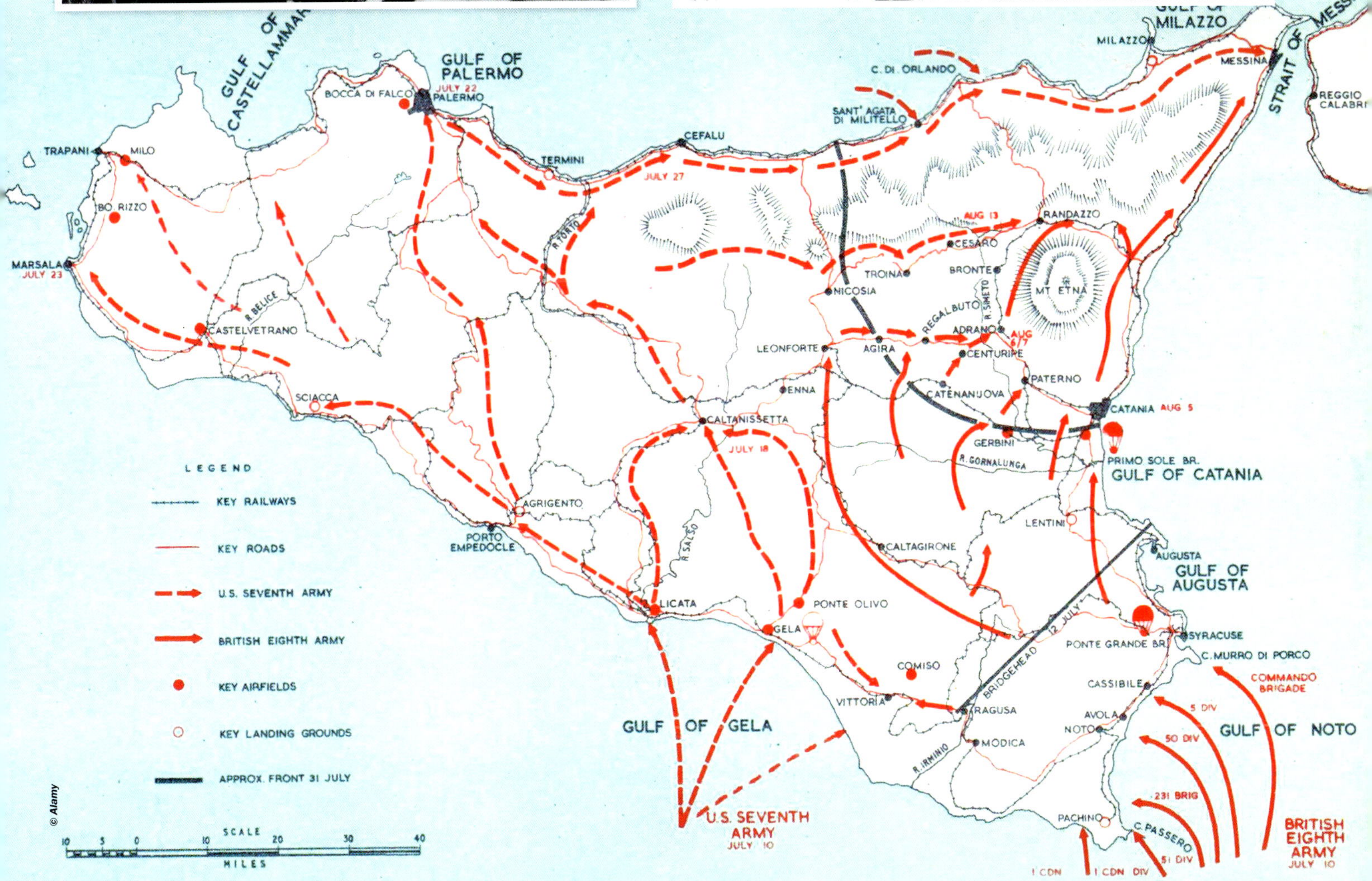

British troops make their way onto the beach using landing craft

Sicilian locals greeting British troops

US troops survey the devastation from Allied bombardments

The town of Centuripe following the battle

British troops wade through the sea during the Allied invasion of Sicily

sea off the coast of Spain armed with highly classified papers detailing an Allied plan to invade Greece and Sardinia in order to distract the Nazis from the real target).

Despite all the drama and intrigue of this highly complex operation, simple logic pointed to Sicily. Certainly, this was what Mussolini and the Italian war leaders thought, and was also what Field Marshal Albert Kesselring, the German commander-in-chief in the Mediterranean, believed. It was true that Hitler accepted the ruse because it conformed with what he believed were the Allies' intentions and reinforced his paranoia about the vulnerability of the Balkans and especially the Ploesti oilfields in Romania, Germany's only source of real – rather than synthetic – oil. In other words, Mincemeat made little, if any, difference.

An unknown quantity

That Sicily was the obvious next target was due to the fact that command of the air was a prerequisite for any amphibious invasion. This meant not only having bombers available but also fighter aircraft too, flying protective high cover. Allied air bases on Malta and in northern Tunisia meant this could only be effectively achieved over Sicily; Sardinia and Greece were too far away.

Planning for Husky began immediately after the Casablanca Conference, even though the British 8th and 1st armies (which included US II Corps) were still battling through Tunisia. The planning team established itself in Room 141

"SECOND GUESSING THE GERMAN AND ITALIAN DEFENSES AND THE REACTION TO AN INVASION WAS PART OF THE PLANNING PROCESS"

of the St George's Hotel in Algiers and was known as 'Force 141'. By the time a plan for the assault was finally agreed, it had already gone through eight different variations. The ninth plan was what was accepted, on Easter Day in April 1943.

Husky was a mind-bogglingly complex operation and drawn up while having absolutely no idea what the enemy reaction might be and while the commanders were still busy fighting the war in North Africa. This was not like Overlord, when the Allies had a fairly clear picture of what German troops were defending France and where they were based; at the time of planning for Sicily, both German and Italian units were still fighting in Tunisia and would continue to do so until May 13, a month after the final plans for Husky were submitted.

Even then it was still unclear what German units might be sent to Sicily. Italian forces were expected to be weak, although the Allies had to be prepared for them to fight harder since they would now be doing so on Italian soil. The Germans, they knew, would fight determinedly and be absolutely no pushover.

The shape of Sicily and the location of its airfields and ports was another thorny matter. It was estimated Allied forces would need 6,000 tons of supplies per day, but the biggest port, Messina, which could handle 2,500 tons a day, was the most heavily defended and furthest away. Palermo could handle 2,000 tons a day but was in the northwest, while Catania could manage 2,000 tons but was halfway up the east coast. The airfields were in the center of the island on the Catania Plain or in the far west or southeast, so at opposite ends of the island. Really, the Allies needed to swarm the entire island, but that wouldn't be possible.

Air power, however, was viewed as absolutely vital, and Air Chief Marshal Tedder, the commander of Allied Air Forces in the Mediterranean, wanted troops to swiftly capture the airfields on the west, south and southeast all at once. On the other hand, the army wanted to land on as narrow a front as possible and quickly build up supplies from there. In other words, the differing Allied forces had entirely contradictory requirements. It was a conundrum that had to be solved.

In the end, a compromise was agreed. The British would land on the southeast coast and head straight to the ports of Syracuse, Augusta and then Catania and from there on to Messina as quickly as possible. Landing on the eastern side made more sense because Messina – and the supply route for the Axis forces from

"THE ALLIES HAD LITTLE CHOICE BUT TO PRISE THE DEFENDERS OUT ONE TOWN AND HILLTOP AT A TIME"

mainland Italy – lay on the northeastern side of the island.

The Canadians would land on the southeast tip, while the Americans would land on the central southern stretch around Gela. It meant the airfields there and on the southeast could be captured swiftly, but not those in the west. Air power alone would have to deal with those.

Tricky conditions

Second guessing the German and Italian defenses and the reaction to an invasion was part of the planning process. The single most important factor at this stage of the war was to ensure the landings were successful – or rather, that they did not fail. There could be no reverses. Not failing trumped every other factor. It also meant that General Alexander agreed with Montgomery to land as many troops as possible to ensure a bridgehead was quickly established and no effective attempt to push them back into the sea could be mounted. That too, however, involved even more compromises, because for all the very impressive build-up of troops and supplies in the Mediterranean, there was still a limit to how much shipping and landing craft were available. Large numbers of troops could only be landed at the expense of large numbers of vehicles – the kind of vehicles that would then transport troops quickly up to Catania and beyond.

It was this decision that lay at the root of the subsequent slow advance inland. As events turned out, the British landings were easier than had been feared, but then the troops had to march north on foot until transport could arrive in numbers over the following days. By that time the Germans on Sicily had been reinforced and regained their balance, and resistance was considerably stiffer as a result.

Consequently, front-loading the landings with troops was the wrong decision, but only with hindsight. At the time, the very real jeopardy surrounding the operation and the risk of failure outweighed the necessity to move north toward Catania and Messina quickly.

It is also this perceived slowness of advance that has clouded the Allied effort in Sicily ever since. At the end of the campaign, nearly 40,000 German troops escaped across the Straits of Messina to fight another day. This, too, has prompted considerable criticism, especially of Montgomery, the commander of 8th Army and in charge of the British effort up the east coast.

Such criticism, however, has been badly misplaced. A very quick tour of the island and its myriad hilltop towns, wide, open valleys and narrow, winding roads is enough to make any modern traveler marvel that the island was cleared of Axis troops in a mere 38 days.

Throughout the campaign the sun beat down on US troops on patrol in the streets of the harbor city of Messina, with temperatures reaching as high as 104 degrees Fahrenheit. The dirt roads kicked up dust that could be seen for miles and which stuck in the throat and made men parched with thirst. Water was not safe to drink and water supply was a constant problem that troubled both sides. British troops caught in the Plain of Catania faced Germans dug in along the southern

The carpet bombing of Castelvetrano

A Martin Baltimore flies over retreating German forces heading for Messina

slopes of Etna, and both sides lost more men to malaria than they did to bullets, mortars or artillery shells.

Unavoidable escapes

Inland, away from the beaches and the Plain of Catania, the island was rocky, mountainous and an extremely difficult place in which to move, and especially so without being seen.

The Germans, as they fell back, did so by taking one town after another. Because the only roads led from one summit to the next up winding, hairpin tracks, the Allies had little choice but to prise the defenders out one town and hilltop at a time. From the summit of each the next could be seen, and the next after that. Assoro, Agira, Regalbuto, Troina and Centuripe – these ancient hill-top towns saw one Herculean struggle after another, in which the Allies were forced to literally inch their way forward yard by yard against an enemy who made each stand on land of his choosing and with the all-important advantage of height from which the advancing Allies could be seen.

While it was left to the Allied infantry to doggedly plow on, their only solace was the fire support they received from the air, especially from the artillery, who pounded the Germans in their positions – invariably the hilltop towns. Each was pummelled into rubble, homes destroyed and civilians killed, wounded or turned into refugees.

Meanwhile, the Germans were struggling with ever-weakening air support and supply shortages and declining morale as it became increasingly clear the island was lost.

The Allies have also been criticized for allowing 39,569 Germans and 62,000 Italians to escape. However, the history of the war shows that evacuations were generally pretty successful. At Dunkirk, 338,000 Allied troops escaped; 42,000 out of 46,000 British troops deployed were evacuated from Greece. Nearly 19,000 of the 32,000 Allied troops on Crete were also evacuated. At the end of the war, more than 2 million Germans were successfully evacuated from East Prussia and Danzig at a time when the Red Army was bearing down upon them. None of these evacuations took place at such a short crossing point as the Straits of Messina, which was little more than a mile wide, nor at a spot that was more densely defended: there were 333 anti-aircraft guns either side of the straits (compared with 135 along the Normandy coast line the following summer). It was literally impossible to stop them, and their escape made almost no difference to the subsequent Italian campaign that followed.

Furthermore, of the nearly 40,000 Germans that escaped, less than 30,000 were fighting troops, and each of the four divisions that had fought on Sicily had been appallingly mauled. Within a matter of months there would be 18 divisions fighting in Italy and some 24 by the following spring; those that escaped Sicily were hardly a decisive number.

Above all, Sicily '43 was an epic of human drama of both combatants and civilians alike. For all those who fought, died and survived this bitter struggle, it deserves to be far better understood today.

American troops of the 1st Infantry Division enter the water under fire at Omaha Beach

HITTING THE BEACHES

On the morning of June 6, 1944, Allied troops came ashore in Normandy, battling German resistance to initiate the ground campaign of Operation Overlord

The skies were overcast and the English Channel waters were rough. Although weather conditions were less than ideal, an Allied armada, poised for hours with troops packed aboard transports, turned for its rendezvous points off the coast of Normandy.

The Allies had not attempted to secure a permanent lodgement in north-west Europe since their disastrous defeat four years earlier. However, on June 6, 1944, the might of Operation Overlord, the carefully planned and orchestrated invasion of Normandy, was underway. It was time to test Hitler's boast that the fortifications he had erected from Scandinavia to the Spanish frontier – the vaunted Atlantic Wall – were impregnable, manned by thousands of soldiers plus studded with artillery, machine-gun emplacements and concrete bunkers. Many of these were designated 'Widerstandsnests' (WN), or 'resistance nests'. Although some defenses were incomplete, the Germans had sown countless landmines and erected beach obstacles that were either topped with mines or designed to rip open landing craft hulls.

Just after daylight, more than 150,000 British, American, Canadian and French soldiers were going to discover whether Hitler's assertion was justified. Bombers delivered payloads and warships pounded targets on-shore, while aircraft carrying airborne and glider troops droned overhead.

WWII was in its sixth year, and the outcome of the conflict hinged largely on the success or failure of this single day, D-Day. Planning and preparation had been underway for months. Along with the three airborne divisions deploying on June 6, five infantry divisions would hit German-held beaches along 50 miles of French coastline in Normandy. Their objectives were ambitious, and the risks were incalculable. Success meant the Third Reich's days were numbered, but failure meant an uncertain future, potentially the ruin of Allied hopes for ultimate victory.

The first waves of Allied troops of the American 1st Army, under General Omar Bradley, and the British 2nd Army, under General Miles Dempsey, were slated to come ashore beginning at 6.30am on beaches codenamed (from east to west) Sword, Juno, Gold, Omaha and Utah. Aboard a transport headed for Juno Beach, the Canadian Broadcasting Company (CBC) reported that a breakfast of scrambled eggs, bacon, coffee, bread and jam was served at about 3.30am. Across the invasion fleet of nearly 7,000 ships, similar activities were underway. The soldiers, heavily laden with equipment, would shortly climb down cargo nets into landing craft, circling as forces were marshalled, and then head toward the beaches, where smoke was rising amid the din of battle.

Mixed fortunes

Overlord's amphibious operations began on the American beaches, Utah and Omaha. The western-most, Utah, three miles long and divided into three sectors – Tare Green, Uncle Red and Victor – had been a late addition to the offensive because of its proximity to the deepwater port of Cherbourg, possession of which could facilitate future operations. The first Allied soldiers to come ashore were men of the US 8th Infantry Regiment, 4th Division, commanded by Colonel James Van Fleet, set to land near the village of Les Dunes de Varreville. When three of four Navy patrol boats guiding the first wave struck mines and sank, the 20 landing craft approaching Utah drifted 5,900 feet east of their intended landing zone, coming ashore in lightly defended Victor sector. When Van Fleet realized the error, he conferred with Brigadier General Theodore Roosevelt, Jr, assistant division commander, and the two decided to "start the war from here!"

Elements of three German divisions, the 91st Airlanding, 243rd and 709th, defended Utah Beach, but the misdirection worked in the Americans' favor. The 4th Division was tasked with capturing four narrow causeways that bridged a flooded, marshy area just off the beach, linking up with airborne troops that were to secure the causeway exits inland, taking control of coastal roads near the towns of Carentan and Sainte-Mère-Église, and preparing for a concerted attack on Cherbourg.

Resistance was sporadic as the Americans encountered some small-arms fire from beachfront houses. They moved rapidly inland after neutralizing German strongpoints WN7 near La Madeleine, WN5 at La Grande Dune, WN4 about 2,000 feet off the beach, and after a brief fight, WN3 at Beau Guillot. They captured three of the four causeways by late morning and made contact with paratroopers of the 101st Airborne Division around Pouppeville at noon.

By the end of June 6, about 23,000 troops of the 4th Division were ashore. They had pushed inland 3.7 miles and were only a mile from Sainte-Mère-Église, where elements of the 82nd Airborne Division awaited relief. The assault at Utah Beach was a resounding

"IT WAS TIME TO TEST HITLER'S 'IMPREGNABLE' ATLANTIC WALL, BUT FAILURE WOULD POTENTIALLY MEAN THE RUIN OF ALLIED HOPES"

success. Casualties were few, with less than 300 troops being killed or wounded.

Elsewhere, though, the Americans found the going extremely rough. Omaha Beach was the longest stretch of Normandy coastline assaulted on D-Day. Much of its six miles was heavily defended by three battalions of the crack German 352nd Infantry Division. A sea wall about ten feet high covered a third of the invasion area while towering cliffs provided strong defensive positions. Omaha Beach extended from the mouth of the River Vire on its western edge to Port-en-Bessin in the east, and five exits led from the shoreline into the towns of Saint-Laurent-sur-Mer, Colleville-sur-Mer and Vierville-sur-Mer. The assault troops were to capture the coastal towns; push across the Bayeux-Isigny road; advance south and west toward the village of Isigny and Pointe du Hoc, where Rangers had been tasked with eliminating a German gun position; then finally make contact eastward with the British 50th Division advancing from Gold Beach.

The assault at Omaha Beach was assigned to the 1st Infantry Division and the attached 116th Regiment, 29th Infantry Division. The Americans divided Omaha into three zones with corresponding sub-sectors from east to west, including Fox (Green and Red sectors), Easy (Green and Red sectors), Dog (Green, White and Red sectors) and Charlie.

The 16th Regiment, 1st Division, was assigned Easy Red and Fox Green, while the 116th Regiment was to hit Dog Green, White and Red. Awaiting them were heavily mined beaches with thickly strewn obstacles and 13 heavily defended strongpoints. Typical of these was WN62, which caused much of the misery experienced by the Americans. Housing two 75mm (3in) cannons, a 50mm (2in) mortar and a 50mm cannon in concrete casemates with numerous machine guns and rifle positions adding to its firepower, WN62 overlooked Easy Red and Fox Green.

The first wave at Omaha clawed toward the beach at 6.30am, immediately running into problems. Accurate enemy fire and strong surf caused some landing craft to disgorge their troops quite a distance from the shore. Soldiers entered the sea with the water over their heads, some drowning under the weight of their packs. Others were shot down as soon as the ramps of their landing craft lowered. Compounding the problems at Omaha, many DD (Duplex Drive) Sherman tanks, which were meant to provide much-needed fire support, foundered when they were released as far as three miles offshore. Only two of the 29 DD Shermans of the 741st Tank Battalion managed to reach Omaha Beach. Others were swamped, sinking to the bottom of the Channel. The 743rd Tank Battalion later landed directly on the beach. In contrast, 27 Shermans made it ashore to support the landings at Utah.

Getting off Omaha

At the Dog beaches, the 116th Regiment ran into interlocking fire from German machine-gun nests, and mortar and artillery rounds blasted craters among them. Bullets rippled through the surf, and soldiers took shelter behind obstacles. One landing craft took a direct hit from a German mortar round and simply

"COMPANY A CAME ASHORE AT DOG GREEN AND QUICKLY SUFFERED HORRENDOUS CASUALTIES, LOSING ABOUT 65 PER CENT OF ITS STRENGTH WITHIN JUST TEN MINUTES"

British troops of No 4 Commando advance house-to-house in Ouistreham with the support of a DD Sherman tank

Soldiers of the US 4th Infantry Division wade ashore at Utah Beach, a relatively quiet area as D-Day progressed

disappeared. Another was lost, along with all 32 men on board. Company A came ashore at Dog Green and quickly suffered horrendous casualties, losing about 65 per cent of its strength in just ten minutes. Twenty-two of its dead hailed from the town of Bedford, Virginia, population 3,200, and they are now forever remembered as the 'Bedford Boys'. The 16th Regiment also ran into heavy German resistance as some troops came ashore in the wrong locations.

At 7am, the second wave headed toward Omaha, but the situation was desperate. Virtually no movement off the beach had been accomplished. The US War Department report stated, "The enemy fire, which had decimated the first waves, was not neutralized when the larger landings commenced." The situation deteriorated to the point that General Bradley, aboard the cruiser USS Augusta, considered withdrawing the troops from Omaha and diverting further landings to other sectors. Around 8am, however, General Norman Cota, assistant commander of the 29th Division, led an advance off Dog Green between strongpoints WN68 and WN70. Elsewhere, non-commissioned and junior officers got small groups to move forward, penetrating less heavily defended areas and taking German fortifications from the rear.

By D-Day's end, the Americans had suffered about 2,500 killed, wounded and missing at Omaha Beach, by far the largest loss on June 6, 1944, but 34,000 American troops had made it ashore. Their shaky lodgement was only 4,500 to 6,000 feet at its deepest, near Colleville, and toeholds had been established around Vierville and St Laurent, far from the assigned D-Day objective of a five-mile beachhead. Some German troops held out among the beach defenses, and a dangerous gap existed between the Americans on Omaha and the British at Gold Beach. The Omaha landings further failed to approach the town of Isigny, where efforts to link up with the 4th Division off Utah Beach were to proceed the following day.

"The long line of beach lay ahead and immediately behind hung a thick pall of smoke as far as the eye could see," remembered wireless operator IG Holley of Company B, 1st Battalion, Royal Hampshire Regiment, as his landing craft approached Gold Beach on D-Day. "Down goes the ramp, out goes the captain with me close behind. We were in the sea to the tops of our thighs. Floundering ashore, we were in the thick of it… The beach was filled with half-bent running figures… A near one blasts sand all over me and my radio goes dead… A sweet rancid smell is everywhere, never forgotten by those who smell it – burnt explosives, torn flesh and ruptured earth."

The five-mile length of Gold Beach was in the center of Allied D-Day operations. To the

RANGERS AT POINTE DU HOC

A handful of US Army Rangers scaled cliffs and assaulted German gun emplacements that threatened Utah and Omaha beaches

Four miles west of Omaha Beach loomed the 100-foot-high cliffs of Pointe du Hoc. Allied reconnaissance had determined that the Germans had placed a formidable battery of six 155mm (6in) howitzers there, capable of bombarding both Omaha and Utah beaches. To deal with the threat that countless air raids had apparently failed to eliminate, 225 men of the 2nd Battalion, US Army Rangers, were ordered to scale the cliffs and silence the guns on the morning of D-Day.

Under the command of Lieutenant Colonel James Rudder, the Rangers trained extensively for perhaps the most hazardous mission of any Allied ground troops on June 6, 1944. Although the mission appeared suicidal, the Rangers borrowed scaling ladders from the London Fire Brigade and employed grappling hooks attached to long ropes that were fired from rocket launchers, intending to climb hand over hand to the summit of Pointe du Hoc.

At about 7am, after a delay of about 40 minutes, the Rangers landed under fire at the base of the cliffs. They soon discovered that several of their waterlogged ropes, now significantly heavier, could not reach the required height. Undaunted, they pressed on, driving the German defenders from the crest only to discover the guns had been removed. Five of them were found hours later, in an orchard, and destroyed by dropping thermite grenades down their barrels.

Maintaining their position at Pointe du Hoc until relieved on June 8, the Rangers fought off numerous counterattacks. By then, only 90 were left uninjured.

west was the port of Arromanches, the village of Longues-sur-Mer, and beyond Port-en-Bessin at Omaha Beach. To the east were the towns of Le Hamel and La Rivière. Gold Beach was divided into four sectors – How, Item, Jig and King. Twenty-nine companies of the German 716th Division manned most defenses at Gold, while elements of the 352nd Division were present. The defenders had fortified houses along the beachfront and constructed concrete strongpoints, including a battery of 155mm (6in) guns at Longues-sur-Mer. Altogether, 500 machine guns, 90 heavy guns and 50 mortars were assembled to contest any landing.

The British 50th Division, including the East Yorkshire, Devonshire, Dorset and Hampshire regiments, along with No 47 Royal Commando, was tasked with cutting the road between the cities of Bayeux and Caen, capturing Arromanches, destroying the Longues-sur-Mer battery, and linking up with the Americans off Omaha Beach to the west, plus the Canadians advancing from Juno Beach to the east.

Less than an hour before sunrise, the pre-invasion naval bombardment of Gold Beach got underway. Combined with earlier air attacks, the naval guns were highly effective. The light cruiser HMS Ajax dueled the Longues-sur-Mer battery just after dawn, silencing the guns with six-inch rounds fired directly through two of its four casemates.

Efforts to clear beach obstacles were stymied as strong winds pushed the tides into the area earlier than expected. Twenty landing craft carrying tanks were damaged during their runs to shore. The first British troops hit the beach at about 7.15am, and the 1st Battalion, Royal Hampshire Regiment, took casualties immediately. Near Le Hamel, a German 88mm (3.5in) gun fired from the cliffs, but British troops assaulted the position with the support of a tank equipped with a spigot mortar.

In Item sector, four of the 14 landing craft carrying No 47 Commando were sunk, but the troops managed to strike west toward Port-en-Bessin. At La Rivière, the 5th Battalion, East Yorkshire Regiment, and 6th Battalion, Green Howards, made steady progress under fire from German 88s.

Gains on Gold

By early afternoon, both Le Hamel and La Rivière were taken. The Commandos captured high ground near Port-en-Bessin by evening, and contact with Canadian forces from Juno Beach was established. About 25,000 British troops were ashore with only 400 casualties. As night fell, the penetration at Gold Beach was six miles deep. Although the Bayeux-Caen road was not cut and no link-up had been made with the Americans, the effort at Gold had produced outstanding results.

East of Gold Beach, the Canadian 3rd Infantry Division was to assault Juno Beach, a length of six miles from Saint-Aubin in the east to La Rivière in the west. The center of Juno was the small village of Courseulles-sur-Mer. The focus of the Canadian landings included two sectors, Mike to the west and Nan to the east. The North Shore Regiment, the Queen's Own Rifles, and the Regina Rifles landed in Nan sector, while the Royal Winnipeg Rifles assaulted Mike. Companies of No 48 Royal Marine Commando and the Canadian Scottish Regiment held the flanks. The Canadians were tasked with cutting the Bayeux-Caen road, taking the Carpiquet airfield west of Caen, and linking up with the British troops at Gold and Sword beaches.

The first Canadian troops landed about 7.55am, slightly behind schedule after contending with difficult tides that left beach obstacles submerged, destroying or damaging about 30 per cent of the landing craft. The

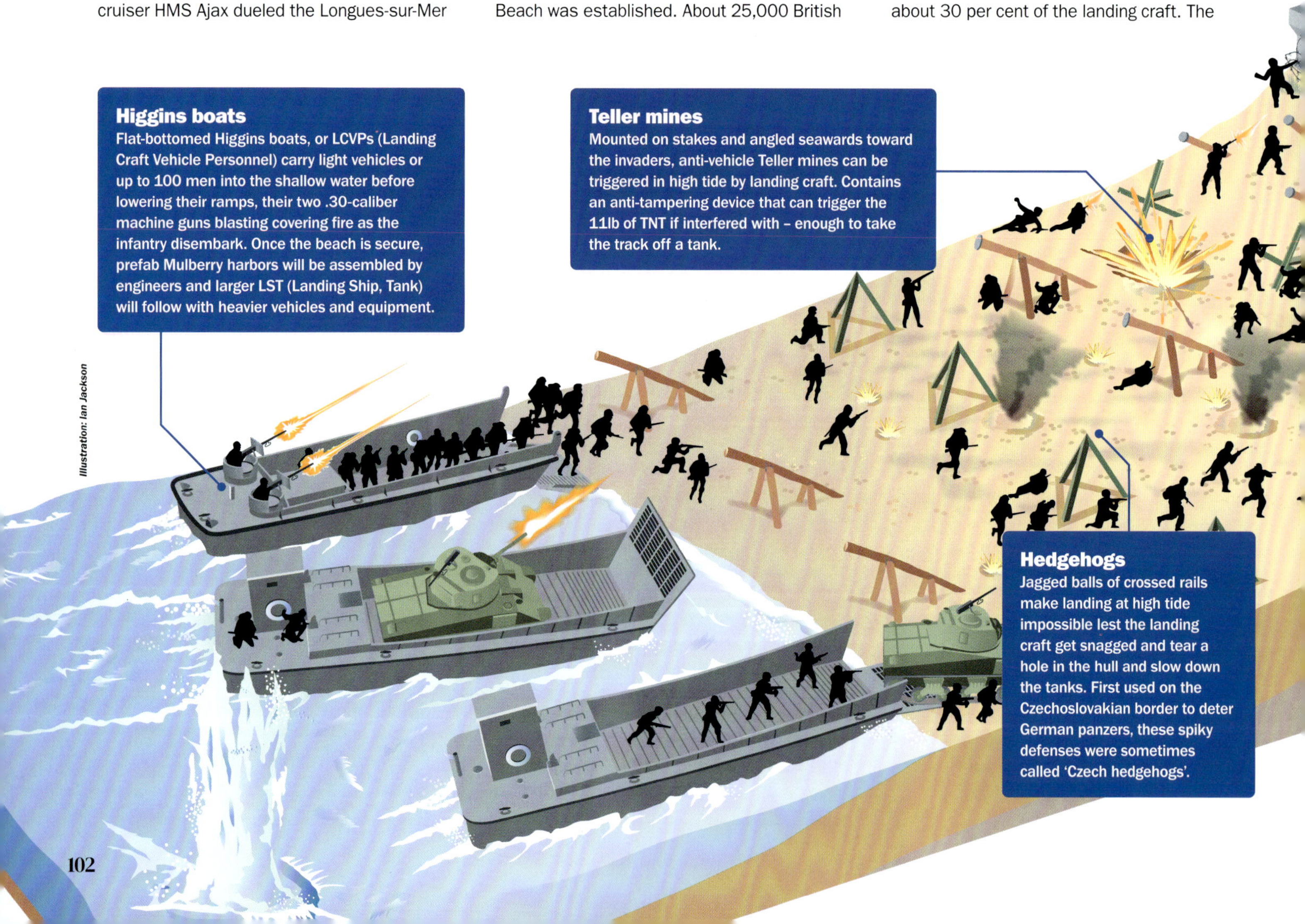

Illustration: Ian Jackson

Soldiers of the British 50th Division rush ashore, at Gold Beach, in the center of the Allied landing area in Normandy

Artillery casement

Safely encased in thick concrete, German artillery positions shell Allied ships approaching the beach. Taking them out prior to landing is a crucial part of the early bombardment from sea or air, as not even light tanks have the firepower to dent their shells. Infantry have to take out casements the hard way, getting under the guns to lob grenades into the closely packed rooms, or by storming the connecting trenches.

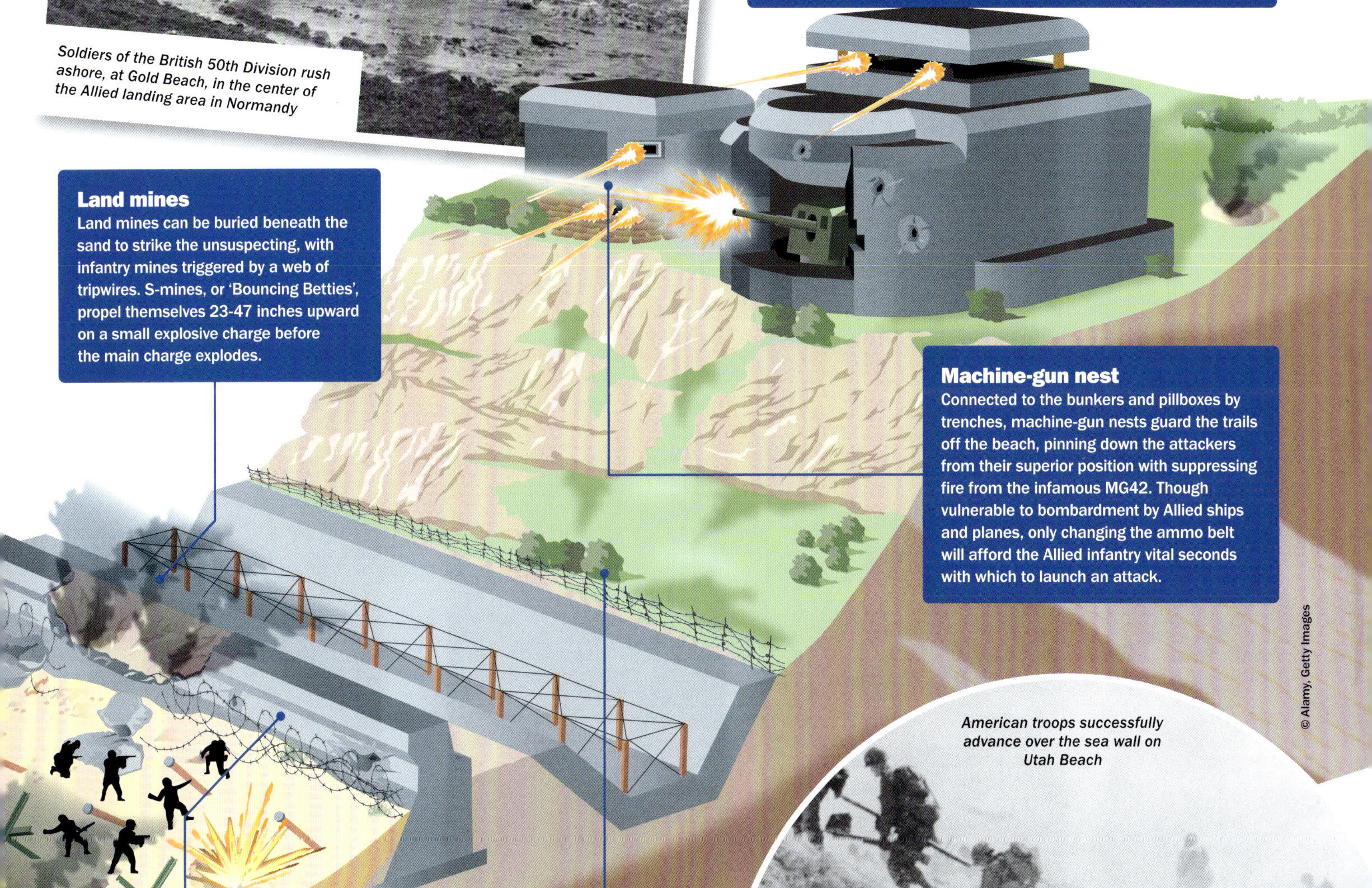

Land mines

Land mines can be buried beneath the sand to strike the unsuspecting, with infantry mines triggered by a web of tripwires. S-mines, or 'Bouncing Betties', propel themselves 23-47 inches upward on a small explosive charge before the main charge explodes.

Machine-gun nest

Connected to the bunkers and pillboxes by trenches, machine-gun nests guard the trails off the beach, pinning down the attackers from their superior position with suppressing fire from the infamous MG42. Though vulnerable to bombardment by Allied ships and planes, only changing the ammo belt will afford the Allied infantry vital seconds with which to launch an attack.

American troops successfully advance over the sea wall on Utah Beach

Barbed wire

Used in vast quantities along seawalls to deny the attackers cover, coils of vicious barbed wire can slow the Allies down as they carefully cut it or flatten it to cross – simple things made more difficult by the hail of machine-gun fire. Loose coils of wire are more difficult to cross as they snare on the unwary.

Seawall

The ten-foot concrete seawall is as much protection against coastal erosion and unseasonably high tides as it is Allied assault, but it can make exiting the beach difficult for infantry and impossible for vehicles. It does, however, provide the attackers with rare shelter from the German guns.

“WHILE LORD LOVAT’S COMMANDOS REACHED THE CRITICAL BRIDGES BY 1.30PM, THE PUSH INLAND MET THE ONLY GERMAN ARMORED COUNTER-ATTACK OF THE DAY”

Men of the 4th Special Service Brigade wade ashore near June Beach

German defenders of the 716th Division fortified houses and buildings close to the shoreline. As the Canadians waded ahead, German fire, zeroed in on the water's edge, intensified. Aside from Omaha, the Canadians at Juno encountered the fiercest enemy resistance on D-Day. For more than two hours, the fighting raged along the beach.

"In the Nan sector, the North Shore Regiment lands under heavy German fire," the CBC reported. "At 8.30am, the Queen's Own Rifles land at Nan sector, held up by high seas. The soldiers have to run 600 feet from the shore to a sea wall under fire from German artillery. Only a few men of the first company survive."

German fire wreaked havoc among the troops coming ashore, and Company B, Royal Winnipeg Rifles, was reduced to one officer and 25 men in their dash for the sea wall. Some units suffered 50 per cent casualties, but by mid-morning the Canadians had taken Saint-Aubin and the village of Bernières. Supported by tanks, they fought house to house in Courseulles. One troop of the 1st Hussars reached and briefly cut the Bayeux-Caen road, the only Allied unit to attain its final objective on D-Day.

As night fell, the Canadians had landed more than 21,000 troops and suffered 1,200 casualties while achieving the deepest penetration of June 6, advancing nine miles. Contact with the British 50th Division off Gold Beach was established, but the Carpiquet airport remained in enemy hands and a dangerous 1.8-mile gap existed between Juno and Sword beaches.

Within 45 minutes of landing across the five miles of Sword, the easternmost invasion beach, the British 3rd Division was pushing inland. Surprisingly, the Germans had constructed light defenses along the most direct route to Caen, a communications and transportation center about nine miles from Sword Beach, but resistance from the German 736th and 125th Regiments, 716th Division and elements of the 21st Panzer Division stiffened as the day wore on.

The body of an American soldier lies where he fell on Omaha Beach during the desperate hours of D-Day

The tides begin to turn

Sword Beach – divided into Oboe, Peter, Queen and Roger sectors – stretched from the town of Lion-sur-Mer in the east to the city of Ouistreham at the mouth of the River Orne in the west. The objectives of the 3rd Division and the supporting 27th Armoured Brigade included capturing Caen and converging on Carpiquet airfield, linking up with the Canadians from Juno Beach in the process.

The 1st Special Service Brigade, including Commando units under Simon Fraser, Lord Lovat, was to advance 3.1 miles to the bridges across the Orne and the Caen Canal, where troops of the British 6th Airborne had seized the spans and awaited relief.

Landing at 7.25am, the British moved rapidly inland. By afternoon, the King's Shropshire Light Infantry and Staffordshire Yeomanry had advanced toward Caen and attempted to link up with the Canadians. While Lord Lovat's Commandos reached the critical bridges by 1.30pm, the push inland met the only German armored counter-attack of the day.

Elements of the 21st Panzer Division advanced late in the day through the gap between Sword and Juno, its 192nd Panzergrenadier Regiment reaching the Channel coast. However, no reinforcements were available to exploit the gain, and the Germans were forced to retire.

At the end of the day, 29,000 troops were ashore at Sword Beach, with only 630 casualties. Still, Caen – a D-Day objective – was out of reach and the junction with the Canadians had not occurred.

Although numerous D-Day objectives were not achieved on June 6, and the beachhead in several areas, particularly at Omaha, was vulnerable to counter-attack, much had been accomplished. Casualties were surprisingly light, with about 4,900 killed, wounded or missing, and the Germans had been taken comprehensively by surprise.

The Allies had returned to northwest Europe in force, but months of difficult fighting lay ahead before France could finally be liberated from its German oppressors, a campaign that would cost thousands of Allied lives. Without doubt, though, the success of D-Day heralded the beginning of the end for Hitler's Third Reich. The course of the war had irreversibly changed.

THE LANDINGS

The deployment of Allied troops on June 6, D-Day

Commander-in-Chief, Air Force:
Air Chief Marshal Trafford Leigh-Mallory

1ST US ARMY

Commander: General Omar Bradley

Speciality Key

- Combat engineers
- Covert intelligence gathering
- Amphibious medium tank
- Light infantry, versatile & reliable
- Air assault, light infantry
- Special forces trained for coastal assault
- Infantry, special forces
- Infantry, Fast tank
- Mine clearance, bridging & transport

US troops look to the shore as their landing craft approaches Omaha Beach

VII CORPS
Commander: Major General J.L. Collins

4th Infantry Division 'Ivy'
Commander: Major General Raymond Barton
Objective: First troops onto Utah Beach

9th Infantry Division 'Old Reliables'
Commander: Major General Manton S. Eddy
Objective: Take and hold Utah Beach

79th Infantry Division 'Cross of Lorraine'
Commander: Major General Ira T. Wyche
Objective: Take and hold Utah Beach

90th Infantry Division 'Tough 'Ombres' **Commander:** Brig-General Jay W. MacKelvie
Objective: Take and hold Utah Beach

30 Commando Assault Unit 'Red Indians' (British)
Commander: Captain G. Pike
Objective: Radar at Douvres-la-Délivrande

70th Tank Battalion 'Thunderbolts' **Commander:** Lt-Colonel John C. Welborn
Objective: Support landing at Utah Beach

237th Combat Engineer Battalion
Commander: Major Herschel E. Linn
Objective: Clear obstacles at Utah Beach

299th Combat Engineer Battalion **Commander:** Colonel Milton Jewett
Objective: Clear obstacles at Utah Beach

UTAH

V CORPS
Commander: Major General Leonard T. Gerow

1st Infantry Division 'The Big Red One' **Commander:** Major General Clarence Huebner
Objective: Take and hold Omaha Beach

29th Infantry Division 'Blue And Gray'
Commander: Major General Charles Gebhardt
Objective: Take and hold Omaha Beach

Ranger assault group **Commander:** Lieutenant Colonel James Earl Rudder

2nd Ranger Battalion **Commander:** James Rudder
Objective: Capture battery at Pointe du Hoc

5th Ranger Battalion
Commander: Lieutenant Colonel Max Schneider
Objective: Capture battery at Pointe du Hoc

743rd Tank Battalion
Commander: Lieutenant Colonel John S. Upham
Objective: Support landing at Omaha Beach

POINTE DU HOC

OMAHA

INLAND

82nd Airborne Division 'All American Division'
Commander: Major General Matthew Ridgway
Objective: Secure left flank and rear of VI Corps

101st Airborne Division 'Screaming Eagles'
Commander: Major General Maxwell D. Taylor
Objective: Secure left flank and rear of VI Corps

US Army Rangers at the cliffs of Pointe du Hoc

Supreme Commander:
General Dwight D. Eisenhower

Commander-in-Chief, Naval Force:
Admiral Bertram Ramsay

Commander-in-Chief, Land Forces:
General Field Marshal Bernard Montgomery

2ND ARMY (BRITISH/CANADIAN)

XXX Corps **Commander:** Lieutenant General Gerard Bucknall

50th (Northumbrian) Infantry Division
Commander: Major General D.A.H. Graham

69th Infantry Brigade **Objective:** Take and hold Gold Beach

151st Infantry Brigade
Objective: Take and hold Gold Beach

231st Infantry Brigade
Commander: Brigadier Sir Alexander Stanier
Objective: Take and hold Gold Beach

56th Infantry Brigade **Objective:** Take and hold Gold Beach

8 Armoured Brigade
Commander: Lieutenant Colonel John S. Upham
Objective: Support the landing at Gold Beach

No. 47 (Royal Marine) Commando
Commander: Lieutenant Colonel C.F. Phillips
Objective: Capture Port-en-Bessin

1st Royal Marine Armoured Support Regiment
Objective: Support Royal Marine assault

89th Field Company, Royal Engineers
Objective: Clear Gold Beach exit of obstacles

90th Field Company, Royal Engineers
Objective: Clear Gold Beach exit of obstacles

GOLD

Commander:
Lieutenant General Sir Miles Dempsey

3rd Canadian Infantry Brigade
Commander: Major General Rodney Keller

7th Canadian Infantry Brigade
Objective: Take and hold Juno Beach

8th Canadian Infantry Brigade
Commander: Brigadier Harry Wickwire Foster
Objective: Take and hold Juno Beach

2nd Canadian Armoured Brigade
Objective: Support landing at Juno Beach

79th Armoured Division [British]
Commander: Major General Sir Percy Hobart
Objective: Clear mines and assist landing at Juno Beach

9th Canadian Infantry Brigade
Objective: Reserves, support landing at Juno Beach

JUNO

Commander:
Major-General T.G. Rennie

9th Brigade
Objective: Take and hold Sword Beach

8th Brigade (Assault Brigade)
Objective: Take and hold Sword Beach

185th Brigade
Commander: Brigadier K.P. Smith
Objective: Take and hold Sword Beach

5th Royal Marine Armoured Support Regiment
Objective: Support landing at Sword Beach

27th Armoured Brigade
Commander: Brigadier George Erroll Prior-Palmer
Objective: Support landing at Sword Beach

1st Special Service Brigade
Commander: Brigadier Lord Lovat
Objective: Capture key German defenses

4th Special Service Brigade
Commander: Brigadier B.W. Leicester
Objective: Secure the flanks of Sword Beach

SWORD

British Commandos ponder the next few moments as they approach Sword Beach during the opening hours of Operation Overlord

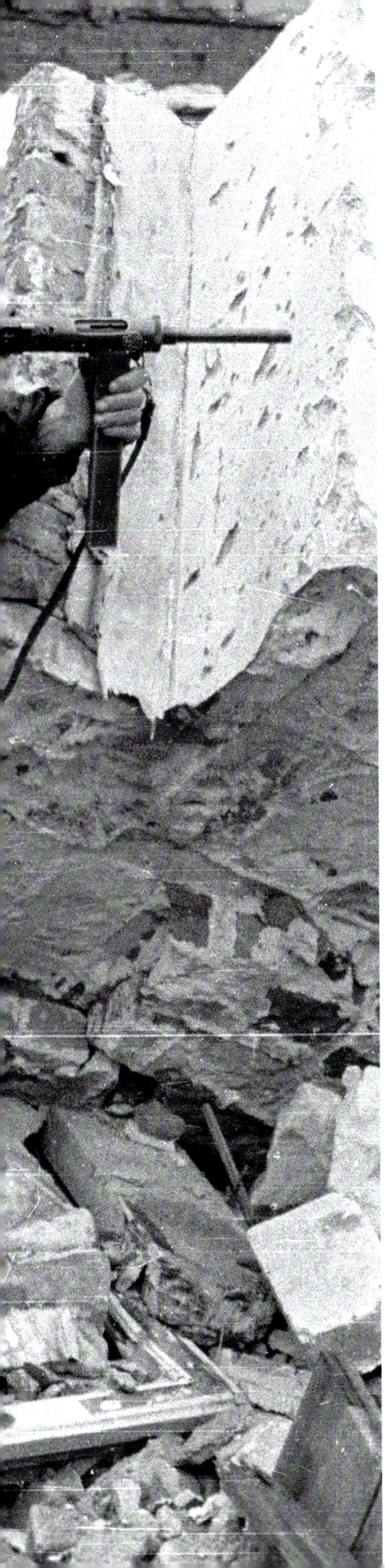

WARSAW RISES

On August 1, 1944, Europe's largest underground resistance, the Polish Home Army, rose up against the Germans as men, women and children fought to liberate Warsaw

In Poland the subject of the Warsaw Uprising of 1944 is seen from many different perspectives and, like all battles, has its own specific circumstances: military, political, social and – seen from Poland's history of uprisings – cultural. Yet, while no longer suppressed, as it was in the bleak years of communism and the Cold War, it still remains a battle relatively unknown outside of Poland today.

Fought from August 1 to October 2, 1944, the outcome of the 63-day battle was a tragedy. An estimated 18,000 Polish insurgents lost their lives and between 180,000-200,000 civilians died during the uprising. Warsaw became a city of ruins. However, despite the catastrophic end, it is also a story of tragic beauty, heroism and fierce resistance against the odds.

A history of uprisings

With the German and Soviet invasion of Poland in September 1939, Polish resistance to the occupiers was instant. Poland had only relatively recently regained its independence at the end of WWI, following 123 years of Russian, Prussian and Austrian partitions, and building underground secret networks against an enemy occupier was something of a second nature. Generations of Poles had fought for independence – in the Kosciuszko Rising in 1794, with Napoleon for the Duchy of Warsaw from 1807-1815, the November Uprising of 1830, the January Uprising of 1863 and in Piłsudski's Legions in WWI, all fighting for the rebirth of the Polish state.

By 1940, Poland's armed resistance movement had formed as the Zwiazek Walki Zbrojnej (Union of Armed Struggle) and developed into the Armia Krajowa (AK or Home Army) in 1942 – the biggest underground army in occupied Europe. By 1944, an estimated 400,000 soldiers were carrying out military training, diversionary activities, sabotage operations and intelligence gathering in preparation for an armed national insurgency.

Occupation

The occupation of Warsaw, Poland's capital city and home to around 1.3 million inhabitants in 1939, was particularly brutal from the very start. Germans confiscated property, renamed streets and put up "Nur für Deutsche" (only for Germans) signs across the city. Every citizen was forced to carry their 'kennkarte' ID card, work and residence permits to show any German official on patrol at any given time.

The German authorities imposed strict food rationing. The average adult in Warsaw lost 22 pounds in weight during the occupation. Monetary depreciation meant loss of any pre-war savings and disproportionately low wages, creating an extortionate black market. Mass arrests and executions of civil servants, doctors, teachers, lawyers, scientists and artists increased and continued throughout the occupation, such as the massacres at Wawer, 1939, Palmiry, 1939/1940, Kabacki Forest, 1939/1940, and Sekocinski Forest in 1942.

From October 1941, under the penalty of death, Jews were no longer allowed to leave the Warsaw Ghetto. Helping or hiding Jews was also punishable by death, not only for the one responsible but also for their entire family. Despite this, many still offered any assistance they could. In 1942, Jan Karski delivered an impassioned plea on behalf of Poland's Jews to Allied officials in London and to American President Franklin D. Roosevelt. In 1943, the remaining Jewish population revolted in the heroic but doomed Ghetto Uprising.

In the fall of 1943 SS-Brigadeführer Franz Kutschera, head of the SS and police in Warsaw, introduced public street executions. The police were allowed to kill anyone at will, on the spot. Round-ups, mass executions and forced deportations as slave labor to Germany became so frequent that when someone left their house they would not know if they would ever come back.

It is impossible for anyone that has not lived through it to understand what it really means to live in constant fear of arrest, torture and death. This terror created a strong unity against the Germans, and sometimes with total strangers, when a glance, a word or some small gesture from someone that just happened to pass on the street could save a stranger's life.

Class of 1920

Many of the young soldiers that would come to fight in the uprising of 1944 were born in the 1920s, and they are known in Poland as the 'Class of 1920'. Born free in the Second Polish Republic, they felt a strong sense of patriotic duty and civic engagement, and as they came of age during the brutality of the occupation, they felt it was their responsibility to fight for Poland's freedom.

As German authorities closed all secondary schools and universities, forbidding Polish history, geography and literature to be taught, teachers took up the struggle against the occupier by providing clandestine study groups. It is estimated that 90,000 students attended these secret schools held in private homes taught by about 5,500 teachers in 1943–1944.

From a young age many joined the 'Grey Ranks' and were very active in the scout movement, learning first-aid skills and military drills. Teenagers spent their free time on conspiratorial activities and small-scale sabotage. Painting the anchor symbol of 'Poland Fighting' on a wall of a house or busy street was very dangerous but boosted morale immensely in the fight against the occupiers.

The iconic PW anchor symbol for 'Polska Walczaca' (Poland Fighting) was designed by Anna Smolenska, a scout and arts history student who would perish in Auschwitz in 1943.

Commanded by Brigadier General Emil August Fieldorf 'Nil' (Nile), the Home Army's Directorate of Diversionary Operations, the KEDYW consisted of elite units and undertook all manner of diversionary and sabotage activities, such as train derailment, arson, blowing up bridges, planting bombs inside SS barracks, sabotage work at German factories and freeing prisoners held captive by the ruthless Gestapo.

"THE GUN USED TO KILL BÜRKL WAS CARRIED IN A SPECIALLY CONSTRUCTED VIOLIN CASE"

One of the KEDYW's special units, named 'Agat' (Anti-Gestapo), and later 'Pegaz' and 'Parasol', carried out the assassinations of exceptionally brutal Nazi officials. The first successful liquidation was of the sadistic deputy commandant of Pawiak Prison, SS-Oberscharführer Franz Bürkl, in September 1943. The Sten gun used to kill Bürkl was carried to the location in a specially constructed violin case. One of the assassins, Bronisław Pietraszkiewicz, pseudonym 'Lot' (Flight), was to become the leader of 'Operation Kutschera', assassinating SS-Brigadeführer Franz Kutschera in February 1944. Similar to the better-known killing of Reinhard Heydrich in Prague, Kutchera died on location. Just as the mass reprisal killings in Lidice had followed Heydrich's death, 300 people were shot in Warsaw by the Germans in reprisal for the Poles' assassination of Kutschera.

17-year-old Wanda Traczyk-Stawska firing her 'Błyskawica' gun during the uprising

Members of the Zoska Battalion. The armband marking the Home Army fighters can clearly be seen

Escaping after the action, one of the cars used by the assassins ran into a German checkpoint at the Vistula bridge, and two of the assassins jumped over the balustrade into the freezing Vistula River. 'Lot' escaped in a second car, but having been wounded during the action, he died later, after surgery, from his wounds. He was only 22 years old.

W-Hour

By June 1944 the Russian offensive in Poland had started, this time on the side of the Allies. The Germans were in retreat and had begun to evacuate Warsaw. Reports were coming in that the Red Army was approaching the Vistula from the eastern suburbs of Warsaw. While diplomatic relations between Poland and the Soviets had not been re-established since the Katyn massacre, when 22,000 Polish officers and intellectuals had been executed by the NKVD in 1940, Home Army Commander General 'Bor' Komorowski was convinced the Soviet attack was continuing toward Germany.

After consulting with the government delegate Jan 'Sobol' Jankowski, he decided to start the uprising to liberate the capital, therefore safeguarding the sovereignty of the Polish state before the Red Army entered. In the words of Jankowski, "We wanted to be free and owe our freedom to nobody."

'W-hour' was set for 5.00pm on Tuesday, August 1, 1944. The uprising was expected to last three days, or a week at most. Victory was very far from certain. Even so, most Varsovians welcomed the Warsaw Uprising with enthusiasm – for the first time in five years of occupation they had a chance to be free. "We were ready to give absolutely everything for freedom," said Wanda Traczyk-Stawska, a 17-year-old girl scout.

Many of the scout groups and units that had formed during the occupation became some of the most famous formations of the rising: Battalion Zoska, Parasol, Koszta, Odwet. With many soldiers being so young, between 16 and 24 years old, the bonds they forged would last for life. Many would choose heroic-sounding or mythological noms de guerre, but some would be nicknamed by their friends. The boys in Traczyk-Stawska's unit named her 'Paczek', meaning rosebud or doughnut. Another characteristic of the uprising was that boys and girls would fight together, side by side.

Traczyk-Stawska would become one of the women who fought as a soldier in a unit under the direct disposition of General Antoni Chrusciel, whose nom de guerre was 'Monter' and who was in command of all the fighting forces in Warsaw.

According to Bór-Komorowski, the Home Army strength amounted to nearly 40,000 underground soldiers in Warsaw. Today it's estimated that on August 1, 25,000 soldiers took up the struggle and, as more joined in, the

GOVERNING IN EXILE AND SECRET

As Germany and the USSR occupied Poland's territories, the Polish state lived on in secret, governed by the Polish government-in-exile

Recognized by the Western Allies, the Polish president, government and commander-in-chief at first held office in Paris, then, after the fall of France in 1940, in London.

Formed under Prime Minister and Commander-in-Chief General Sikorski, Poland's armed resistance movement was organized as ZWZ Union of Armed Struggle in 1940. It became the AK Home Army in 1942 – the biggest underground army in occupied Europe.

In Poland, the plenipotentiary delegate to the government in London held the highest authority, directing all clandestine civil administration. This included the judicial system, with courts that conducted trials and passed verdicts, including death penalties for traitors and collaborators. Clandestine radio stations informed the West of events in Poland.

Underground printing presses published newspapers and leaflets, providing vital information and helping to keep up morale. Over 700 press titles were published during the occupation. As German authorities closed all secondary schools and universities, teachers took up the struggle against the occupiers by providing clandestine study groups. Many teenagers were also active in the scout movement, learning skills that would prove vital for a chance of survival before the war's end.

Władysław Sikorski was prime minister of the Polish government-in-exile until his death in 1943

German captives, made to wear marked uniforms by Polish resistance fighters

number would rise to nearly 50,000. However, only around ten per cent of them had guns. Every imaginable weapon that could be found was used. One of the most recognized guns of the rising was the 9mm sub-machine gun 'Błyskawica', meaning 'lightning', that was designed by Polish engineers and assembled in underground workshops. Much would depend on taking weapons off the enemy and on the supply of ammunition, of which there was a great shortage from the start.

In comparison, at the time of the outbreak of the rising, the German garrison in Warsaw had almost 20,000 well-armed and highly trained soldiers, yet at first the Germans sustained heavy losses.

Soldiers of the resistance

A Home Army soldier's uniform was a red and white armband. Although the uprising started in the summer heat of August, those who were able to prepare dressed in what suitably durable clothing they had. Many soldiers wore a mixture of civilian and any military clothing that they could find, making each soldier's uniform rather individual and unique. But as the battle went on civilian clothing tore and wore out fast.

When the Home Army secured larger areas they also took over German warehouses and storage facilities, and so large quantities of German uniforms came into their possession, which they would use. Any soldier will attest to the importance of wearing boots and a helmet, as well as clothes with pockets and belts in battle. German belts with an eagle swastika on the buckle were worn upside down. Photographs of young smiling nurses and couriers wearing Waffen-SS camouflage anoraks over summer dresses and sandals create a striking contrast.

Ask any veteran soldier, and they will likely say that the bravest in battle were the nurses and first-aid girls. They would run straight into the raging battlefield with stretchers, and under fire from Germans they would try to save the

"THE GERMANS KILLED HOME ARMY SOLDIERS AS 'BANDITS' AND CONSISTENTLY BROKE THE RULES OF WAR"

lives not only of Polish soldiers but also of severely wounded Germans.

Couriers and liaison girls were vital in coordinating information between different units, which was exceptionally dangerous, as it meant having to run through enemy territory in order to do so. Unarmed due to the lack of weapons, they had no guns to protect themselves – when captured, they would often be raped before they were executed.

Adam Borkiewicz was the first historian of the uprising. In the opening lines of his book are the now legendary last words of courier Maria Comer, who upon capture was asked, "Bist du Banditin?" (Are you a bandit?), to which she replied, "I am a soldier of the Home Army", before she was executed on the spot.

Recognized by the Allies as a combat force, the Home Army was protected under the Geneva Convention. Yet the Germans killed Home Army soldiers as "bandits and terrorists" and consistently broke the rules of war with the continuous mass murder of civilians.

Civilian front line

As news of the Warsaw Uprising reached Himmler, he appointed the command in Warsaw to Erich von dem Bach-Zelewski, chief of German anti-partisan formations. On Himmler's order all combatants and non-combatants, including women and children, were to be shot and Warsaw was to be razed to the ground.

Under the command of SS-Gruppenführer Reinefarth, the notorious RONA brigades of Kaminski and Dirlewanger started the assault on the Warsaw neighborhoods of Ochota and Wola on August 5. When they advanced, they would use women and children as 'human shields' in front of their tanks. As mass rape and systematic murder of civilians continued, during the course of a few days over 40,000 civilians were slaughtered.

The mass killings in Ochota and Wola count among the worst atrocities of the war. This only reinforced the Home Army soldiers' belief that now the rising had started, there was no turning back – it was a battle to the end. Every street, every house, was fought for.

The Germans used heavy rocket launchers, which civilians nicknamed 'cows' due to the moaning sound they made when the missiles were launched. People caught in their range as they exploded became 'living torches' coated in flammable liquid. Another terrifying German weapon was the so-called 'Goliath', a small remote-controlled tank filled with explosives.

Many civilians lived in basements throughout the uprising and only went out on street level when absolutely necessary, moving through underground passages and basement tunnels

created by demolishing the walls between cellars. The longer the rising went on, the harder their situation became.

At times, in certain areas the relationship between the civilian population and Home Army soldiers became understandably strained. Nevertheless, they held out. The truth is that without the support of the civilian population the uprising could not have continued. It was the civilians that helped to set up and worked in hospitals treating the wounded, built barricades, cooked food and collected water, put out fires and provided shelter for soldiers. It was with their help that the battle continued for as long as it did.

Battlefield Warsaw

The insurgents adopted defensive tactics and achieved significant success in the city center, capturing the PAST state telephone company building, the Holy Cross Church and the police headquarters. They also mounted offensive actions in the Zoliborz area, attempted assaults on the railway station and tried to establish a link between the city center and the old town area. Unfortunately, these attempts proved unsuccessful and became some of the bloodiest battles of the uprising.

The insurgents ultimately failed to capture the most essential military targets and were locked in an uneven battle against continuous German reinforcements of heavy weapons, which were used to Polish positions with artillery fire supported by air raids.

The Germans systematically killed civilians following any retreat by the Home Army. Knowing that civilians would be murdered once the Home Army had been forced to abandon its positions was the absolute worst part about the uprising, said Traczyk-Stawska. "A soldier, when he is firing, when he is in battle, he does not feel pain even when he is wounded," she said. "Pain comes later, and even when a soldier is dying, then that death is a very different situation – compared to civilians, who suffer much worse deaths than soldiers. A soldier has a different mindset. He is armed. He is fighting. He is in a state of euphoria and the adrenaline is very high. But civilians… they were dragged out and executed… defenseless." The suffering of civilians is something that Wanda Traczyk-Stawska thinks about constantly to this day.

Home Army soldiers were a motley crew. One soldier in Traczyk-Stawska's unit, 'Kruczek', forever the avid reader, would crawl along a torn barricade on his back, his jacket bulging up, filled with books that he had found along the way in some bombed out, abandoned buildings. Another soldier in their unit was unwilling to be separated from his wife and child and brought

Polish fighters take aim across a street from behind a wall of tiles

Wanda Traczyk-Stawska, pictured at her home in Warsaw at the age of 97

them along with him – crawling through the torn barricade, the wife would carry their wrapped up new-born baby in her mouth, like a lioness. Scenes like this would seem improbable in a film, and yet in real life they happened. The Warsaw Uprising was filled with many surreal or miracle-like experiences.

The fall

After fierce fighting, German units captured the last defenses of the old town on September 2. With the fall of the old town no single building was left standing, and the conditions of the insurgents worsened with each day. The catastrophe forced Colonel Karol Ziemski to begin an evacuation. Every attempt to break through the German lines and connect with the city center had failed, and the only way out of the siege was through the sewer tunnels. The municipal sewer system ran under most of the city and had been used by couriers throughout the uprising. The conditions in the sewers were very difficult: insurgents waded in darkness through toxic waste, with the risk of Germans hearing them from above and releasing poison gas or explosives into the tunnels. It took around four hours to cover 1.2 miles.

For two days, over 5,000 insurgents escaped through the sewers. On September 2 the last Home Army units left the old town. Behind them they left some 40,000-50,000 civilians. The old, sick and wounded were shot by the Germans, and the rest where transported to Mauthausen and Sachsenhausen.

This is one of the most tragic chapters of the uprising. The fall of the old town also prevented the city center insurgents from connecting with units in Zoliborz and Kampinos Forest and allowed German forces to concentrate on suppressing each individual stronghold of resistance. Despite the insurgents' great determination, the Germans had an overwhelming advantage, both in manpower and military resources. The Karl-Gerät 040 siege gun caused huge devastation, along with shelling by German artillery and the Luftwaffe, which made nearly 1,400 sorties over Warsaw, fighting the insurgents and destroying the city.

In the end, all the insurgents could do was to hold onto their positions. With time the conflict reached a virtual stalemate. Despite the brave efforts of Allied airmen, the Warsaw Airlift had not been successful. The route from Italy was too difficult, and by the time some airdrops were conducted most supplies fell into enemy hands. Churchill couldn't persuade Stalin to give Allied flights landing rights in the USSR to help get supplies and ammunition to the insurgents in time. Western assistance had failed. The conditions for civilians became

The Warsaw Uprising involved many combatants, including women and children. These Polish boys participated in the fighting

unbearable and the Home Army had no resources left with which to fight. The situation was unsustainable. It is still remarkable that the rising lasted for as long as it did – 63 days.

Capitulation

The last shot of the uprising was fired on October 2. In the final capitulation terms, agreed between representatives of the Home Army command and Von dem Bach-Zelewski, Home Army soldiers were to be treated as POWs according to the Geneva Convention. Civilians were not to be killed or persecuted.

Around 11,600 Home Army soldiers surrendered, along with about 2,000 women. Wanda Traczyk-Stawska was one of the 1,800 women that would end up as a POW in Stalag VI-C Oberlangen, where in a beautiful twist of fate, they would later be liberated by the Polish First Armoured Division led by General Maczek. Elsewhere, many Home Army soldiers would be freed or escape German captivity and continue to fight before the war's end.

The mass evacuation of the civilian population from Warsaw, which the Germans insisted upon, is an unprecedented event in Europe's history and remains one of the most tragic and haunting scenes of the war. First taken to a transit camp, in contradiction to the capitulation agreement, over 100,000 Varsovians were sent as slave labor to Germany, and tens of thousands were sent to concentration camps, including Mauthausen, Ravensbrück and Auschwitz. The exact number of people who perished in the uprising will remain unknown.

An estimated 18,000 Polish insurgents lost their lives, while German deaths are estimated

"THE DEMOLITION OF WARSAW WAS COMPLETED METHODICALLY... AROUND 85-90 PER CENT OF THE CITY WAS RAZED TO THE GROUND"

to be similar. It was the civilians that suffered the most incomprehensible loss: between 180,000-200,000 civilians died during the 63 days of battle. At the Warsaw Insurgents Cemetery in Wola, over 100,000 people are buried, most of them in mass graves.

The landscape after battle

During the three months that followed, the demolition of Warsaw was completed methodically, house by house, on Adolf Hitler's orders; around 85-90 per cent of the city was razed to the ground.

As the Red Army finally entered Warsaw in January 1945 they 'liberated' a pile of rubble. In their wake, the NKVD arriving from the east had been disarming and arresting Polish insurgents all along. Many of the labor and concentration camps established under German occupation retained similar functions under the new Soviet occupiers. Poland's borders were changed and fell under the Soviet sphere of influence. The legitimate Polish government-in-exile in London didn't return to Poland, where Stalin had a Soviet-friendly government installed.

The geopolitical landscape had changed – the rest of the world moved on. However, some Polish soldiers continued to fight, joining WiN and different partisan groups in forests. From a more academic point of view, fighting at this stage may seem irrational, if not suicidal, but it had an emotional logic. In Poland, one occupying force had simply been replaced by another. Some describe this period as a civil war. The last of the 'doomed soldiers', Józef Franczak, was killed in 1963.

Even those who tried to rebuild or start 'normal' civilian lives were rarely able to do so: the majority of Home Army soldiers were persecuted and imprisoned at some point, and many were executed in the years of Stalinist repression that followed. Polish soldiers returning from the West did so at their own peril, and they too were often arrested and prosecuted as 'traitors'.

Reading about the lives and profoundly unjust fates of Emil 'Nil' Fieldorf, executed in 1953, or Captain Witold Pilecki, executed in 1948, and so many others, is heartbreaking. But in the years that would follow, speaking publicly about the Warsaw Uprising was not allowed. "Not a word about the rising. Not a word about the Home Army. As if we never existed," Wanda Traczyk-Stawska recalled. Only with the fall of communism did this change.

In Poland today the rising is a subject of constant, passionate debate and public discourse, yet it still remains relatively unknown in the West, despite the many films and books that have documented it.

The Warsaw Uprising and its aftermath remains not only crucial to understanding WWII and Poland today, but it is also part of Europe's shared history: it is the story of the Allies who fought for freedom – and lost.

SIEGE OF BASTOGNE

In one of the coldest winters on record, German forces mounted a desperate final roll of the dice to drive the Allies back. Cut off and encircled by the enemy, one city and its defenders held the line for over a week

When American and German forces clashed in the Belgian city Bastogne during the winter of 1944-45, in the most inhumanely freezing conditions, both sides incurred high losses. The fight was a bitter struggle, a desperate slogging match of attrition and decimation, but the bonds forged between local inhabitants and American soldiers back then are still commemorated and celebrated annually to this day.

Contrary to what has been claimed, there was never really any significant danger at any given time that the German forces would actually capture Bastogne. Initially it wasn't even a German objective, but as the situation deteriorated it became precisely that.

Commander of the 5th Panzer Army, General Hasso von Manteuffel, led one of the three German armies that attacked west at 5:30am on December 16. He was a seasoned tactician who had learned some of his craft while serving under General Erwin Rommel, with the Deutsches Afrika Korps (DAK) in the Western Desert of North Africa. Manteuffel was initially more interested in the Belgian/German-speaking town of Saint Vith, to the northeast of Bastogne, which still had 14 operative rail links to the Reich.

The primary objective of the 5th Panzer Army was to strike out to the west, cross the Meuse River and head for Antwerp before the Allies had the opportunity to reinforce and prevent their progress, a mammoth task for the Germans. That said, the strategic significance of Bastogne had been acknowledged by both Oberkommando der Wehrmacht (OKW) and Supreme Headquarters Allied Expeditionary Force (SHAEF) because the city rests on a high plateau where seven roads converge.

It's fair to state that Manteuffel's 5th had the most favorable terrain, a series of rolling hills interspersed with pastureland and planted woodland, which was most conducive to tank and troop maneuvers. Moreover, he had studied maps of the region, understood the topography perfectly, and acknowledged that Bastogne was a city that would have to be contained to preserve his supply lines to the east, but not necessarily taken. It would transpire later on that some of his subordinates had other ideas on the subject.

A gruesome gamble

While the Allies prepared to sit out the winter in the 86-mile-long 'Honeymoon' sector, throughout late November and early December there had been numerous indicators of an imminent breakout to the west by Nazi forces, which they simply chose to ignore.

General Omar Bradley was dismissive of reports from Bletchley Park, to the point that he often forgot, intentionally or unintentionally, to share the information with his subordinates. Then there were reports from the Luxembourg/German border where two German soldiers had been taken prisoner by the 28th Infantry Division, who revealed the extent of the Nazi build-up. The two POWs were duly taken to Bradley's HQ, but again he shelved the intelligence with the off the cuff remark: "The Germans know we're going to attack them so they're building their defenses."

The London Meteorological Office weather forecast for the south of Belgium for December 18 said that the day would begin with dense fog and intermittent light snow showers, combined with a mild northeasterly wind. The expected temperature was 12 degrees Fahrenheit. The Ardennes are always blanketed in fog

Men of B Company, 101st Engineers, emerge after holding a woodland position all night against a German counterattack near Wiltz, Luxembourg, January 14, 1945

The bitterly cold conditions made life hell for the American troops as they maneuvered to stem the Nazi advance

throughout the winter months, but it wasn't snowing when the first American reinforcement units began arriving in Bastogne, and it would be a few days before the snow would begin to settle. Between early December 1944 and late January 1945, Bastogne would experience one of the coldest winters ever recorded – conditions that would make the fight to come an even crueller struggle.

The city had been officially liberated by the Allies on September 10, 1944, and from that point on it was garrisoned by soldiers of the 28th Infantry Division, who were part of VIII Corps, commanded by the very capable General Troy Middleton.

On December 18, Colonel Roberts, commanding the 10th Armored (Tiger) Division, met with Middleton at his VIII Corps HQ, formerly the Heintz Belgian Army barracks in Bastogne. Middleton had been seriously preoccupied during those first days, organizing defenses in the east along the Luxembourg/Germany border with what meagre forces he had at his disposal to resist the Nazi tsunami.

A tactical genius, he accurately deduced that Manteuffel's 5th Panzer Army was advancing in the direction of Bastogne from the north, northeast and east on the main approaches to the city. Manteuffel would later lament that "the impetus was lost during those first 48 hours."

Race to the front

Ludwig Lindemann of the 26th Volksgrenadier Division (VGD) recalled how the early promise of the offensive rapidly dissipated:

"At midday, December 18, 1944, the Americans surrendered and we took 16 officers and 365 men prisoner. Seven tanks were destroyed and a lot of war materiel was captured. This action opened the route to Bastogne. But what started as a military success would end in torrents of blood."

On their arrival in Bastogne on December 18, the 10th Armored Division's Combat Command B (CCB) was divided into three teams. Team Cherry at the head of the column, commanded by Lieutenant Colonel Henry T Cherry Jr, was ordered to head northeast to Longvilly to cover the northeasterly approach. Team O'Hara, commanded by Lieutenant Colonel James 'Smiling Jim' O'Hara, was assigned a sector along the Bastogne-Wiltz road to prepare for an assault from the east. Team Desobry, commanded by young, gangly Major William Desobry, Commanding Officer of the 20th Armored Infantry Battalion, was dispatched to Noville, roughly four miles north of Bastogne. The purpose of the CCB was to establish defensive blocking positions to hinder or prevent the advancing enemy forces from capturing this key city, with specific instructions from Middleton to "hold at all costs". It was a fairly wide perimeter, but the most important aspect at this juncture centered on buying time. Meanwhile things had been stirring down south.

Artillery commander Brigadier General Anthony C McAuliffe, who in the absence of Major General Maxwell D Taylor had been put in charge of the 101st Airborne division for the duration, had received a phone call from XVIII Airborne Corps' General Matthew B Ridgway, ordering him to prepare for immediate departure to join Middleton in the Ardennes. The 101st Airborne Division would leave as early as possible on December 18.

Ralph K Manley of the 501st Parachute Infantry Regiment (PIR) 101st Airborne Division was on a brief period of leave when the Germans made their move:

"I was in Paris on a 24-hour pass just after we returned from Holland when a loudspeaker announced: 'Report to your units immediately.' So we returned from Paris back to our unit and immediately got on what clothes we had. I still had on my class A, of course, for being in Paris, and we loaded onto port battalion trucks, without overcoats and without overshoes, these semi-trucks that had four-foot sidewalls on them and open tops, and we headed toward the Bulge. And at zero degrees you can imagine [what it was like] in open air trucks,

"THIS ACTION OPENED THE ROUTE TO BASTOGNE. BUT WHAT STARTED AS A MILITARY SUCCESS WOULD END IN TORRENTS OF BLOOD"

Left: (From left) Lieutenant General Omar Bradley, Supreme Allied Commander Dwight D Eisenhower and General George S Patton survey the damage in Bastogne, February 5, 1945

going there, put in like cattle you might say, on trucks that weren't covered. That's what we rode to Bastogne on. Once we got there, of course, it was just dismount and head up the road to the city, on foot. We had our rifles, our hand grenades, our anti-tank mines and things of that nature, and each demolitionist had 25 pounds of composition C."

Desperate but determined

The German troops heading toward Bastogne were not as well provisioned as previously assumed, and they were not all seasoned veterans. The Volksgrenadier divisions had only been formed in the fall of 1944 and were subsequently regarded as 'below average' by the German high command. Not one single Volksgrenadier division in the west was considered capable of autonomously launching a sustained, all-out attack. They were encumbered by lack of mobility and equipment, and many of the recently formed divisions hadn't even experienced basic training.

The American forces tasked with the defense of Bastogne, on the other hand, were mostly seasoned veterans. While the 10th Armored Division had experienced vicious fighting as part of General George Patton's 3rd Army around Metz, the 101st Airborne had earned their colors in Normandy and the Netherlands.

The prospect of facing off against the 101st Airborne certainly incited consternation from General von Lüttwitz, commander of the German 47th Panzer Corps:

"We had intercepted a radio message to the effect that the 101st Airborne Division was ordered to Bastogne in a fast, motorized march. I personally heard this message and was trying to get into Bastogne before the 101st Airborne Division got there."

Despite running low on ammunition, US troops dug in on the perimeter held off the German assaults

Another stark difference between the two opposing sides was that German units in the field rarely operated independently below regimental level. They needed orders. This was to a large extent the antithesis of the US Army, which could take the initiative, improvise and act on the hop all the way down to squad level.

At zero hour when the German attack commenced, beneath low clouds and swirling mist, the landscape was still shrouded in darkness. From the German/Luxembourg border in the east, the 26th VGD advanced on the left flank and the 2nd Panzer Division on the right; the notorious but much depleted Panzer-Lehr were earmarked to follow in their wake at 6am. They were inevitably delayed by roads that had become unnavigable and inundated by mud, which caused delays to the 5th Army timetable.

Another cause for delay was due to the blocking tactics of American units in the east. These soldiers were primarily from the 28th Infantry Division, the Pennsylvania National Guard, who found themselves directly in the path of the German attack. In spite of their numbers having been reduced by 80 per cent in the previous Battle of the Hürtgen Forest, supported by elements of the 9th Armored Division their courageous delaying tactics and staunch defensive lines bought invaluable time for the American forces to get troops and armor into Bastogne but, again, it was Middleton's

Images: Alamy, Getty

An American Sherman tank and infantrymen advance over open ground near the besieged Bastogne

General Dwight D Eisenhower, (left), Major General Maxwell D Taylor (second left) and Lieutenant General Lewis R Brereton (third left) during a review of the 101st Airborne Division, March 14, 1945

The bravery of the US servicemen who defended Bastogne is celebrated to this day

quick thinking and remarkable grasp of the strategic situation that helped protect the city.

Good friends Private First Class William F Greenplate and Private First Class Joel W Rauls, both attached to the 9th Armored Division, had already experienced some hard fighting as they attempted to repel the Germans. As the situation deteriorated they decided to make a run for it. Greenplate never talked about his experiences at Bastogne, until one day he told his daughter, Virginia, about a very close shave:

"I survived the war – it was being married that almost killed me. While retreating into Bastogne, I accidentally caught my wedding ring on a barbed-wire fence. The radio man was right behind me and cut me loose, but he forgot to hold the tension in the wire, so it snapped back on me and nearly took my damned finger clean off."

By the time American defenses in the east began to disintegrate and fall back, reinforcements had already arrived in Bastogne. The first German shell landed outside the town's Church of Saint Peter during the early afternoon of December 18.

Driven back

Supported by American artillery units and paratroopers, the 10th Armored teams held on for a good few days against sustained German attacks, before they gradually began to fall back piecemeal toward Bastogne. The weather played a significant part here too. Some soldiers on the frontlines observed that the freezing fog was incredibly dense, severely limiting visibility. This so-called 'Hitler weather' actually worked in the Allies' favor, because despite not being able to use their superior air power, the attacking Germans were never entirely sure of the size of the opposing forces, and vice versa. Roads in the east quickly became congested due to the interminable flow of American stragglers from the 9th Armored Division's Combat Command Reserve (CCR) and 28th Infantry Division falling back west. These men would be formed into a defensive reserve that became known somewhat ominously as Team SNAFU.

101st Airborne paratroopers from A company, 1st Battalion, 506th, commanded by Lieutenant Colonel James L LaPrade, were

US forces refused a German ultimatum to surrender and fought on in the appalling conditions

Commander of the 5th Panzer Army, General Hasso von Manteuffel, 1944

ordered up to Noville to provide support for Team Desobry. When LaPrade arrived at the 20th Armored Infantry Battalion's command post at 11:30am on December 19, there ensued a furious altercation between him and Major Desobry concerning who would be in overall command. The one thing Desobry and LaPrade agreed on was that this ship didn't need more than one captain, so with LaPrade being senior, he assumed the assignment.

This detail would shortly become superfluous because later that day a German shell landed in the street just outside the Team Desobry command post in Noville. The explosion killed LaPrade outright and Desobry, who was in the same room, was peppered with fragments of white-hot shrapnel. Despite the severity of his wounds, and with one of his eyes resting on his bloodied cheek, Desobry was taken to Roberts' headquarters in Bastogne to report on the situation in Noville. Roberts was shocked at the appearance of his young major's blood-covered visage, and wasted no time ordering him to report immediately to the 101st Airborne Division's medical facility northwest of Bastogne at Barriere-Hinck. It was a fateful decision because later that same evening the facility was attacked from the northeast and captured by elements of the German 116th (Windhund-Greyhound) Division.

Fog of war

Sergeant Paul Bebout, 1st Battalion, 501st Parachute Infantry Regiment (PIR), 101st Airborne Division, said, "When I arrived in Bastogne the fog was so thick you could hardly see in front of you. At first it rained but then it started snowing, and I think we had about three to four inches. The only place to go was the foxhole. We had nothing with us, no warm winter clothing and not enough weapons, so we had no choice back then – we had to bum these things off the guys that were falling back."

On December 20, German artillery began raining down on Team O'Hara's position at Wardin, roughly two miles east of Bastogne. The previous day had seen a vicious running battle during which fog had effectively masked all potential observation. Fearing that an infantry assault was imminent, O'Hara's men hit out with every gun and mortar that they could bring to bear on the Germans. The supporting 2nd Battalion, 327th Glider Infantry, in Marvie almost adjacent to Wardin, also began to receive concentrated enemy artillery fire and had heard the throaty rumble of enemy tanks moving toward them. While Team O'Hara was tentatively holding out against the flow of German troops and vehicles heading westward, Team Cherry could no longer impede the approaching enemy due to the sheer weight of numbers. It was time to retire to safer positions closer to the perimeter of Bastogne. Team Hustead (previously Team Desobry) ran the gauntlet returning to Bastogne.

On December 20, McAuliffe was officially placed in command of all the US forces in and around Bastogne. His final meeting with Middleton occurred that same day at Middleton's newly established VIII Corps HQ in Neufchateau. They discussed the current situation at some length, and as Middleton left his parting remark to McAuliffe was: "Don't get yourself surrounded, Tony." Approximately 11,000 airborne troops and auxiliaries had made it to Bastogne. This was numerically about the same as the German troops who were attacking.

The people of Bastogne were a special breed. Tenacious, generous and stoic, they were no strangers to conflict. Roughly two-thirds of Bastogne's citizens had already fled the city before the first German bombs fell. With its meagre population reduced to around 9,000, they opted for a subterranean existence in private and communal cellars beneath the city.

One of these cellars was located beneath the Notre-Dame school a few hundred yards up the street from the church. During the artillery exchanges it became a refuge for more than 600 civilians and around 50 nuns. As bombs and ear-shattering explosions impacted in close proximity, clouds of asphyxiating dust shook loose from those ancient rafters, rendering the foul air in the cellar almost unbreathable. With water and electricity supplies disconnected, this sizeable underground space was only illuminated by sparse candles and the few narrow shafts of light that occasionally pervaded the murkiness below.

The incessant screams of panicking children intermingled with the agonized wails and

An American soldier moves cautiously toward the prone figure of a German infantryman

moans of the wounded and dying, creating a cacophony that would've tested the resilience of even the sturdiest observers.

One of the temporary residents was a young nurse named Augusta Chiwy, who had returned home to Bastogne on December 16 in order to spend Christmas with her father and aunt. As her profession demanded, she volunteered to help care for those confined in the cellar beneath the Notre Dame school. Later on she volunteered to assist in caring for wounded GIs under the auspices of 20th Armored Infantry Battalion medic Dr John 'Jack' Prior.

Heroic defense

As the perimeter around Bastogne began to contract, American soldiers and civilians adopted a siege mentality. The weather report for south Belgium from the London Meteorological Office for Wednesday, December 20 forecasted persistent fog, with heavy snow showers expected on the high ground. It would remain cloudy, overcast and with a mild northeasterly wind. Temperatures were expected to fall below a bone-chilling five degrees Fahrenheit. Ralph K Manley, who was on the perimeter defending the city, recalled the horrendous conditions:

"I was out on the edge, in a foxhole. The ground was frozen. We disabled some tanks that were coming through with the bazooka, but they got very close. Often you maybe had two in a foxhole, but in this case it was just one because the ground was so hard to dig, at least on the surface with the snow. Also, you didn't want to reveal your position."

"GUNFIRE FROM TURRET-MOUNTED .30-CALIBER MACHINE GUNS SATURATED ENEMY POSITIONS WITH DEVASTATING SPEED"

By December 21, Bastogne was surrounded, but this in no way diminished the fighting spirit of its American defenders. Outside the city in hurriedly dug foxholes and slit trenches, shivering GIs desperate stave off the mind-numbing cold drew up blankets donated by the civilians. Some artillery units were reporting that they were down to their last shells and all stocks of ammunition and medical supplies were becoming seriously depleted.

Second Lieutenant Everett 'Red' Andrews of the 377th Parachute Field Artillery Battalion said, "I hold the record for the shortest time spent as a forward observer ever. I peeked my head above the foxhole to see if we hit the targets, and next thing I knew I was clutching the blood from my mouth in my hands and trying to put it back. I thought I was going to die. I was 22 years old."

The following day, December 22, McAuliffe received an audacious ultimatum from the enemy. At around 11:30am, four Germans emerged out of the fog on the Arlon Road southeast of Bastogne to present a bare-faced bluff. When the ultimatum was presented to McAuliffe he was initially confused: "They want to surrender?" Lieutenant Colonel Ned Moore, the division's acting chief of staff, explained the Germans' meaning: "No, sir, they want us to surrender." When McAuliffe heard that he laughed out loud: "Us surrender? Aw, nuts."

He pondered for a few minutes then said, "Well, I don't know what to tell them." He turned to his staff and asked what they thought. G-3 Lieutenant Colonel Harry Kinnard said, "That first remark of yours would be hard to beat."

McAuliffe replied, "What do you mean?"

Kinnard answered, "Sir, you said: 'Nuts.'"

All members of the staff present applauded enthusiastically. McAuliffe then carefully wrote his response: "To the German Commander, Nuts! The American Commander."

It became one of the most famous ripostes in military history, and to this day it's commemorated every year in Bastogne during 'Nuts' weekend.

The December 23 would become a seminal day in the history of the siege, when the skies above Bastogne finally cleared. By mid-morning US Pathfinders had parachuted in from two C-47s to mark the landing zones (LZs) and drop zones (DZs). Codenamed Operation Repulse, it was one of the most accurate air resupply drops of the WWII. The C-47s were followed by fighter planes that swooped in from the azure skies to hammer Manteuffel's panzers, trucks and assault guns with bullets, napalm and high-explosives, their tracks in the fresh snow making them easy targets. A further 240 tons of supplies were dropped the following day, Christmas Eve.

By December 24, the defensive perimeter was 12.5 miles in circumference. In Bastogne the streets were practically deserted. The smell of smouldering embers permeated the air, mingling with the stench of decaying corpses literally stacked outside American aid stations. Somewhere on the Rue Neufchateau, one of the seven roads that lead from the main square, Bing Crosby's 'White Christmas' crackled mockingly on a requisitioned gramophone. The city had reached its nadir, but the fighting continued almost unabated.

In the 20th Armored Infantry Battalion Aid station on the Rue Neufchateau, surgeon Jack Prior was using five-star cognac to disinfect wounds, and his two volunteer Belgian nurses had bathed in champagne because there was no running water.

Festive fighting

In the early hours of Christmas Day, the Germans launched a fresh offensive. The village of Champs, the furthest outpost of the 101st located to the northwest of Bastogne, was deemed a prime target for this yuletide assault. Generalmajor Heinz Kokott, commander of the 26th VGD, assembled depleted battalions of the 15th Panzergrenadier Division and the 26th VGD, and issued orders to the effect that Bastogne would have to be taken before 8pm. It was a daunting task, but relatively unmoved by the fact that most of his troops were cold, exhausted and operating on empty stomachs, he prepared the assault. He would first strike at the 502nd Parachute Infantry Regiment

Infantrymen from the 4th Armored Division in the advance to relieve Bastogne, December 27, 1944

US troops supported by Shermans established a narrow corridor through German positions south of Bastogne

Private Adam H Davis and Milford A Sillars during a break in fighting in Bastogne, December 19, 1944

(PIR) in Champs, through a small breach in the line between the 327th Glider Infantry Regiment on the left and the 506th PIR on the right. A force of M18 tank destroyers from the 705th concealed in nearby woods had been designated to provide support. The Americans were ready.

The attack commenced at 2:45am under cover of darkness to avoid Allied air attacks. A powerful barrage by the entire artillery battalion of the 26th VGD was quickly followed at 3:30am by an attack of the 115th Panzergrenadier Regiment and the 15th Panzergrenadier Division, supported by two battalions of the 77th Regiment of the 26th VGD. The valiant American forces repulsed every attempt to break through to Bastogne. Within hours the offensive had ground to a shuddering halt and none of the German objectives had been achieved.

The following day, sometime around noon, McAuliffe received word that some soldiers of the 326th Airborne Engineer Battalion were reporting contact with "three light tanks believed friendly". Along the ice-covered road from Assenois, just a few miles southeast of the Bastogne perimeter, three American Sherman tanks and a half-track rumbled forward, followed by two more Shermans sweeping the rear. The three lead Shermans were commanded by First Lieutenant Charles P Boggess and his crew. He ordered covering fire into the tree line.

Patton punches through

During the ensuing melee, a 900-foot gap developed between the first three tanks and the last three vehicles, giving the enemy just enough time to throw a few mines out on the road in front of the half-track, which rolled over the first mine and promptly exploded, throwing burning metal, shrapnel and body parts across the freshly fallen snow.

Gunfire from turret-mounted .30-caliber machine guns saturated enemy positions with devastating speed and, after a short while, the two rear tank crews hastily disembarked, cleared the remaining mines and radioed for more elements of their column to follow on. At 4:50pm (recorded in 4th Armored Division dispatches), Boggess, commanding officer of C Company, 37th Tank Battalion, spied what turned out to be Airborne engineers from A Company of the 326th preparing to assault a pillbox near the highway . Boggess told the driver of his Sherman to take his foot off the gas. As daylight dithered and the light faded, a single engineer from the 326th shouted, "I'm Lieutenant Webster, 326th Airborne Engineers. Glad to see you guys."

Patton had broken through and pried a narrow corridor through German forces to the south of Bastogne. It was only one-mile wide in some places, but it was enough to effectively reinforce the defenders and remove the many wounded GIs to a safer haven. The fighting around Bastogne was far from over, and the weather would deteriorate even further, but despite OKW committing what feeble reserves they had, it was all going to be in vain.

Elements of the US 1st and 3rd Armies met on January 16, 1945, in the small, devastated town of Houffalize a few miles north of Bastogne. The war would continue for five more months, but this crushing defeat of Nazi forces in the winter of 1944-45 sapped all their remaining offensive capability and handed the tactical and strategic initiative to the Allies.

The battle ended with the Nazi swastika flag on the Reichstag roof being replaced by the Soviet hammer and sickle

ENDGAME

THE FALL OF THE — THIRD REICH —

The Battle of Berlin between Hitler's Germany and Stalin's Russia was history's bloodiest showdown, and its shockwaves echoed for decades...

© Alamy, Getty Images

Hitler's mesmeric speeches were heightened by the theatricality of their setting. His followers frequently responded rapturously

In October 1941, four months after the Wehrmacht invaded the Soviet Union, Adolf Hitler stood before a packed auditorium at the Sportpalast, Berlin. The largest meeting hall in the city, with some 14,000 spectators, was festooned with swastika banners and further 'Nazified' by way of a dramatically lit, 65-foot-wide theater prop in the shape of a golden eagle. It hovered over Der Führer, seemingly radiating power and purity. This was Hitler's altar and before it he delivered the following sermon.

"Today, I can say that the enemy is broken and will never rise again! Her power had been assembled against Europe, and would have been a second storm of Genghis Khan. That this danger has been averted, we owe to the bravery, endurance and sacrifice of the German soldier!" His histrionic version of events was met with fanatical applause. His enemy, though, was far from broken.

By May 1945, the "Sieg Heils" that had echoed around that room had been replaced by the chilling war cries of Soviet infantrymen as they smashed their way into Hitler's sacred temple and onto the very stage he had preached from. "Ura!" they screamed as they hunted down the last of his disciples holding out in the building, going about their murderous work with bayonet, grenade and rifle butt. The Red Army wanted vengeance for the bloodletting at Stalingrad.

For the soldiers of the Red Army that stage, more so even than the Reichstag, symbolized Nazi power. Its capture meant not just the end of the war but also the death of National Socialism – the ideology that had been responsible for the slaughter of 27 million Russian citizens. For the Soviet leader Joseph Stalin, however, the real prize was the capture of the prestigious German capital itself.

The idea that the Soviets might seize Berlin and bring an end to WWII in Europe had become a distinct possibility by the start of 1945. The success of the Red Army's January offensive had seen it smash through 300 miles of German-held territory in just 20 days. By February 5, its troops began to cross the Oder river, the last great natural barrier before Berlin. Once on the other side, however, and just 37 miles from Hitler's capital, they stopped.

The Soviet advance had been so rapid and the fighting so intense that the successes had left the Red Army short of ammunition and fuel. It would take more than two months before it was resupplied sufficiently for the final push.

The pause in slaughter gave the Nazis time to reorganize, too. Reserve units were cobbled

"THE SOVIET ADVANCE HAD BEEN SO RAPID AND THE FIGHTING SO INTENSE THAT THE SUCCESSES HAD LEFT THE RED ARMY SHORT OF AMMUNITION AND FUEL"

The final offensive against Berlin opened with a bombardment of the Seelow Heights by some 9,000 Russian guns

HITLER'S LAST LINE OF DEFENSE

The boy fanatics and citizen militia of Berlin's Volkssturm

Foundation

By the end of 1944 the German war machine was running on empty, its manpower almost spent. Hitler ordered all German men aged between 16 and 60 to join Volkssturm units, and with the regular army disgraced by defeat, overall command was given to Reichsführer-SS Heinrich Himmler, who announced the birth of the People's Storm over the radio waves on October 18 while a studio audience sang 'Volk ans Gewehr!' (People to Arms!)

Recruitment

With most adult men already serving in the Wehrmacht, most of the total 6 million-strong Volkssturm were old men - with 1.4 million physically unfit and suitable only for guard duty. Approximately 600,000 were 16-19 year-old members of the Hitler Youth, with some volunteers as young as ten. Even the women of the Nazi Women's League were drafted in to provide rear-echelon support. On March 23, 1945, the women were issued firearms.

By April 25, 24,000 Volkssturm were still trying to save the doomed Germany capital, with 18,000 of that number part of the 'Clausewitz Levy' mobilized from essential war workers.

Newly mobilized members of the Volkssturm and their weapons

Training

Volkssturm recruits were rushed through a 48-hour training program covering the use of rifle, Panzerfaust and Panzerschreck anti-tank weapon, and grenades. If the situation warranted it they were also schooled in the use of pistol, sub-machine gun and landmine.

Equipment

Units assigned to guard duty were expected to use hunting rifles or weapons taken from the enemy, but even combat units found supplies hard to come by and some were only issued a trench spade by way of self-defense. In Berlin, supplies were so scarce that units were issued with Italian or Danish rifles and only a couple of rounds each. Only single-shot Panzerfaust rocket launchers seemed plentiful.

Uniform

An order issued on December 1, 1944, required recruits provide their own, resulting in a mixture of paramilitary, Hitlerjugend, police and even old WWI uniforms, but many had to make-up with cast-offs, captured British fatigues or simply civilian clothes. All insignia had to be removed except Volkssturm rank pips on the collar and the black Volkssturm armband on the upper left sleeve. The lack of a consistent uniform led to many facing summary execution as guerrillas by the Red Army.

Leadership

Command roles in the Volkssturm were often held by senior members of the Hitler Youth, civilian police and non-combat paramilitary groups such as the motoring association NSKK, the flying club NSFK and military engineering/slave labor force Organization Todt. The Berlin District Volkssturm was under the direct command of Propaganda Minister Joseph Goebbels who was also Gauleiter, or head, of the regional branch of the Nazi Party.

Effectiveness

While many Volkssturm units were as farcical as you'd expect from such an ad hoc collection of OAPs and inexperienced ideologues, some of them – such as the Siemensstadt Volkssturm Battalion 3/115 fighting in the eastern suburbs of the city – held out until the surrender. The Hitlerjugend – representing a generation that had known only National Socialism – fought with a level of zeal that terrified even battle-hardened soldaten, and one Russian account describes a column of 400 Hitlerjugend marching down Kolonnenstrasse toward them as if they were on parade. The stupefied 5th Shock Army paused briefly before opening fire.

Hitlerjungend 'tank-hunting units' armed with Panzerfausts terrorized the Soviet advance through the Wilmersdorf District, while a counter-attack launched from the Ruhleben U-Bahn saw 1,000 German troops reinforced by 2,000 Hitlerjugend – many completely unarmed – that actually drove back the advance of the 55 Guards Tank Brigade.

Perhaps the most infamous tribute to their tragic fanaticism came on April 23, when Volkssturm battalions made up entirely of Hitler Youth tried to hold the Pichelsdorf bridges across the Havel River for a relief army that never arrived – one of the many phantoms commanded by Germany's ailing despot as he raged in his bunker. Five thousand boys in adult uniforms and oversized helmets fought for five days against the Red Army advance, with 4,500 of them killed or wounded.

KEY PLAYERS

Thousands died as Berlin fell, many believing their cause was a noble one. These are the men they followed

Georgy Zhukov
USSR 1896-1974

The key Soviet commander, having driven the Germans from Moscow, defeated them at Stalingrad and routed them at Kursk, Zhukov was known as 'the man who never lost a battle'. While he did capture Berlin, his tactics cost many casualties.

Gotthard Heinrici
Nazi Germany 1886-1971

Considered the best defensive tactician in the Wehrmacht, Heinrici managed to delay the Soviet advance at Seelow despite overwhelming odds. A non-Nazi, he also refused to carry out Hitler's more suicidal orders.

Ivan Konev
USSR1897-1973

As commander of the 1st Ukrainian Front, Konev was encouraged by Stalin – who admired his ruthlessness – to 'race' Zhukov to Berlin. Attacking from the south, his forces were also the first to link up with advancing US troops.

Helmuth Weidling
Nazi Germany 1891-1955

On April 22, Hitler ordered Weidling's execution. The next day he appointed him commander of Berlin's defense. On learning of his promotion, Weidling said: "I'd rather have been shot."

together from whatever troops were left and whichever civilians could be press-ganged into service. Wounded soldiers were ordered from their hospital beds and army clerks sent to combat units, while men as old as 60 and boys as young as 13 were drafted into the newly formed Volkssturm militias. Those who refused were executed.

In the end, the Nazi high command managed to sweep together about 760,000 troops. Many were sent to join the 9th Army at Seelow Heights, the highlands east of Berlin, to help build elaborate defenses there. In the plains before them as these troops worked, the Soviets gathered together an army of 2.5 million men, more than 6,000 tanks and 40,000 artillery pieces. The clock was ticking on what would be the bloodiest showdown in history. By the time Berlin fell, hundreds of thousands of people lay dead.

British Prime Minister Winston Churchill also wanted to capitalize on this brief pause. He saw it as an opportunity for the West to seize both the initiative and Berlin itself. By late March, the Western Allies had crossed the Rhine, and were themselves just 60 miles from the city. "If the Russians take Berlin," Churchill warned US President Franklin D Roosevelt on April 1, "may this not lead to grave and formidable difficulties in the future?"

Churchill, as it would transpire, was very much focused on the future and what a post-war map of Europe should look like. He urged the Americans to take the city. The US high command, though, under General Dwight D Eisenhower, wasn't keen. The mauling his troops had taken during the Battle of the Bulge that winter, when Hitler had launched his final counter-offensive in the west, had left him wary. When Eisenhower asked what casualties he could expect if he attacked Berlin, one of his generals, Omar Bradley, told him 100,000. It was an unthinkable figure. Had it transpired, it would have constituted one-fifth of all US casualties for the entire war. Eisenhower instead deferred to Stalin, who told him that Berlin was strategically unimportant and that his efforts would be better focused on preventing the Nazis from regrouping in the south. It was advice that Eisenhower was quite happy to take.

Yet neither Stalin nor Churchill was being transparent. It had already been agreed at February's Yalta Conference that when the Nazi regime toppled, the Allies would divvy up Berlin between them. So why then did it matter to Churchill who took the city first? Similarly, if Berlin was strategically unimportant, why was Stalin so keen for the USSR to single-handedly suffer such high casualties capturing it? After

1. ZHUKOV LAUNCHES SEELOW HEIGHTS OFFENSIVE
April 16, 3am
After more than two months of intensive preparation, the 1st Belorussian Front under Marshal Zhukov attacks the well-fortified German position at Seelow Heights. The objective is taken after three days of fierce fighting. It proves to be Germany's last significant position of organized resistance to her inevitable defeat.

2. ZHUKOV REACHES THE OUTSKIRTS OF BERLIN
April 20, 8pm
After having raced 37 miles from Seelow to the eastern edge of Berlin, Zhukov's 1st Belorussian Front announces its arrival with an artillery barrage that continues until the city falls two weeks later.

3. THE BATTLE OF HALBE
April 24, 10am
The 9th Army, escaping from Marshal Konev's 1st Ukrainian Front, is pinned down by SS troops after being mistaken for a Soviet column. The hold-up allows Konev to envelop them. Over the next few days, the 9th Army is annihilated.

4. BERLIN ENCIRCLED
April 24, 6pm
Forward elements of Marshal Konev's 1st Ukrainian Front link up with men from Zhukov's 1st Belorussian Front, to the west of Berlin. With Marshal Rokossovsky's 2nd Belorussian Front pushing down on it from the north, the Nazi capital finds itself completely surrounded.

5. SOVIET AND US TROOPS MEET
April 25, 4pm
Elements of Konev's 1st Ukrainian Front make contact with men from the US 69th Infantry Division at Torgau on the Elbe, 84 miles southwest of Berlin.

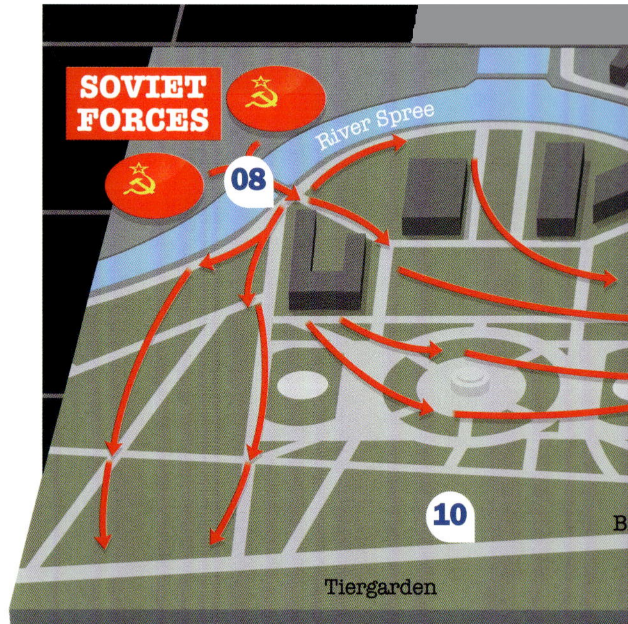

6. HITLER'S BUNKER IS SHELLED
April 27, 10am
Soviet artillerymen on Schlesingerstrasse are ordered to fire on the Reichstag; they comply even though Berlin's so engulfed by flames they can't see it. After hitting their own troops, they switch targets to the Reich Chancellery, where Hitler's bunker is located.

6. THE CAPTURE OF TEMPELHOF AIRFIELD
April 28, 11am
With much of Berlin's southern suburbs now in Soviet hands, Tempelhof airport is seized. With the city completely surrounded, Hitler's last exit route has been closed off. He now knows his fate lies with either death or capture in Berlin.

THE RED ARMY'S INVASION

At 2.5 million strong, Stalin's war machine was an irresistible force hell-bent on avenging the Nazis' murderous campaign of the previous four years

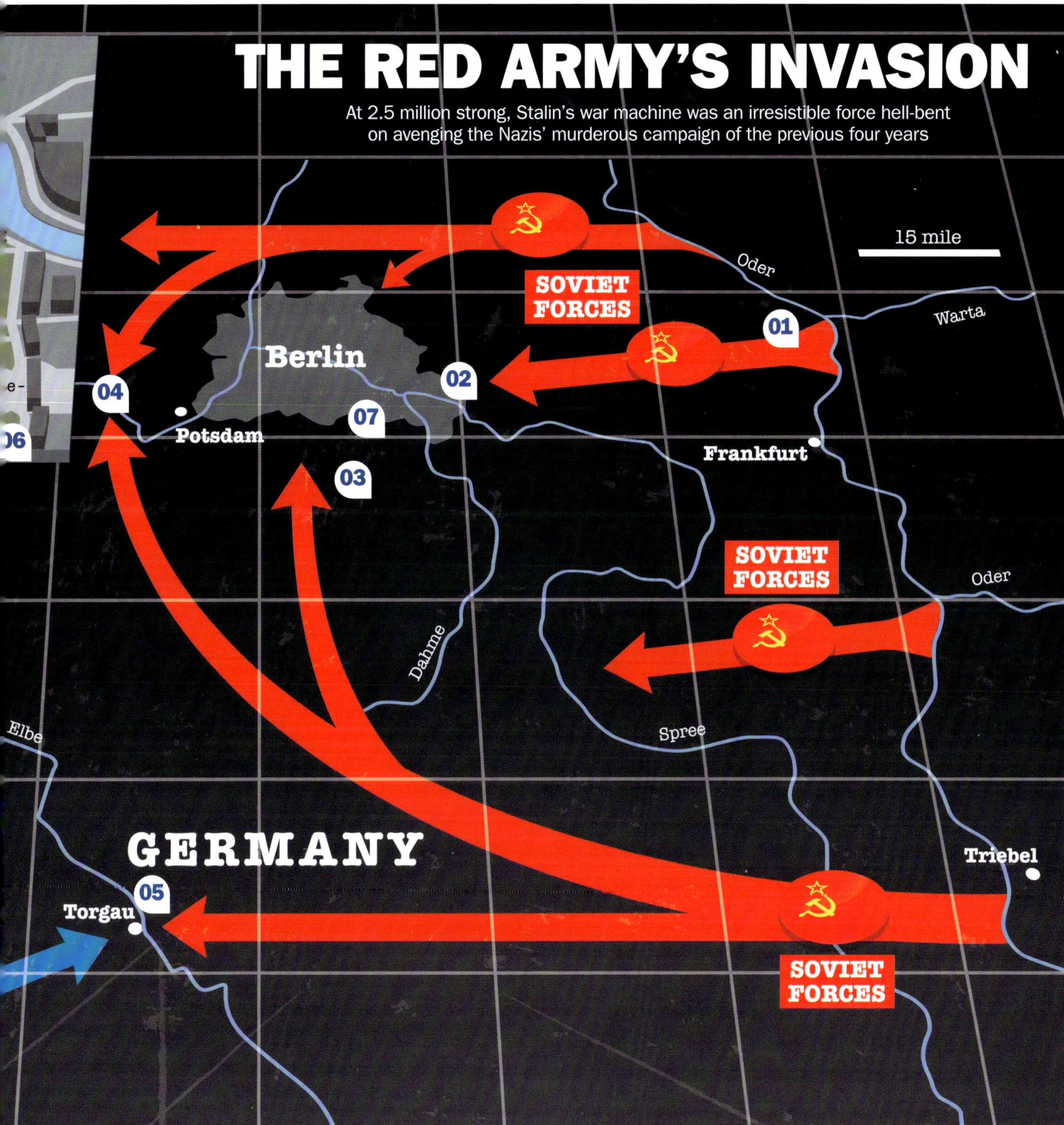

8. THE CAPTURE OF THE MOLTKE BRIDGE

April 28, 5pm

This last intact crossing over the River Spree was the gateway into central Berlin. About 5,000 German troops barricaded it at both ends and wired it up for demolition. Soviet forces assault the bridge at dusk and capture it.

9. THE CAPTURE OF THE REICHSTAG BUILDING

April 30, 10.40pm

After two days of fighting, Soviet forces finally place their flag atop the Reichstag in time for May Day, as ordered by Stalin. By May 1, the Reichstag is in Soviet hands, and news of Hitler's suicide prompts the German surrender.

10. KROLL OPERA HOUSE IS CLEARED

April 30, 11.30am

Soviet infantrymen just 26,620 feet from the Reichstag are attacked from the rear by SS diehards in the Kroll Opera House. The building is taken after several hours of bitter hand-to-hand fighting.

all, he'd spent much of the war prior to D-Day haranguing his allies for not dying enough while Russia was being bled white. Surely now was the time for them to make up for that in this common crusade against fascism? Militarily it would have made more sense, too – a ready-made pincer movement that would save one side from having to surround the city on its own. The answer to these questions lies in what would appear to be a giant game of chess being played out between Churchill and Stalin, only with real-life pawns and potentially catastrophic consequences on the world stage.

At the start of April, Churchill, fixing his gaze well beyond Hitler's imminent demise, ordered the drafting of Operation Unthinkable. Documents declassified in 1998 reveal that a month before the end of hostilities in Europe, Churchill was plotting a war against the Soviet Union. In his secret plan, 47 British and US divisions were to launch a surprise attack against the Soviets on July 1, 1945. Moreover, this offensive was to be supported by ten German divisions with the intent not merely of driving the Soviets out of Eastern Europe but of invading the USSR itself. According to official documents, the aim was to seize "such vast areas of Metropolitan Russia that the war-making capacity of that country would be [rendered] impossible."

Did Stalin know what Churchill was up to? Almost certainly. By 1945, the Soviets had so successfully infiltrated British intelligence that notorious double agents like Kim Philby and Guy Burgess had been feeding the Kremlin secrets for years. It also explains Stalin's desire to flood Berlin and its surrounding area with his troops. Control Berlin, as Karl Marx once pointed out, and you control Europe. And if you're Joseph Stalin, you also put an awful lot of territory between your borders and any newly-drawn battle lines.

Whatever the truth, there's little doubt that Roosevelt's sudden death on April 12 prompted Stalin to finally attack. In Roosevelt he'd had

COUNTDOWN TO THE END

A blow-by-blow account of how the Red Army dragged Hitler's Third Reich to the execution block and finally killed it off

The Battle of Berlin begins
The Red Army begins its assault on the German Army's last major defensive line at Seelow Heights, 37mi west of Berlin. It falls just three days later.
April 16, 3am

Bombardment of Berlin begins
It's Hitler's 56th birthday. He emerges from the Führerbunker for the last time to award medals to boy soldiers. On the same evening, the Soviet bombardment begins.
April 20, 8pm

First counter-attack ordered
Hitler orders a force under General Steiner to repel the encircling Soviets. When it fails, Hitler announces that he's going to kill himself.
April 21, 11am

General Weidling appointed
With the Soviets closing in on all sides, Hitler appoints Artillery General Helmuth Weidling commander of the Berlin Defense Area.
April 23, 2pm

Retreating 9th Army surrounded
General Busse's 9th Army, heading to Berlin after withdrawing from Seelow Heights, is encircled at Halbe. Trapped, the Soviets destroy it.
April 24, 10am

Second counter-attack
General Wenck's 12th Army is pulled off the line facing US troops and sent to relieve the encircled 9th Army. It proves impossible.
April 24, 9pm

As the siege went on and the street fighting became more intense, Berlin's once beautiful city streets were shattered by flames and shellfire

The onslaught arrives
About half a million Soviet troops swarm into Berlin from all directions. Fierce street fighting starts to see almost every building damaged or destroyed.
April 26, dawn

Himmler discusses surrender
Hitler learns that his most trusted ally, Himmler, has approached the Western Allies to discuss peace terms. Hitler declares him a traitor.
April 28, 3pm

Moltke Bridge is captured
Demolition charges fail to properly destroy the last bridge over the Spree. It falls into Soviet hands, taking access to central Berlin with it.
April 29, 5pm

Weidling's last report
Weidling informs Hitler that the Soviets are just yards from his bunker, that the Reichstag is under fire and the Nazi ammunition is very nearly exhausted.
April 30, 10am

Hitler's suicide
Hitler kills himself in the Führerbunker by simultaneously biting into a deadly cyanide capsule and shooting himself in the head. His remains are later cremated by his bodyguards.
April 30, 3.30pm

Walter Doenicke lies dead next to a portrait of Hitler

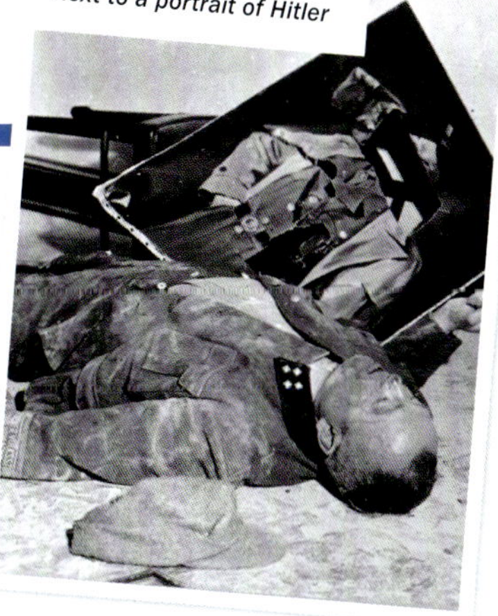

The Volkssturm militias, mostly made up of old men and schoolboys, were hastily trained and poorly equipped. Casualty rates reflected this

SURRENDER AND PEACE

After triggering the most devastating war in history, Germany finally signed a peace settlement with the Allies

Although Weidling surrendered Berlin to the Russians on May 2, effectively ending hostilities, Germany's official surrender didn't take place until six days later, on May 8, 1945, at a ceremony in the Soviet Military Administration in Berlin-Karlshorst.

This was actually the second act of surrender the German authorities signed. The first at the Western Allies HQ in France the day before was deemed unacceptable to the Soviets, who argued that the surrender should take place at the seat of the German government. The terms of both documents, however, were the same – the surrender was to be unconditional, although Germany could expect to be treated a lot better than she had been in 1918.

Various German leaders, Himmler included, had earlier made several attempts to surrender conditionally to the Western Allies. But the condition was always the same – that the regime be allowed to continue its fight against the Soviet Union. To his credit Eisenhower refused to accept any of them. Like Roosevelt, he was a man of his word and he insisted Germany surrender to all the Allies – the USSR included – so that the war that had ravaged Europe for six long years could finally be brought to a close.

Field Marshal Wilhelm Keitel signs Nazi Germany's unconditional surrender to the Allies on May 8, 1945

an ally he could trust. His replacement, Harry S Truman, offered no such assurances and, rather than wait to be stabbed in the back by those who'd soon be his enemy, Stalin acted decisively. The Battle for Berlin began just four days later.

In the early hours of April 16, Soviet propaganda officers announced in German over loud speakers that the assault on Seelow was imminent. The message that drifted across no man's land was designed to terrorize the Germans waiting there into putting their hands up. But for troops in those trenches and dugouts, surrender was not an option. The SS men who held guns to their backs made sure of that.

Shortly after this, at 3am, 9,000 guns fired half a million artillery shells into the German line. The bombardment lasted 35 minutes, and when it finally ended there was a chilling silence. Then the earth began to shake as 3,000 tanks rattled and clanged their way toward the German positions, among them tens of thousands of Soviet infantrymen ready for a merciless fight to the death.

The Russians expected to take Seelow Heights within hours, but its German commander General Gotthard Heinrici, had prepared well. Anticipating the bombardment, he'd pulled his troops back for its duration. Casualties had been minimal and they now raced back to their positions. Prior to the assault, he'd also ordered engineers to open a dam on the Oder river, flooding the land the Soviets now struggled to cross as anti-tank fire thundered down on them. The Soviet commander, Marshal Georgy Zhukov, had also made a critical error. Hoping to dazzle the German defenders, he'd lit his men's advance with 143 high-powered searchlights. His bombardment, however, had created an enormous wall of smoke that their beams couldn't penetrate and instead bounced back from, blinding his own troops and silhouetting them in the glare. The Germans couldn't have hoped for better targets to aim at. By dawn the Soviet advance had stalled.

It would take Zhukov three days to dislodge Heinrici's defenders, and even then only after his great rival Marshal Ivan Konev began to outflank the Germans from the south. The defensive position at Seelow fell on April 19. About 12,000 of its defenders had been killed and the rest now fled. It had cost the Soviets more than double that and nearly 750 tanks, but there was now nothing left between them and Stalin's ultimate prize – Berlin.

Zhukov's 1st Belorussian Front raced toward the city from the east, and by April 20 was on its outskirts. Zhukov marked what was to be Hitler's final birthday by launching a huge artillery barrage against the city. Cowering in his Führerbunker, Der Führer, by now deranged and deluded, ranted wide-eyed about how the German people had betrayed him. If he was going to die, he shrieked, then they would die with him. The war was lost, and Hitler knew it, but he'd make Berlin's three million inhabitants suffer terribly. The following day Zhukov's ground troops began their assault.

To the south, meanwhile, Konev's 1st Ukrainian Front was also making rapid progress. It'd broken into open country and was chasing what was left of the German 9th Army. By now, these German troops, who'd fought so bravely at Seelow, were slowly being encircled.

"THE SIEGE THAT WOULD ENGULF THE CITY FOR THE NEXT TWO WEEKS REDUCED THE ONCE SPLENDID CAPITAL TO THE INNER CIRCLE OF HELL"

Soviet troops proved they were there by tagging the Reichstag walls. Some of their graffiti is still visible today

Source: Wiki Commons / Public domain

With nobody to bury the dead, corpses crowded the streets. About 400,000 people died during fighting in the city alone

They fled toward Berlin where there was still an opening in the front but, on April 24, were halted at the town of Halbe. Not by Russians, however, but by fantaical SS troops holding the line there.

Mistaking the approaching Germans for a Soviet column, the SS opened up on them. The men from the 9th scurried for cover, and by the time the SS realized their mistake, Konev's troops were swarming all over them, assaulting the SS defenses. The 9th were trapped between the two sides and when fighting eased six days later, 60,000 Germans lay dead, some by the hands of the comrades they were supposed to defend.

The rest of the 1st Ukrainian Front swept forward, driving relentlessly toward Berlin. By nightfall it had made contact with Zhukov's troops west of the capital. With the 2nd Belorussian Front hemming the city in from the north, Berlin was now surrounded.

Hitler attempted a counter-offensive. He ordered the German 12th Army facing US troops in the west to smash through the Russian lines, link with the beleaguered 9th and drive northward to Berlin. It was a wild gamble that had no chance of success. Halted 20 miles from the city, the 12th was soon sent back by overwhelming firepower.

The Russians now tightened the noose, and the siege that would engulf the city for the next two weeks reduced the once splendid capital to the inner circle of hell. The air became poisoned with the stench of burning buildings and rotting flesh, the streets busy with twisted corpses, the cellars and subways filled with untreated wounded. As the food ran out and the water supply dwindled, those in uniform ran amok. The civilian population was terrorized by both the Russians – who hunted in packs for the city's females, raping whoever they found regardless of age or medical condition – and those supposedly defending them.

By now the mask of respectability had slipped from the faces of those who wore the swastika, the Death's Head or SS lightning bolt badges. The slavering faces of the monsters beneath were revealed as they roamed the city in gangs murdering anyone they deemed cowardly or defeatist. The corpses of old men and children alike swung creaking from the city's scorched lampposts and trees.

A doomed last stand was prepared. General Helmuth Weidling, the man to whom Hitler had given the impossible task of defending the Nazi capital, established a defensive perimeter around the city center. His 85,000-strong force, made up of literally the last men (and boys) standing, faced an onslaught from 500,000 Soviet troops.

In the early hours of April 26, the final battle began. The streets quaked and crumbled as Soviet armor rumbled through them, while artillery and aircraft rained down fire from above. Every street was contested by infantry, with much of the fighting conducted house to house and hand to hand.

By April 28, Tempelhof Airport was in Soviet hands. There was now no way out, and the German lines were collapsing fast. The following evening, Soviet troops captured the Moltke Bridge over the River Spree, giving them direct access to the Nazi heart. Within hours they'd captured Gestapo Headquarters. They were now less than a mile from the Reichstag and just 2,300 feet from Hitler's bunker. The brutal end was, now, inevitable.

Weidling delivered the news to Hitler on the morning of April 30, also informing him that his garrison only had enough ammunition to last 24 hours. He begged Der Führer to allow him to attempt a breakout, but there was to be no escape. Hitler dismissed Weidling's request and later that afternoon blew his own brains out, abandoning the Third Reich he had led to war to a horrific fate.

Whether or not this news would have persuaded the die-hard Nazis defending the Reichstag to surrender is doubtful. What isn't, though, is that many of the men the Russians exterminated as they fought their way to the top of the building weren't German. The voices the Russians heard echoing along the burning corridors, in smoke-choked offices and even in the grand auditorium were French, Norwegian, Danish, Dutch and Latvian – members of the SS's various foreign legions, dying in Berlin while fighting for their twisted ideology.

By 10.40pm that night, the swastika had been taken down from the roof of the Reichstag and replaced with the red flag of Soviet communism. The symbol of one defunct political ideology was replaced by that of what would eventually be another.

The Battle of Berlin may have helped end WWII, but it also marked the start of a new global conflict, one that would last for 45 years and stretch around the world. For it was in the rubble of the Reichstag that the next global ideological conflict – the Cold War – was born.

"EVERY STREET WAS CONTESTED BY INFANTRY, WITH MUCH OF THE FIGHTING CONDUCTED HAND TO HAND"

OKINAWA

The last campaign of WWII in the Pacific required an arduous 82 days for the Allies to claim victory

It was a curious coincidence – Operation Iceberg, the Allied invasion of Okinawa, was scheduled for April 1, 1945, both Easter Sunday and April Fool's Day. Short of an invasion of Japan itself, the island in the Ryukyu archipelago was the last objective of the Allied campaign across the Pacific Ocean during WWII. Only 340 miles from the Japanese Home Islands, Okinawa would provide the sternest test of the war for the Marine III Amphibious Corps and the US Army's XXIV Corps, comprising the 10th Army under Lieutenant General Simon Bolivar Buckner, the son of a Confederate general from the American Civil War.

The invasion date was designated Love-Day (L-Day) to avoid confusion with D-Day. Actually, the Allied build-up was larger than that of D-Day. The US and Britain brought 1,300 warships and support vessels along with 750,000 tons of supplies to the waters off Okinawa.

Buckner's 10th Army included more than 180,000 troops. Marine Major General Roy S Geiger led the III Amphibious Corps, including three divisions – the veteran 1st Marine Division, the 6th, and the 2nd in reserve. Major General John R Hodge commanded the XXIV Army Corps, including four infantry divisions – the 7th, 77th, 96th and reserve 27th.

The recent carnage at Iwo Jima remained fresh in American minds and a bloodbath was also expected at Okinawa. During the week before L-Day, navy guns fired 13,000 shells and carrier-based aircraft flew 3,095 missions. The L-Day landings were to hit the Hagushi beaches on Okinawa's southwestern shore. After the anticipated fight to gain a foothold, the Americans intended to advance eastward across the Ishikawa Peninsula, seizing Yontan and Kadena airfields. Splitting the island in two, they would swing north and south, fighting their way to opposite shores, completing the conquest of Okinawa. Another worrisome aspect of Operation Iceberg was the kamikaze threat to the host of Fifth Fleet ships obliged to remain offshore. Japanese suicide planes were expected to assault these rich targets with unprecedented vigor.

Eighty-two days of fighting on Okinawa and the nearby cluster of small islands also seized yielded an immense harvest of destruction. By the time the island was declared secure on June 22, 1945, American deaths totalled 7,374, while 31,807 were wounded and 239 were missing. The navy suffered 4,907 casualties, 120 ships were damaged and 29 had been sunk. Marines and soldiers earned 23 Medals of Honor, sadly many of them posthumous. Victory had come at a huge cost.

The Japanese garrison, under Lieutenant General Mitsuru Ushijima, commander of the 32nd Army, fielded over 100,000 troops – only

Crouching as low as possible, an American soldier races across an open stretch of ground while under machine-gun fire

11,000 prisoners surrendered. A total of 2,373 Kamikaze pilots died and thousands of sailors perished in the Imperial Japanese Navy's last substantial offensive of the war. Many died when the battleship Yamato sank under a fusillade of explosives. An estimated 150,000 Okinawan civilians also perished.

Under a canopy of aircraft and naval bombardment, the invasion rolled forward on the morning of April 1, landing craft engines stirring white wakes over seven miles across. Virtually no resistance was encountered. By the end of L-Day, 60,000 American troops occupied a beachhead 15,000 feet deep and almost 46,000 feet wide. Twenty-eight men were killed, 104 wounded, and 27 missing.

Ushijima watched the awe-inspiring sight from his command post at Shuri Castle, the ancient abode of the kings who once ruled the Ryukyus, as the Americans put 16,000 troops ashore in an hour. A firm advocate of defense in depth, he conceded the beachhead and airfields to draw the Americans inland, where he would defend the island to the last man. His forces included the 9th, 24th and 62nd Divisions. Independent brigades and artillery, engineer and naval troops were also attached. For the death struggle, the Japanese constructed three defensive lines across southern Okinawa.

Early progress was swift. In four days, American troops took territory they thought would require three weeks of combat. Both airfields were captured on the first day. By April 3, the 1st Marine Division crossed the Ishikawa Isthmus, captured the Katchin Peninsula and cut Okinawa in half. The airfields were quickly operational. Marine Air Groups 31 and 33 flew in from aircraft carriers and an Army Air Force fighter wing also arrived.

Paying for every inch

Soon enough, the Marines found stubborn resistance. Five battalions of the 4th and 29th Marines attacked the 1,200-foot Mount Yae-Take and 2,000 enemy troops under Colonel Takesiko Udo. The Marines were stonewalled by enemy machine guns and mortars. The 14-inch guns of the battleship USS Tennessee barked, and Corsairs of Marine Fighter Squadron 322 (VMF-322) bombed and strafed. The Udo Force was slaughtered while the Marines took 964 casualties clearing the area.

The 7th and 96th Divisions hit the first defensive line on April 19. The 27th Division was soon committed. Minimal gains could not be held and the attack faltered, meaning that Sherman tanks got separated from supporting infantry while advancing near Kakazu and enemy guns knocked out 22 of the 30 that were sent forward. On April 23, Admiral Chester W Nimitz, commander in chief of the Pacific, arrived on Okinawa and voiced his concerns for the Fifth Fleet as kamikaze attacks intensified.

Marines of 2nd Battalion, 1st Marines maneuver at Wana Ridge. One fires his Thompson submachine gun; the other carries a Browning Automatic Rifle

Torpedo bombers and fighters of the Royal Navy Fleet Air Arm occupy the flight deck of the carrier HMS Implacable

Hammering Buckner to energize the offensive, Nimitz snarled that if Buckner was not up to the task, "We'll get someone here to move it... I'm losing a ship and a half each day out here."

Nimitz was blunt for a reason – Japanese Operation Ten-Go was unleashing 4,500 kamikazes against the Fifth Fleet, filling the skies with ten mass sorties nicknamed Kikusui, or Floating Chrysanthemums, each including 350 or more aircraft. The sailors of the Fifth Fleet endured, earning the nickname of 'the fleet that came to stay'. Two kamikazes ripped into the aircraft carrier USS Bunker Hill on May 11, its 58th day on station.

American fighter pilots shot down scores of kamikazes. On April 22, three Marine Corsairs of VMF-323 flamed 16 in 20 minutes. Nevertheless, some suicide planes got through. The stand of the Fifth Fleet (redesignated Third Fleet when Admiral William F 'Bull' Halsey relieved Admiral Raymond A Spruance on May 27) wrote a stirring chapter in US naval history.

After three weeks of fighting, Ushijima pulled surviving defenders out of the first line, cloaked under steady rain and thick fog. In early May, the 10th Army was poised to assault the second, or Shuri Line, four divisions abreast across a 26,900-foot front. On May 2 , the 1st Marine Division assaulted the Awacha Pocket. The 5th Marines advanced through a downpour but ran into enemy fire from concealed positions. It took a week to clear Awacha.

Private Dale M Hansen of the 2nd Battalion, 1st Marines, lost his rifle as it was shattered by an enemy bullet during his single-handed destruction of a Japanese pillbox on May 7. He picked up another weapon and ran up an adjacent ridge but six Japanese soldiers blocked his path. Hansen shot four – but then his rifle jammed. The two survivors pounced. Hansen swung the rifle's butt and slipped away. Grabbing a third rifle and a clutch of grenades, Hansen charged forward again, killing eight enemy soldiers and smashing a mortar position. More Marines followed, claiming the ridgeline. Hansen was killed by a sniper four days later. On May 30, 1946, his parents accepted his posthumous Medal of Honor.

The 1st Battalion, 7th Marines, reached the top of Dakeshi Ridge twice on May 11 but was forced to retire in the face of ferocious resistance. A day later, three Sherman tanks, two mounting flamethrowers, charged ahead of the riflemen spitting flame and machine-gun bullets and claimed the high ground. The Marines atop Dakeshi Ridge looked southward toward the rocky jumble of Wana Draw and nearby Wana Ridge. The 1st Marine Division flung itself against the outcroppings, cliffs and caves. Progress was measured in yards. Through 19 days of horror, Marine casualties averaged 200 for every 300 feet advanced.

Marine and army tanks fired 5,000 75mm (3in) shells and 175,000 rounds of .30-caliber ammunition on May 16 alone. The 3rd Battalion, 7th Marines lost a dozen officers in four days. The 7th Marines took 700 casualties at Dakeshi Ridge and 500 more in five days at Wana Draw.

Storming Sugar Loaf

Five hundred replacements reached the 1st Marines, which relieved the 7th Marines, and renewed the attacks on Wana Draw, 1,200 feet wide at its mouth but narrowing southward toward Shuri Ridge, funnelling Marines into interlocking fields of fire. By May 20, the 5th Marines had taken Hill 55 west of Wana Draw but at the end of the month, the 1st Marine Division was bogged down one ridgeline short of Shuri.

Meanwhile, to the west, the 6th Marine Division crossed the Asa River on May 10, advancing 2,950 feet in 36 hours. By May 12, it had drawn up around a nondescript hill rising precipitously 230 feet. The riflemen nicknamed it Sugar Loaf.

Sugar Loaf was flanked by two more small hills dubbed Half Moon and Horseshoe. The Marines did not initially realize that the complex was the western command nexus of the Shuri Line. Two thousand Japanese soldiers

American ships unload supplies on the shores of Okinawa after a foothold had been secured

defended Sugar Loaf and another 3,000 held Half Moon and Horseshoe.

The battle for the Sugar Loaf-Half Moon-Horseshoe triad extended for ten harrowing days. Captain Owen G Stebbins of Company G, 2nd Battalion, 22nd Marines, led his command toward Sugar Loaf. In seconds, two platoons were pinned under a torrent of enemy fire. Stebbins and executive officer Lieutenant Dale W Bair kept the third platoon moving. Twenty-eight of the 40 men were quickly killed or wounded in a hail of metal.

Stebbins was hit in both of his legs. Bair was shot in the left arm but still he persevered, gathering 25 Marines and charging to Sugar Loaf's crest although he was ultimately unable to hold it. Five attempts had come up short. Just 75 of the original 200 Marines in Company G were unscathed.

After dark on May 14, the 29th Marines reinforced the 22nd Marines. Forty-four men were marooned on Sugar Loaf's slope with at least 100 bodies lying around them. Major Henry A Courtney Jr, executive officer of the 2nd Battalion, 22nd Marines, decided that his men could not remain where they were but withdrawal would invite a hostile response. He reasoned that the best option was to attack so he roused Marines of Companies F and G and asked for volunteers. Courtney led all 44 Marines again to Sugar Loaf's crest. They held until after dark, when 15 survivors scrambled down. Courtney, however, died when a mortar fragment slashed his neck. He received a posthumous Medal of Honor.

Corporal James L Day's seven-man squad from Company F, 2nd Battalion, 22nd Marines, had followed Courtney up Sugar Loaf. Quickly, five men were shot. Day and Private Dale Bertoli were alone on the western slope. For four days and three nights the pair peppered rifle bullets and tossed grenades at the Japanese – Day was wounded and Bertoli was killed later. In 1984, Major General James L Day would return to Okinawa and take command of its Marine garrison. The 22nd Marines had lost 400 casualties, nearly half its number, in three days.

Hold at all costs

On May 17, Company E, 2nd Battalion, 29th Marines, charged Sugar Loaf four times, losing 160 men but holding the hill for several hours before withdrawing at dusk. On May 18, Company D, 2nd Battalion, 29th Marines, under Captain Howard L Mabie, assaulted Sugar Loaf while suppressing fire, keeping Japanese heads down on Half Moon and Horseshoe. Mabie's Marines skirted both flanks, negotiated minefields and emptied their weapons into clusters of Japanese soldiers emerging from bunkers on the reverse slope. Company D's grip on Sugar Loaf held.

The 4th Marines relieved the 29th, and by May 20 its 3rd Battalion controlled most of Horseshoe, while the 2nd Battalion held most of Half Moon. The 6th Marine Division had lost nearly 2,700 casualties during the bitter fighting for Sugar Loaf.

While the Marines battled in the west, the 96th Division took Conical Hill and the 7th Division were able to secure Yonabaru. Ushijima's flanks were vulnerable and his positions at Shuri Ridge and Shuri Castle were untenable. He finally withdrew to the final line across the Kiyamu Peninsula under a cloak of steady rain and fog.

Foul weather slowed the American advance – nevertheless, 6th Marine Division tanks probed the village of Naha on May 28. The next morning, Company A, 1st Battalion, 5th Marines, managed to reach the crest of Shuri Ridge without firing a shot, crossing into the 77th Division zone to occupy the much-coveted Shuri Castle.

Ushijima's four-mile front then stretched across Kunishi Ridge in the west to Hill 89, the site of his last command post, and to Hill 95. Meanwhile, the 6th Marine Division secured the Oroku Peninsula and Naha Airfield in a joint land and amphibious craft assault, decimating 5,000 Japanese defenders under the command of Rear Admiral Minoru Ota.

The 7th Division's 32nd Regiment captured Hill 95 on June 12, while the 17th Regiment took the eastern end of the Yuza Dake escarpment, unhinging Ushijima's right flank. The 96th Division claimed the rest of Yuza Dake the next day and the 1st Marine Division concurrently began its assault on the western

Two kamikazes smash into the USS Bunker Hill during the Battle of Okinawa

© Alamy, Getty Images

anchor of the Japanese line. With Colonel Edward Snedeker's 7th Marines in the lead, initial assaults on Kunishi Ridge on June 11 were repulsed. Snedeker ordered a night attack and two Marine companies reached the crest near sunrise, mowing down surprised Japanese troops who were cooking breakfast and preparing for the day.

The Japanese mounted some heavy counterattacks. Three attempts to reinforce the Marines atop Kunishi Ridge were thwarted but the 1st, 5th and 7th Marines slowly made gains. In five days, the last heavily defended ridgeline on Okinawa was finally subdued. On June 18, the 7th Marines finally trudged rearward to be relieved by the 8th Marines, 2nd Marine Division.

General Buckner climbed Mezado Ridge to observe the 8th's deployment. Five Japanese artillery shells crashed down, spraying rock and shrapnel – a splinter the size of a dime struck Buckner in the chest. One of the highest-ranking American officers killed in action in WWII, he died in ten minutes. General Roy Geiger handled the 10th Army for five days until Army General Joseph Stilwell arrived to take over the command.

Geiger declared Okinawa secure on June 22, while elements of the 7th Division took Hill 89, and the 77th Division captured Hill 85. That same day, as 7th Division troops neared the entrance to his headquarters in a cave on Hill 89, General Ushijima committed ritual suicide along with Rear Admiral Ota. The 6th Marine Division turned south from the Oroku Peninsula, occupying Ara Saki, Okinawa's southernmost point. Company G, 2nd Battalion, 22nd Marines, raised the Stars and Stripes.

The great battle of Okinawa, the climax of the Pacific land campaign, was finally over. Until that time, suffering on such a scale had seemed impossible.

The Japanese sometimes pressed teenagers and young boys into service. Here, an American soldier attempts to communicate with two of them

OKINAWA

April 1 - June 22, 1945

06 Savagery at Sugar Loaf In late May, American forces finally capture the Sugar Loaf-Half Moon-Horseshoe complex of mutually supporting hills, significant progress against the Shuri Line. After losing nearly 3,000 men, the Americans compel the Japanese to abandon strong positions at Shuri Ridge and Shuri Castle.

05 First Line Breached For three weeks, the Americans batter the first of three Japanese defensive lines, finally forcing an enemy withdrawal and proceeding toward the second, or Shuri Line, where determined defenders have fortified a labyrinth of caves, crevices, hills, and valleys. By the first week of May, casualties begin to mount on both sides.

04 Rapid Run Northward The Americans bisect Okinawa and then turn north and south. Japanese resistance in the north is sporadic and sacrificial, and many enemy troops are bottled up and annihilated in the Motobu Peninsula. By April 13, the 22nd Marines have occupied thumb-shaped Hedo Misaki Peninsula at the extreme northern tip of the island.

07 Kamikaze Rain Of Steel For weeks, the US Navy's Fifth Fleet and British warships are subjected to Operation Ten-Go, an onslaught of Japanese suicide planes that ravages Allied ships, including picket line destroyers and aircraft carriers. More than 300 ships are damaged before Ten-Go blows itself out. The fleet remains on station.

03 Capturing Key Airfields Kadena and Yontan airfields, keys to continuing support of the American ground offensive, are captured on the first day. Marine, navy and army aircraft are soon flying combat air patrol, interdiction, and ground support missions from these airfields, facilitating the advance, which nevertheless grows sluggish as enemy resistance intensifies.

02 Storming Ashore On April 1, 1945, US Marines and Army troops splash across the Hagushi beaches on southwestern Okinawa, while the 2nd Marine Division creates a diversion at sea. Although a tough battle is expected at the water's edge, the Japanese have withdrawn to the south, and early progress is brisk.

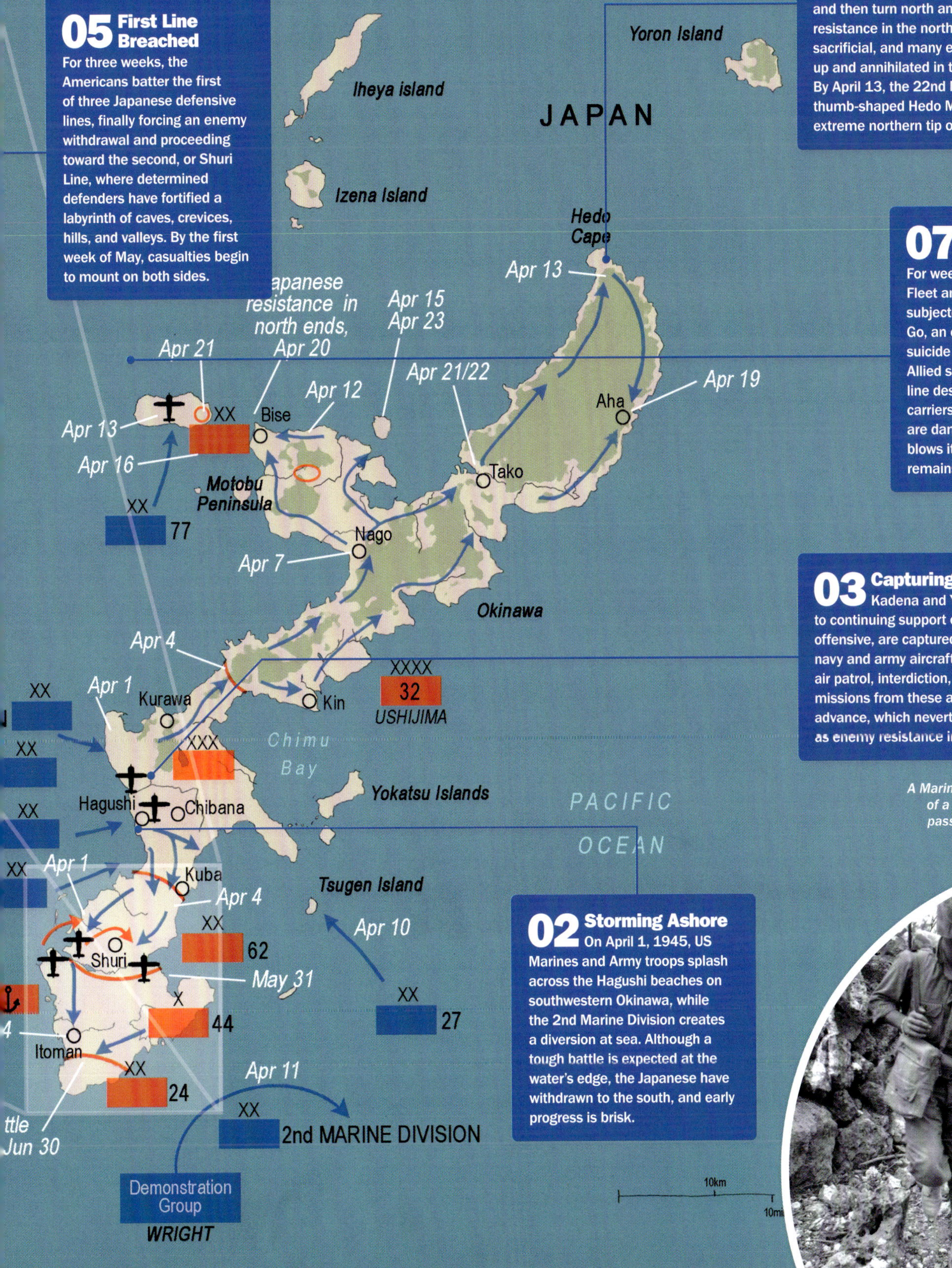

A Marine glances briefly at the body of a dead Japanese soldier as he passes with comrades through a shattered Okinawan village

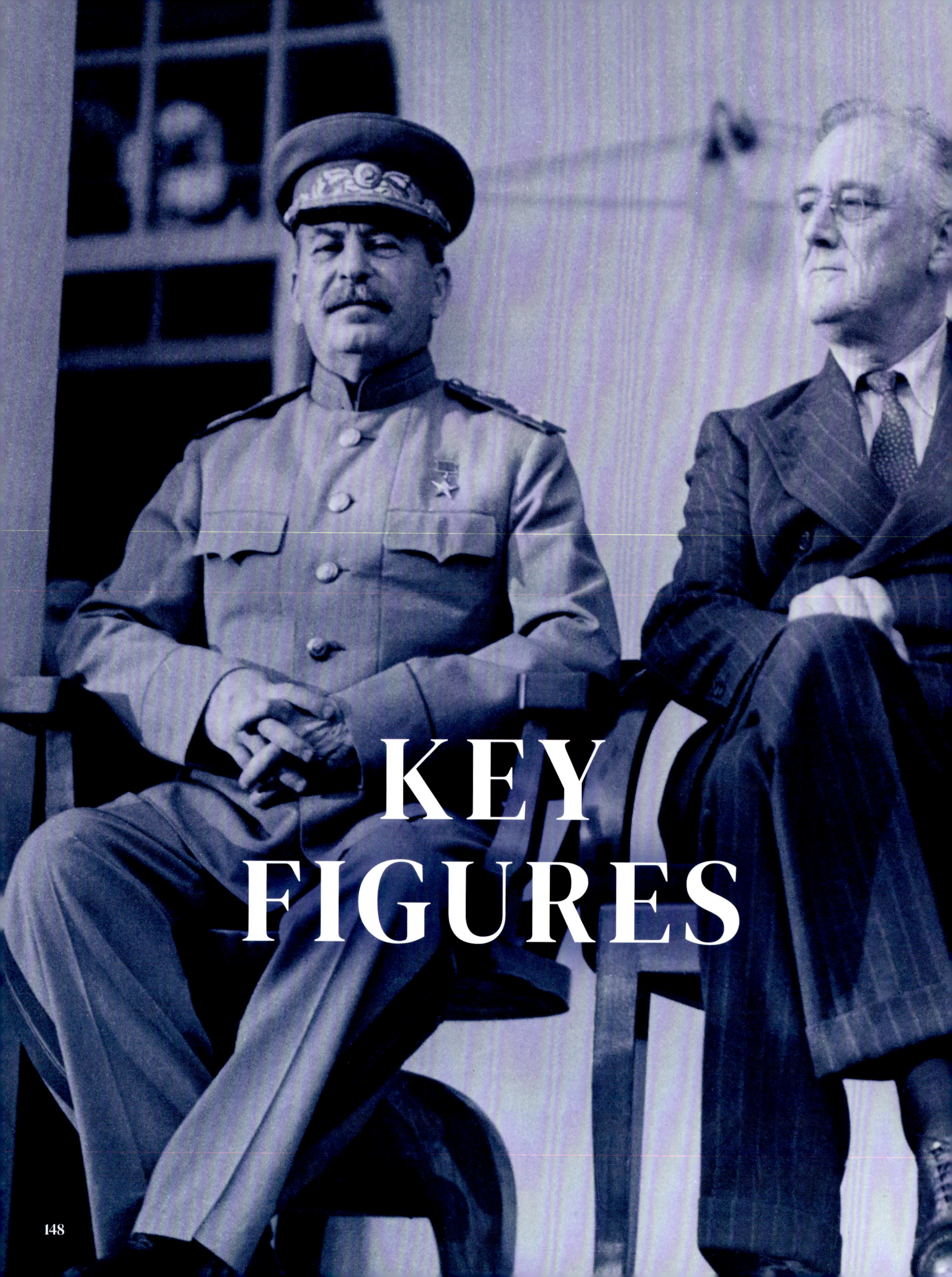

KEY FIGURES

CHURCHILL

For five years Winston Churchill stood as a beacon of freedom in the darkest days of WWII. Discover how this unlikely champion picked up the skills to take on his Axis foes

In the blustery summer of 1940, British Prime Minister Winston Churchill gazed across to the distant shores of continental Europe, where the Nazi war machine had brought down Europe's great democracies, and said, "No more." Britain was battered and bruised, the Commonwealth and empire stretched to breaking point, and a humiliated rag-tag of defeated armies pulled from the burning wreckage of conquered states stood in opposition to a nigh-on-unstoppable totalitarian Axis of Nazi Germany, Fascist Italy and Imperial Japan. Standing tall against this, Churchill was as powerful and enduring a symbol of the free world's defiance as the leonine roar of the Spitfires above the green patchwork of southern England.

A determined young man

That they were fighting on was testament to Churchill's abilities as a leader – he cajoled and convinced, bullied and hectored and played the rousing symphony of public opinion like a master conductor. Even the British establishment, panicked by the fall of France in June 1940 into contemplating surrender, needed to be picked up, dusted down and pushed back into the fight, and Churchill proved to be the perfect man for the job.

The former prime minister is widely regarded as one of the 20th century's defining world leaders, yet Churchill's legacy hinges almost entirely on his performance during WWII. However, in truth, every great decision he made between 1940 and 1945 had already been foreshadowed by a long, distinguished and even chequered career that saw him influence the tide of history from the ministries of the British state, the back benches of the Commons, the officer's saddle and even the pages of the national press.

Britain's WWII leader was born in 1874, the son of Lord Randolph Churchill, a larger-than-life parliamentary figure in his own right who became secretary of state for India, chancellor of the exchequer and leader of the House of Commons by the time Winston was 12. Their relationship was distant, with Winston recalling later in life that they hardly spoke, but they shared many of the same qualities. Both men had a reputation for fantastic oration, with Randolph's childhood friend Lord Rosebery remarking, "His wit, his sarcasm, his piercing personalities, his elaborate irony, and his effective delivery, gave astonishing popularity to his speeches."

They also shared radical mood swings, a driven work ethic and a taste for alcohol. Lord Randolph's death in 1895, aged 45, instilled in his 21-year-old son a fear that he too would die young, adding to his ambition and enduring reputation as 'a young man in a hurry'.

Winston spent four of the first six years of his life in Dublin where his grandfather, John Spencer-Churchill, was the Lord Lieutenant – effectively the monarch's representative in the then British-ruled Ireland. This is where the bulldog-to-be may have first found himself fascinated by troops, as he watched them parade outside his window. Lord Randolph would later prove a fierce opponent of any sniff of Irish nationalism, coining the slogan, 'Ulster will fight, and Ulster will be right' beloved of

Churchill, with his Chiefs of Staff in the garden of No 10 Downing Street

Lenin instigated the Bolshevik Revolution in Russia

Churchill gives his final address during the 1945 election campaign

Source: Public Domain

WAR ON COMMUNISM

How Churchill's Russian folly made an enemy of Stalin

Following the Bolshevik Revolution and the sudden collapse of the Eastern Front in 1918 as Lenin's newly red Russia made peace with Germany, Churchill – as minister of munitions, and as of January 1919, Secretary of State for War and Secretary of State for Air – was determined, "To strangle at birth the Bolshevik State." The British North Russian Relief Force landed at the sea port of Arkhangelsk to aid the 'White' anti-communist faction in the Russian Civil War, but between June 1918 and March 1920 little gains were made. However, this campaign was the scene of the first ever intricately co-ordinated aerial and naval bombardment and amphibious landing, a neat foreshadowing perhaps of one of the greatest such operations in history – D-Day.

Outlasting WWI, it became an increasingly bitter affair, motivated by rabid anti-communism that saw the press dub it 'Mr Churchill's private war'. On the ground court martials and disobedience were common, along with threats of strike action as soldiers realized that while their comrades on the Western Front had headed home, they were trudging through the snow being peppered with sniper fire.

Though Churchill and Stalin wouldn't meet until 1942, Stalin would come face to face with British forces in June 1919 when the 41-year-old ex-seminary student and bank robber from Georgia was leading the fighting against British troops. In honor of Stalin's defiance, Tsaritsyn would be renamed Stalingrad in 1925, and come WWII would be the scene of a bigger and bloodier battle.

Future influence

Though Churchill was quick to support the Soviet Union when Nazi Germany invaded in 1941, mutual suspicion between the two leaders always remained, in no small part because of Churchill's anti-communism stance. Throughout the war, Churchill and Stalin had a strained relationship, and after the war's end Churchill advocated a pre-emptive attack using the re-armed remnants of the German army.

Churchill and Soviet leader Joseph Stalin meet in 1942

©Getty

the Protestant Unionists in Northern Ireland. In 1914, as Britain attempted to soothe the nationalists in the run up to WWI, Churchill would campaign vociferously in favor of the Home Rule Bill – using his role as First Lord of the Admiralty to order a squadron of battleships to Belfast as a threat to the mobilizing Protestant paramilitaries, the Ulster Volunteers.

On the front lines

This was arguably the first time that Churchill's now-legendary immobility and refusal to compromise – which would be an enormous benefit during WWII – came into play. The government opted to negotiate, rescinding Churchill's order and entering a dialog that would in 1914 lead to the partition of Ireland. This sort of compromise was anathema to Churchill, foreshadowing his dogged criticism of appeasement of Nazi Germany in 1937, his brutal response to the general strike in 1926, his dispatch of the infamous Black And Tans to Ireland and his belligerent denial of the Indian independence movement under Mahatma Gandhi. Churchill outlined his stance in his memoirs, writing, "I have always urged fighting wars and other contentions with might and main till overwhelming victory and then extending the hand of friendship to the vanquished… I thought we should have conquered the Irish then given them Home Rule, and that after smashing the General Strike we should have met the grievances of the miners."

As a blue blood growing up in the shadow of the British Empire, Winston Churchill seemed destined for the military, and with his poor academic record, it was one of the only viable routes available to him. The entrance exams for officer cadets at the Royal Military Academy at Sandhurst were considerably less trying that those of an Oxbridge undergraduate, and Churchill soon found himself a young officer in the 4th Queen's Own Hussars, fighting to enforce the will of the empire across territories like South Africa, India and Sudan. Using his family connections, he secured postings in the most dramatic conflict zones of the day, earning extra money and building his public image through journalism with a view to "Return with two more decorations… and beat my sword into an iron dispatch box."

Churchill's war reporting was particularly jingoistic and spoke loudly of his view of Britain's place in the world and of his attitudes to the empire.

"The British Army had never fired on white troops since the Crimea, and now that the world was growing so sensible and pacific – and so democratic too – the great days were over," he wrote.

"Luckily, however, there were still savages and barbarous peoples. There were Zulus and Afghans, also the Dervishes of the Sudan. Some of these might, if they were well-disposed, 'put up a show.'"

These crude caricatures could be put down to the ignorance of youth, but in 1920 he mused on the links between Judaism and Bolshevism (a union that Hitler not only believed in passionately but vowed to wage total war against), and later still, in 1937, he spoke of the

"CHURCHILL GENUINELY BELIEVED IN THE BRITISH EMPIRE AS A CIVILIZING FORCE THAT WOULD BRING CRICKET, DECENCY AND THE ENGLISH LANGUAGE"

Native Americans and Australian Aboriginals, saying, "I do not admit that a wrong has been done to these people by the fact that a stronger race, a higher-grade race, a more worldly wise race to put it that way, has come in and taken their place."

The British Empire might have been at the height of its influence and prestige while Churchill galloped about, but over the decades that followed his entry to the Commons for the first time in 1900 as the MP for Oldham in Lancashire, it would swell to its geographic limit, creaking under its own weight and throwing up a set of challenges that would flow like tributaries into the churning oceans of the two world wars. Whether fighting for Britain with his thunderous rhetoric from the green benches of Parliament or with his cavalry sabre on dusty Sudanese slopes, it's clear Churchill saw it as one calling, saying to a journalist in 1906, "Politics are almost as exciting as war and quite as dangerous."

Controversial opinions

As the dogged defender of an empire mostly gained and largely maintained through force of arms, through modern eyes Churchill had disquieting commonalities with fascist regimes. His brushes with racism and anti-Semitism speak for themselves, but unlike the future Axis powers, who saw expansion as purely for the betterment of their own people, Churchill genuinely believed in the British Empire as a civilizing force that would bring trains, civil service, cricket, decency and English language

A seven-year-old Winston Churchill poses for the camera

CHURCHILL'S MEDALS

What Churchill's battle experiences reveal about the future leader of Britain

The 'rebellious' Pashtun Tribe

India Medal (1898)

Churchill's first experience of the empire in action, he served at Malakand in the lawless north-west frontier of India to put down rebellious Pashtun tribes. His experiences were recorded through various newspapers and his book The Story Of The Malakand Field Force.

Victory Medal (1920)

Following the Gallipoli backlash, Churchill headed to the Western Front to redeem himself. Though he disapproved of the overall strategy, he continued to exhibit daring and made 36 trips into No Man's Land. He wrote in his diary, "I have found happiness and content such as I have not known for many months."

Soldiers take a break from fighting during fighting in Gallipoli in WWI

The cavalry charge at the Battle of Omdurman

The Queen's Sudan Medal (1899)

Transferred to Sudan with the 21st Lancers, Churchill took part in the decisive Battle of Omdurman against the rebels in one of the world's last significant cavalry charges.

Khedive's Sudan Medal (1899)

Resigning his commission for a failed shot at the Oldham by-election in 1899, he returned to the field the same year for the Second Boer War as a war correspondent. Ambushed while traveling, he escaped captivity and traveled 300 miles to safety.

Churchill as a prisoner of the Boers in 1899 before he mounted a daring escape

Future influence

Churchill's vast experience in the field shaped his policies during WWII and provided a solid grounding of military tactics. Perhaps due to his earlier career, Churchill would favor decisive and daring campaigns during WWII.

UPBRINGING

How Churchill's early years molded his later career

With a family line that stretched back to John Churchill, the first Duke of Marlborough and commander in the 1701-14 War of the Spanish Succession that led to the acquisition of Gibraltar from Spain and Newfoundland and chunks of Canada from France, Winston seemed fated to serve as the British Empire's most ardent defender.

He was raised in the shadow of his grandfather and father, both career statesmen in the governments of Benjamin Disraeli and Lord Robert Cecil, the 3rd Marquess of Salisbury. Disraeli, credited with the formation of the modern British Conservative Party, also made it a party indivisible from the greater glory of the British Empire – bartering ownership of the Suez Canal and kicking off unpopular wars in South Africa and Afghanistan to pacify rebels – a mission continued by Cecil, who presided over the First Boer War. It was in this most blue-blooded brotherhood and against this constant backdrop of overseas expansion that three generations of Churchills served in office and Winston himself was raised.

His relationship with his father was distant, and young Winston's upbringing was largely entrusted to a nanny at the Marlboroughs' ancestral Blenheim Palace, a seven-acre stately home in Oxfordshire, which in true Churchill family fashion has a prominent statue of Britannia presiding over two French captives.

Following a number of schools ill-suited to Winston's difficult and distinctly non-academic temperament, he was sent to Harrow aged 13, where he found his true calling amid the dusty Latin rote learning – the Harrow Volunteer Rifle Corps. Other students recalled the Harrow Rifles as not being a particularly popular group until at least the late 19th century, so that Churchill joined within weeks of his arrival speaks volumes about his enthusiasm for military matters. In fact, despite his unease with education, the Harrow Rifles seemed to trigger a passion for knowledge

Future influence

Churchill was brought up in an era in which the British Empire was the dominant force on the planet. Aligned to his aristocratic upbringings, it is no surprise that Churchill was brought up utterly confident in his, and his country's place in the world. This confidence – unshakeable and at times unjustifiable – would strongly influence how he led the country after 1940.

2nd Lieutenant Winston Churchill, 1895

in Churchill, who wrote to his father in 1889 that "I bought a book on drill, as I intend going in for the corporal examinations next term." With many of the traditional careers set aside for his social class – law, civil service, and through them a route to politics – conditional on university education and so firmly out of Churchill's reach, Sandhurst beckoned, and with it a chance to fulfil that most ancient imperative of the Dukes of Marlborough – the defense of the empire.

On a return home, the young Winston enjoyed a rare encounter with his father as Lord Randolph thoughtfully inspected his son's vast collection of lead soldiers. "He spent 20 minutes studying the scene, with a keen eye and captivating smile," Winston recalled in his autobiography. "At the end he asked me if I would like to go into the army. I thought it would be splendid to command an army, so I said 'Yes' at once; and I was immediately taken at my word."

"THE MAN WHO WOULD ONE DAY STARE DOWN THE AXIS ADVANCE PRAISED MUSSOLINI"

to those unfortunate enough to have been born without them. The real overlap, though, was a shared pathological hatred of communism, which could so easily have seen him become Hitler's cheerleader instead of implacable foe. He warned in 1929 of "a poisoned Russia, an infected Russia, a plague-bearing Russia, a Russia of armed hordes not only smiting with bayonet and with cannon, but... political doctrines which destroyed the health and even the souls of nations." Earlier still, in 1919 he heaped the blame for WWI's catastrophic loss of life on not the German Empire or Austro-Hungary, but on the "baboonery" of Russian Bolsheviks who had pulled the country out of the war, saying, "Every British and French soldier killed last year was really done to death by Lenin and Trotsky."

The man who would one day stare down the Axis advance even praised Mussolini, saying in 1927, "If I had been an Italian, I am sure I would have been entirely with you from the beginning to the end of your victorious struggle against the bestial appetites and passions of Leninism." He also showed Hitler begrudging respect. As late as 1935 he wondered, "Whether Hitler will be the man who will once again let loose upon the world another war... or whether he will go down in history as the man who restored honor and peace of mind to the Great Germanic nation."

Whatever overlap existed between Britain's brand of imperialism – for all its misuse, still tethered to the principles of parliamentary democracy – and that practiced by the racist and totalitarian regimes of Italy, Germany and Japan grew increasingly slimmer on the march to war. In parallel, Churchill's anti-red rhetoric also softened, and the bulldog not only attacked Prime Minister Neville Chamberlain's appeasement of Hitler but criticized him for not seeking a rapprochement with Stalin – an unlikelier U-turn is harder to image.

No surrender

This shift in position, the one that ultimately placed Churchill at the helm of Britain in her

KEY MOMENTS THAT SHAPED CHURCHILL

Army service
Churchill joins the 4th Hussars, and goes on to serve in India, Sudan and Egypt.
1895

Daring escape
Churchill is captured in the Second Boer War, becoming a celebrity, and a year later is elected as a Conservative Party MP
1899

Party defection
After opposing a government bill, Churchill is de-selected by the Conservatives and joins the Liberals.
1904

Real power
He becomes Home Secretary, sends troops to support the police against striking miners and proposes a referendum on women's voting rights.
1910

Naval reforms
Churchill is promoted to First Lord of the Admiralty, where he undertakes sweeping reforms.
1911

Resignation
Churchill resigns from the cabinet following the Gallipoli campaign and rejoins the army. He would return to parliament the next year.
1915

Churchill poses with an elephant he has shot

Sir Winston, his son Randolph and grandson Winston

Churchill during a visit to Egypt in 1910

A year after being appointed first lord of the Admiralty, Churchill meets with the Canadian prime minister

Election failure
Fails to retain his seat in the general election and rejoins the Tories, saying, "anyone can rat, but it takes a certain ingenuity to re-rat."
1922

Wilderness years
With the Conservative government defeated in the General Election, he becomes estranged from the party and his 'wilderness years' begin.
1929

Appeasement
As Germany annexes Austria and overruns Czechoslovakia, Neville Chamberlain holds fast to his policy of appeasement, with Churchill a strong critic.
1938

War cabinet
War is declared and Churchill appointed First Lord of the Admiralty and a member of the War Cabinet, advocating a pre-emptive occupation of key ports.
1939

Blood, sweat and tears
Chamberlain resigns following the invasion of Norway, and Churchill is the agreed upon successor. He delivers his iconic 'blood, sweat and tears' speech.
1940

Churchill inspects a British tank

Churchill the war correspondent during the Boer War

darkest hour, was nothing to do with political ideology and everything to do with political reality. Churchill the enemy of communism had been trumped by that first love – Churchill the imperialist. His early fears of Soviet-backed mischief in India and Ireland had been replaced by Italian ambitions in the Mediterranean, Japanese ambitions in Asia and growing German naval power, which brought them sharply into Britain's dimming spheres of influence. This rabid defense of the empire, a product of his upbringing and his life serving this ideal, would shape his strategies in WWII, as well as transform him from an authoritarian avatar of the old order to the champion of freedom. The decision to fight primarily in North Africa, the Middle East and then Italy at the expense of other theaters – to the irritation of both the US and the USSR – was primarily to safeguard the Suez Canal, a vital artery of the empire through which valuable raw materials from India to Britain were shipped, and protect the oil fields of Iraq and Persia.

Naval command

Churchill's stubbornness, belligerence and refusal to negotiate under threat helped keep the Allies fighting in their dark days, but they would have been nothing without his innovative approach to military technology, which his entire life had shaped him for. Churchill may have been a poor student back when he was in short trousers, but he devoured Alfred Thayer Mahan's The Influence of Sea Power Upon History, and told his mother in 1898 that "command of the sea is everything." Fittingly for such an absolute proclamation, when he was appointed as first lord of the Admiralty in 1911, he went about perhaps the single most radical campaign of his career to date, the one that says the most about the kind of prime minister he would eventually become. Fearing growing German naval power, he immersed himself in naval lore and tactics.

It wasn't just the machinery and the rules of conflict that fascinated him but the organization, and he established a new Naval War Staff to co-ordinate strategy more fully with the government's War Office, much to the alarm of the high-ranking sea lords, who prized their independence – not that their opinions mattered much, and by the end of his first year in office he'd replaced three out of the four with more pliant figures.

Churchill rolled out a new line of 'super dreadnoughts' – the largest warships ever built at the time – and began to explore the potential of submarines, launching planes from ships and switched the fleet from coal to oil-powered, which increased their speed and decreased the plumes of smoke that frequently betrayed their positions. He also threw his support, along with naval research funds, behind another promising new contraption – the tank, a machine bizarrely

AMERICAN CONNECTION

Establishing the special relationship

Churchill always had one eye on the United States of America, and through his American-born mother, the New York socialite and alleged inventor of the Manhattan cocktail Jennie Jerome, he had a trans-Atlantic connection that he would later play up to its full, with maternal ancestors who fought in the Revolutionary War against Britain, and even, according to family legend, some Native American blood.

Even as early in his career as 1903, he told the gathered occupants of the House of Commons, "I have always thought that it ought to be the main end of English state-craft to cultivate good relations with the United States," and his epic *A History of the English Speaking Peoples*, which he started in 1937 and finally published well after WWI, seemed contrived to create a sense of kinship between the US and the British Commonwealth. In 1939, Churchill, in his capacity as First Lord of the Admiralty, began corresponding with President Theodore Roosevelt (who'd met him once before, having been told by his advisers that Churchill was a "drunk and a windbag") – who was determined to keep the US well out of any conflict. However, Churchill did have a role to play in not only bringing the US and Britain closer together, but also in paving the way for a future conflict with Imperial Japan.

As of 1902, Britain had been allied with the newly modernized Japan in order to checkmate their shared rival, Tsarist Russia, and, renewed in 1905 and 1911, this treaty also entrusted the defense of Australia and New Zealand to the Japanese navy during WWI so as to free up British ships for European combat.

The 1921 Imperial Conference was called in part to negotiate their collective stance toward the United States and Japan, who many believed were on a collision course for dominance of the Pacific. Churchill attended in his capacity of secretary of state for the colonies, and the end result was to allow the Japanese alliance to lapse in the hope of gaining American goodwill, the latter an increasingly powerful entity.

Japan's isolated position from the other world powers increased its belligerence, ending its participation in the Washington Naval Treaty that capped the size of battleships in 1936 and walking out of the League of Nations in 1933 over criticism of its annexation of Manchuria. "Japan is on the other end of the world," Churchill wrote in 1924. "She cannot menace our vital security." It seems optimistic, but undercutting Churchill's stance was the belief that there was nothing Japan could do without provoking a reaction from the United States. He was ultimately right, but proving it would cost many lives.

Churchill worked hard to build a relationship with Roosevelt

Future influence

Churchill worked the American connection hard in an attempt to build a close relationship but, nevertheless, soon after the outbreak of WWII, Britain was isolated. However, when Pearl Harbor was attacked, Roosevelt was persuaded to adopt a 'Germany first' strategy to relieve Britain before they turned their full attention to Japan, a justification of Churchill's work before the war. The 'special relationship' has dominated Anglo-American foreign policy ever since.

The Washington Naval Treaty capped the size of battleships

Allied leaders, including Roosevelt and Churchill, confer in Quebec during WWII

GALLIPOLI

How Churchill recovered from disaster

Despite British naval supremacy, WWI had yet to see a decisive naval engagement when Churchill posited an ambitious plan to take the Dardanelles, the first of two channels through Ottoman Turkey (a German ally) that would link up France and Britain in the Mediterranean with Tsarist Russian in the Black Sea.

The plan was to have British and French warships simply charge through the Turkish blockade via sheer power and then land troops (including many members of the Australia and New Zealand Army Corps, the ANZACs) at Gallipoli. Betting on brute force proved to be disastrous gamble.

The heavily mined coast and unexpectedly high number of gun emplacements took their toll on the attackers, and when the troops landed, they were largely unsupported by the panicked high command at sea, who refused to move to close to the shore. Early gains weren't exploited, allowing the Turkish time to reinforce their position, turning this hoped-for quick campaign into another entrenched slog, only up a cliff face instead of over a Belgian field.

Between April 25, 1915, and January 9, 1916, 252,000 Allied soldiers were killed before an evacuation could be carried out, and an Australian war reporter broke the censorship to smuggle out a damning report of the commander on the ground, General Hamilton. The problem was in the planning and the divided chain of command. Churchill, who insisted the Ottomans would crumble, and General Hamilton, who was slow to take the initiative, bore the brunt of the blame, both castigated in the press and forced from their positions, but others too should have been held to account. Admiral John de Robeck refused Churchill's order to bring his ships in and provide support, while military planners in London had cut the numbers of troops set aside for the mission.

Future influence

Churchill's enthusiasm for decisive action (and greater control over commanders in the field) was bolstered – something that would influence how much responsibility he took on during WWII. Even if he did not deserve all of the blame he bore, the setback hardened his resolve.

V Beach at Cape Helles, Gallipoli, May 6, 1915

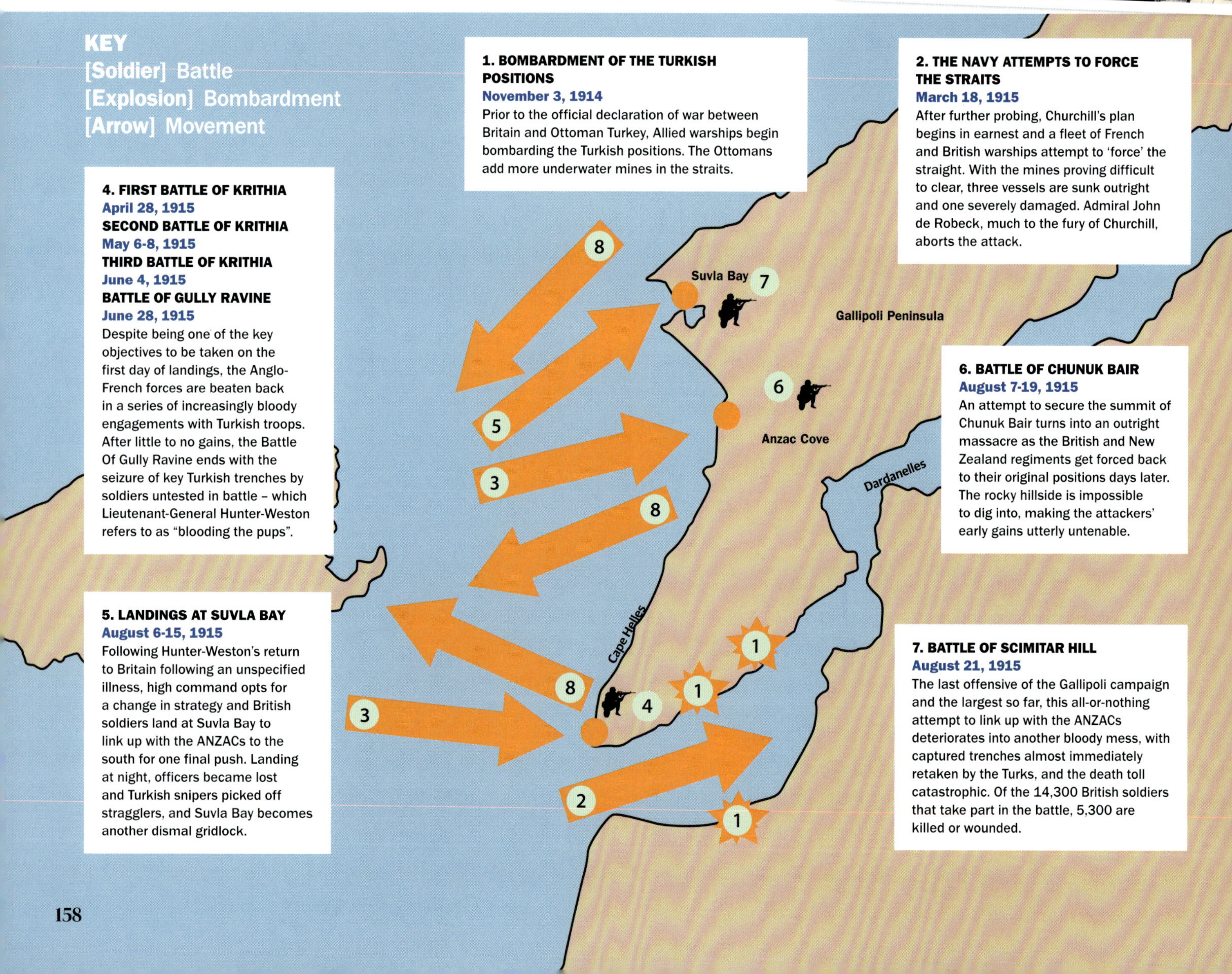

KEY
[Soldier] Battle
[Explosion] Bombardment
[Arrow] Movement

1. BOMBARDMENT OF THE TURKISH POSITIONS
November 3, 1914
Prior to the official declaration of war between Britain and Ottoman Turkey, Allied warships begin bombarding the Turkish positions. The Ottomans add more underwater mines in the straits.

2. THE NAVY ATTEMPTS TO FORCE THE STRAITS
March 18, 1915
After further probing, Churchill's plan begins in earnest and a fleet of French and British warships attempt to 'force' the straight. With the mines proving difficult to clear, three vessels are sunk outright and one severely damaged. Admiral John de Robeck, much to the fury of Churchill, aborts the attack.

4. FIRST BATTLE OF KRITHIA
April 28, 1915
SECOND BATTLE OF KRITHIA
May 6-8, 1915
THIRD BATTLE OF KRITHIA
June 4, 1915
BATTLE OF GULLY RAVINE
June 28, 1915
Despite being one of the key objectives to be taken on the first day of landings, the Anglo-French forces are beaten back in a series of increasingly bloody engagements with Turkish troops. After little to no gains, the Battle Of Gully Ravine ends with the seizure of key Turkish trenches by soldiers untested in battle – which Lieutenant-General Hunter-Weston refers to as "blooding the pups".

6. BATTLE OF CHUNUK BAIR
August 7-19, 1915
An attempt to secure the summit of Chunuk Bair turns into an outright massacre as the British and New Zealand regiments get forced back to their original positions days later. The rocky hillside is impossible to dig into, making the attackers' early gains utterly untenable.

5. LANDINGS AT SUVLA BAY
August 6-15, 1915
Following Hunter-Weston's return to Britain following an unspecified illness, high command opts for a change in strategy and British soldiers land at Suvla Bay to link up with the ANZACs to the south for one final push. Landing at night, officers became lost and Turkish snipers picked off stragglers, and Suvla Bay becomes another dismal gridlock.

7. BATTLE OF SCIMITAR HILL
August 21, 1915
The last offensive of the Gallipoli campaign and the largest so far, this all-or-nothing attempt to link up with the ANZACs deteriorates into another bloody mess, with captured trenches almost immediately retaken by the Turks, and the death toll catastrophic. Of the 14,300 British soldiers that take part in the battle, 5,300 are killed or wounded.

3. LANDINGS AT ANZAC COVE AND CAPE HELLES

April 25, 1915

Two divisions of the Australian and New Zealand Army Corps and a larger Allied force land on key points at the foot of the Gallipoli peninsula. The Cape Helles landings are mismanaged, and the Allied force suffers 6,500 casualties.

8. EVACUATION OF SUVLA BAY AND ANZAC COVE

December 10-19, 1915

EVACUATION OF CAPE HELLES

December 10, 1915 – January 9, 1916

With public opinion thoroughly against the campaign and damning reports in the Australian press, a harsh winter sets in, bringing frostbite and flooding as respite from the summer heat. Evacuation begins.

American President Harry Truman and Winston Churchill shake hands, 1945

considered a 'landship' and therefore falling under his remit.

It would be the possibilities of air power that stuck with him the most though, warning parliament in 1933, "Not to have an adequate air force in the present state of the world is to compromise the foundations of national freedom and independence." It is therefore no surprise that Churchill proved himself to be a talented leader of Britain's air force, and the thirst for new technology and tactics he showed throughout his life would lead him toward sponsoring such celebrated pieces of wartime ingenuity as the Bletchley Park code breakers and the birth of commando warfare.

Churchill's overthrow of the sea lords and his mission to bring the navy into a more central decision-making process was a dry run of sorts for his War Cabinet during WWII, in which he held the key positions of both prime minister and minister of defense, as well as his personal contact and sporadic micro-management of commanders in the field.

This, along with his bold – and often unrealistic – strategies would infuriate his commanders in WWII as regularly as they had during the previous war. Captain Osmond de Beauvoir Brock, then the assistant director of naval mobilization, observed Churchill's appointment in 1911 with apprehension: "Whether all his schemes are quite sound I shouldn't like to say, but I do know that those which have come this way bear traces of great haste and little thought."

Perhaps influenced by the cavalry officer he once was, Churchill favored bold, headline-grabbing actions that would decisively turn the tide of battle, and it was four years later in 1915 where he was knocked bloody-nosed from the saddle.

The disastrous Gallipoli landings wound up as an inglorious failure, and he was ignominiously ousted from office, choosing to serve at the front to rehabilitate his reputation. His experience of the mud and squalor doubtless hardened his commitment further to grand strategies like Gallipoli, and in WWII he would drag his heels over an invasion of France, instead focusing on 'peripheral' campaigns, some more successful than others.

To say Churchill was the right man at the right time sounds disingenuous, but it's tough to imagine that his indomitable strength of character, willingness to tightly grasp the reigns of power, sometimes cynical pragmatism, hawkish approach to foreign policy and fundamental belief in the primacy of the British Empire could be found in any other form.

Churchill's career had more than its fair share of tragedies, missteps and moments of outright hypocrisy, but all of his past was little more than a canvas with which he would sketch out his future glory. Churchill at his worst could have been little better than the vicious tyrants whom he fought, but the alchemy of circumstance made the most fantastic virtues of his vices, and by 1940 the world saw Churchill at his very best.

"CHURCHILL'S CAREER HAD ITS SHARE OF MISSTEPS... BUT ALL OF HIS PAST WAS LITTLE MORE THAN A CANVAS WITH WHICH HE WOULD SKETCH OUT HIS FUTURE GLORY"

Churchill at his seat in the Cabinet Room at No 10 Downing Street

FRANKLIN D ROOSEVELT

At the height of the Great Depression an unlikely candidate stepped forward to help the US through some of its darkest years

When Franklin D Roosevelt won his first presidential election in 1933 he was taking command of a country in crisis. He ran on the Democratic ticket with a desire to help the average American citizen. He had his job cut out for him as the national average rate for unemployment was one in four, but in some cities and industries that figure was as high as 50 per cent. A staggering 13 million Americans were without work and some were going hungry. To make matters worse, the country was also in dire financial straits. Since the crash on Wall Street 4,000 banks had closed for good, and by 1933 that number rose to more than 9,000, with $2.5 billion in lost deposits. This resulted in millions of Americans losing their savings – if they arrived at the bank too late, there would simply be no money to withdraw. The panics raised troubling questions about credit value and many started to question capitalism itself. Something needed to be done to avert catastrophe. Acting as soon as he entered office, Roosevelt and Congress declared a four-day 'bank holiday' and emergency banking acts to help stem the outpouring of the nation's wealth. He also managed to instill confidence in the country with his rousing inauguration speech featuring the quote, "The only thing we have to fear is fear itself".

Roosevelt sought to rectify these problems with a range of domestic programs called the New Deal. It focused on what were known as the 'three Rs', relief, recovery and reform. Relief was the immediate action that was taken to halt further economic failure. Recovery saw temporary programs implemented to restart consumer spending and reform saw more permanent programs put in place to avoid another crash and safeguard savings. With these actions the American people began to see hope in the new Democratic Party. The Republicans under Hoover had said the worst was over and only hard work and determination would see the United States though, but these had actually turned out to be either dismal lies or woeful predictions.

Some of Roosevelt's more conservative supporters felt betrayed by his actions, however. Indeed many of those from inside his own party viewed him with disdain, seeing him as rich, spoiled and unwilling to cooperate. Here was a man who was taking money away from big business and then reinvesting it into the working man. Under Roosevelt, a huge federal bureaucracy would grow that was designed to prop up the average American who was down on his luck. This might seem a little surprising considering his childhood and background.

Franklin D Roosevelt was born into an old, prominent and above all rich, Dutch family in the Hudson Valley town of Hyde Park. Being tutored at home from a young age he did not interact with many other children his own age. His mother Sara was a particularly prominent influence throughout his childhood, but he was also close with his father and the family took frequent trips together to Europe.

While his schooling and higher educational years would bring him little joy he flourished as a lawyer, passing the bar exam in 1907. Becoming heavily involved in politics, he

The last photograph of FDR, taken the day before his death

LIFE IN THE TIME OF FRANKLIN D ROOSEVELT

Dance to forget

Some of the Roaring Twenties' nightlife carried over into the next decade, with flocks of young people descending on ballrooms and dance halls where the swing bands would play. This would serve as a welcome distraction from the realities of real life.

A call to serve your country

For the first time in its history the US initiated a peacetime draft for men from 21-36 years of age in 1940. FDR was famous for promising the mothers of the United States that he would not send their sons to fight in foreign wars, WWII would change that.

The United States had become isolationist

After WWI many Americans were in favor of adopting an isolationist policy. Keen to avoid more bloodshed that they had witnessed just a few years previously, anti-war feelings were strong even as the Axis powers ravaged Europe. It would take the attack on Pearl Harbor to bring the US into WWII.

The world was changing

In just a few short years between the wars, people saw technology jump forward in leaps and bounds. Machines like airplanes, which at the turn of the century were little more than a curiosity, would evolve massively in people's lifetimes to revolutionize global travel, trade and warfare.

Mouths to feed

Aid for citizens hit hard by the Great Depression could come from many directions, not just the government. Notorious gangster Al Capone opened one of the very first soup kitchens in Chicago in 1931, feeding the masses of unemployed who were on the street desperate to find work.

THE FIRST LADY OF THE WORLD

Eleanor Roosevelt, fifth cousin once removed and wife to Franklin D Roosevelt, was a formidable political figure in American politics. From her support of FDR through his illness, serving as first lady through his four terms, to her work at the UN she was not someone to live in her husband's shadow.

She had met Franklin on a train in 1902 and from there they had begun a secret correspondence that turned into a romance. Although Franklin's mother disapproved of the match the pair were married on March 17, 1905. Unfortunately it was not to be happily ever after as Franklin's affair with a secretary would force Eleanor to give him an ultimatum: end the relationship or divorce. He chose to end the relationship but the episode had shown Eleanor that she should pursue her own happiness in public life.

As a staunch supporter of civil rights she helped sway the African-American vote, that were usually pointing Republican, to become a consistent base for the Democratic Party.

After her husband's passing Eleanor became the first chairperson for the United Nations Commission of Human Rights and stayed in the position until 1947. In the 1950s she embarked on an exhaustive touring schedule both at home and abroad on behalf of the UN and the work she did there. In 1962 she passed away after a battle with a rare bone marrow disease.

Roosevelt walks with James M Cox during their failed presidential campaign of 1920

served as assistant secretary of the navy under Woodrow Wilson and ran as the vice president on the Democratic ticket for the 1920 election. It was a dismal failure and the Democratic Party lost by a wide margin.

A defining factor in Roosevelt's life, and one that almost made his political aspirations come crashing down, was his battle with polio. Diagnosed from 1921 he completely lost the use of his legs and took measures to not appear in public in a wheelchair, feeling self-conscious and thinking that it would make him look weak. Although he was never able to recover the use of his legs, he did manage to walk short distances with the help of some crutches and steel braces, though that is not to say he didn't try every possible cure available to him, even going so far as to purchase Warm Springs resort in Georgia, which would later be open to other patients. While his personal efforts were unsuccessful his work would help thousands of other sufferers battle the affliction and he would also later help fund a vaccine.

While still struggling with health issues FDR was convinced to make a return to politics and in 1928 he became the governor for the state of New York. From here he had a great opportunity to win the presidential election in 1932. He was inaugurated in 1933 as the 32nd president of the US.

Roosevelt is often praised for his foresight into future events, the most significant example being the rise of Nazi Germany and the danger this posed to the world. As the US had adopted a strict isolationist policy he could not openly help the Allied powers of Europe fight against Germany without risking the wrath of Congress and the American people. He wanted to ready the country for war without going against American neutrality. In 1940, a peacetime draft called the Selective Training and Service Act was enforced. To quell rising fears from the population he promised the parents of the United States that he would not send their sons

Defining moment

Diagnosed with polio

August 1921

It would be in Campobello Island, Canada where FDR would hear this life-changing news. Losing the use of his legs dashes his political aspirations and Roosevelt resigns himself to living the life of a patient, but Eleanor persuades him to continue on his career path. Although the many forms of treatment he would try would not return his leg function, he teaches himself to walk short distances with leg braces and a pair of crutches. For the rest of his life he would be a strong supporter of polio research and would open a treatment center for patients at Warm Springs, Georgia.

TIMELINE

A rude awakening
After being home schooled for years FDR is sent to board at Groton School in Massachusetts. Due to this, and his privileged upbringing, he found it difficult to fit in and make friends.
1896

Graduated Harvard University
Surprisingly Roosevelt did not excel while at Harvard and was by all accounts a rather average student. After taking four years of economics classes Roosevelt reportedly said "Everything I was taught was wrong".
June 24, 1903

Tying the knot
FDR marries his sweetheart, Eleanor Roosevelt, a niece of ex-president Theodore Roosevelt and his fifth cousin once removed. The two would have a marriage complicated by an overbearing mother and Franklin's infidelities.
March 17, 1905

Passes New York state bar examination
After graduating and passing the bar exam Roosevelt takes a position at Carter Ledyard & Milburn, a highly prestigious Wall Street law firm that deals mainly with corporate law cases.
1907

Appointed assistant secretary of the Navy
A firm believer that the US needed a larger naval presence, Roosevelt took to this position with fervor, earning him a reputation as an energetic and hard-working Democratic man.
April 1913

Nominated to run as vice president
Roosevelt is named as the Democratic vice presidential candidate alongside James M Cox, but the pair lose the 1920 election to Republicans Warren G Harding and Calvin Coolidge.
1920

The official poster for Roosevelt's 1944 campaign with Harry S Truman. He would go on to win a landslide victory and secure his fourth term in office

to fight in foreign wars. However when the US finally entered WWII he claimed that it didn't count as a foreign war as it encompassed the globe – this was thought to be a rather Machiavellian move by his critics.

Roosevelt also began a constant stream of correspondence with British Prime Minister Winston Churchill so that he was kept up to date with events across the Atlantic. Not wanting to wait to take action, he decided that the United States would be the 'Arsenal of Democracy' – if the country couldn't openly fight, it could at least supply those that did. Roosevelt achieved this goal via the lend-lease program, in which the United States supplied aid in the form of oil, food, war planes, ships, munitions and materials with terms stating that the supplies be used until returned or destroyed. A total of $50-billion worth of cargo was shipped out of the US, mostly to Britain but also to China, France and the USSR.

This aid would have to reach Europe by ship, and so began a huge operation where tons of supplies were ferried across the Atlantic. Roosevelt knew these convoys were tempting targets for prowling German U-boats, but if an American ship was attacked then it would enable him to declare war without fear of a backlash. On December 7, 1941, however, Japan bombed the American navy at Pearl Harbor. This single act immediately galvanized the public and put the whole country behind the president when war was declared the next day.

"HIS INFLUENCE WAS CEMENTED AS THE US ESTABLISHED ITSELF AS A WORLD POWER"

After 12 years in the White House, Roosevelt's influence was cemented as the US emerged from the ashes of WWII to establish itself as a world power. His foresight would come into play again, as he was instrumental in the construction of the United Nations. Unfortunately he would never see it come to fruition as he died on April 12, 1945.

During his final years FDR cut a gaunt figure as his health rapidly deteriorated. He was kept from the public eye so as to not cause panic or lower morale in the war years, and so when his death came just months after the commencement of his unprecedented fourth term in office it shocked the nation.

This was a man who had taken the reins during the Great Depression, stood up for the working man and given the country jobs, financial security and most importantly, a future. Hailed as a hero of the American people, he won the hearts of the population by promising and delivering fast and effective action time and time again. Today he is regarded by many as one of the finest US presidents in history.

Defining moment

Elected president of the United States

November 8, 1932

Having a strong political base in the most populated state put Roosevelt on good footing for the presidency. In his nomination speech, he stated "This is more than a political campaign. It is a call to arms." Focusing on the citizens hit hardest by the recession, the Democratic Party found new allies in the workers' unions, minority groups and the more impoverished US citizens. With this charged electorate Roosevelt went on to win in all but six states and with 57 per cent of the vote, making him the 32nd president of the United States.

Defining moment

A date that will live in infamy

December 7, 1941

With the surprise attack on the US naval base of Pearl Harbor by the Empire of Japan, the United States loses interest in its isolationist policy and rallies behind its president. Having already signed the lend-lease to other allied countries, the US had forgone its neutrality with entering into army conflict. The unprovoked attack on US sovereignty, however, could not be ignored and whatever dealings that Roosevelt had previously been making under the table were no longer necessary. The United States were now fully committed to the war effort and it would be four costly years until the hostilities would cease.

Elected governor of New York state
Roosevelt sets out as a reform governor and establishes new social policies. Some of these prove unpopular as a bomb was found addressed to him but was defused before it went off.
November 4, 1928

Champions the 'First Hundred Days' program
By closing the banks on a special 'bank holiday' and convening Congress to pass the Emergency Banking Act, FDR helps to stabilize the recession and restore some measure of public trust.
March 5, 1933

Re-elected for a second term
Buoyed by his successes and public support Roosevelt smashes the election with 60 per cent of the vote and carries all but two states: Vermont and Maine.
November 3, 1936

Astoundingly re-elected for a third term
At the time, presidents serving for two terms was an unwritten rule, so to run for a third was a great risk. Roosevelt says he will only run if he has the backing of the party. "We want Roosevelt… the world wants Roosevelt" was the reply.
November 5, 1940

Successfully re-elected for a fourth term
With WWII raging the American people once again choose the leader who has seen them through some of the darkest times in US history, with the knowledge that he would continue to do so.
November 7, 1944

A death that shook the nation
The death of Franklin D Roosevelt is felt both at home and abroad. It rocks the country to its very foundation and a great sense of loss is felt by every American.
April 12, 1945

JOSEPH STALIN

The world's fate was decided by the contest between a butcher and a monster. This is the story of the butcher: Joseph Stalin

On December 18, 1878, the man who would be known to history as Joseph Stalin was born Ioseb Dzhugashvili. The name is Georgian, for this most implacable of Russian rulers was not himself Russian. His father was a cobbler and his mother a washerwoman. Stalin's father was a drunk who beat his son. The family spoke only Georgian and Stalin himself only learned to speak Russian at school; he never lost his thick accent. The young Stalin was bullied, while the smallpox he contracted at the age of seven permanently scarred his face and an accident at 12 left his left arm shorter than his right arm. But the boy was immensely strong and tough, and he learned to hide his feelings, while storing revenge in his heart. The culture into which he was born had a strong tradition of blood feuds and the young Stalin took its lessons to heart: never forget and never forgive, but wait, sometimes for years, to take revenge.

Stalin's devout mother wanted him to be a priest and in 1895, aged 16, sent him to the Russian Orthodox Seminary at Tiflis, capital of Georgia. It didn't work: the young Stalin became an atheist, saying, "You know, they are fooling us, there is no God." But in losing one religion, Stalin gained another: communism. At the seminary, he read the works of Lenin and Marx, and joined one of the proto-Bolshevik groups. The seminary finally expelled Stalin in 1899 and his involvement in revolutionary politics deepened, leading him to become, in 1902, a full-time revolutionary, living off crime and hand-outs. As an agitator and revolutionary, the young Stalin came often to the attention of the Tsar's secret police: he was arrested seven times between 1902 and 1913, being sent into internal exile within the vast boundaries of the Russian Empire. Stalin always seemed able to escape, however, leading to rumors that he was in fact working as a double agent for the Tsarist secret police.

In 1906, Stalin married for the first time. His wife, Ketevan Svanidze, gave birth to a son, Yakov, but died from typhus in 1907. Stalin was grief-stricken. At her funeral he said, "This creature softened my heart of stone. She died and with her died my last warm feelings for humanity." And when it came time for Svanidze to be buried, Stalin threw himself into the grave; only the approach of the secret police brought him to himself, and he fled.

It was after his wife's death that Ioseb Dzhugashvili took the name Stalin. In Russian, it means 'man of steel'.

Stalin's rise up the Communist Party hierarchy was slow but steady. In between periods of exile, he edited the party newspaper *Pravda* and in 1917 he was elected to the party's Central Committee. With the abdication of the Tsar on February 15, 1917, the future of Russia was up for grabs and Lenin was determined to grasp it. Launching the second phase of the Russian Revolution, Lenin made his bid for power.

In the battle of colors, the Reds defeated the Whites (communists against anti-communists) and Lenin assumed control. In the confused fighting and in-fighting of the next five years, Stalin did little to distinguish himself beyond

Joseph Stalin at the Potsdam Conference on August 1, 1945

LIFE IN THE TIME OF JOSEPH STALIN

The Gulags

The Gulags were the forced-labor camps where Stalin incarcerated political opponents and petty criminals. Estimates vary, but it's likely that 14 million were imprisoned in the camps, and an additional 10 million sent into labor colonies and exile. The work was so brutal and the conditions so tough that about ten per cent of the inmates of the Gulags died each year.

The NKVD

The People's Commissariat for Internal Affairs, or NKVD, was formed in 1934 and merged into successor secret police organizations in 1946. But during those 12 years it was the chief instrument of Stalin's repression, running the Gulags, conducting show trials and executing anyone whom Stalin saw as a threat. Their favored method of execution was a bullet in the back of the head of a man made to kneel.

Show trials

A key feature of the Great Terror were the show trials held in Moscow between 1936 and 1938. In these trials, the most high-profile of the men Stalin wished to destroy – all the Bolsheviks who had fought alongside him in the 1917 Revolution – were put on public trial accused of increasingly outlandish crimes, including plots to assassinate Stalin. The trials were characterized by public confessions, protestations of recovered loyalty to Stalin and the execution of the defendants. At the time, many Western observers believed the trials to be fair, unaware of how the NKVD had broken down the defendants by interrogation and torture before the trials.

HOW STALIN DID BUSINESS

Stalin's Soviet Union was probably the most thoroughgoing autocracy in history, but he still needed people to convey his will to the country. As Stalin aged he conducted more business from his dacha, his country house outside Moscow, or over dinner at the Kremlin. Stalin preferred to sleep through the day and work through the night, so his inner circle was often summoned to begin their day in the evening - often starting with a cowboy film in the Kremlin movie theater. As the movies were in English, a Politburo member translated the film into Russian as they watched. The film over, Stalin would have dinner with his officials after midnight and then demand that they stay with him through the night.

While Stalin himself drank in moderation, he would insist his party comrades knocked back the vodka - drunkenness revealed weaknesses that he could later use against them. As part of his rituals of control, Stalin would humiliate his officials in front of the gathering, on one occasion forcing the 60-year-old Nikita Khrushchev to dance a Ukrainian folk dance. Khrushchev would later succeed Stalin as ruler of the Soviet Union but, as he said, "When Stalin says dance, a wise man dances."

Another reason for Khrushchev's survival was that he took day-time naps to make sure not to fall asleep during these late-night sessions. As he noted later, "Things went badly for those who dozed off at Stalin's table."

Dressed up to watch an athletic parade through Moscow in 1936, a beaming Stalin stands out from his foreign minister, Molotov (far left) and his eventual successor, Nikita Khruschev (center)

When Nikolai Yezhov (right), head of the NKVD, was purged, all traces of him were expunged from records

displaying a particular ruthlessness toward deserters and enemies, but nevertheless Lenin appointed him General Secretary of the Communist Party in 1922. This enabled Stalin to place allies into many important positions in the party.

Lenin was forced into semi-retirement by the strokes he suffered in May and December of 1922. Although he turned against Stalin in the final two years of his life, Stalin was able to suppress Lenin's criticism of him so that when Lenin died, on January 21, 1924, he was able to win the subsequent power struggle, gradually concentrating power in his own hands.

Initially, Stalin saw the main threat to his power as coming from the Old Bolsheviks: the committed communist revolutionaries who had helped Lenin push through the Russian Revolution. Stalin moved to isolate them: Trotsky was exiled, while others were stripped of power. But even removed from power, Stalin's paranoia still saw the Old Bolsheviks as possible centers of opposition and between 1934 and 1939 he moved to liquidate every possible opponent to his rule, in a period that came to be called the Great Terror. The Old Bolsheviks were, one by one, arrested, tortured and then put on show trials where they confessed to a series of bizarre crimes against the Soviet Union, while professing their undying love for Stalin. Their encomiums to Stalin were given in return for promises that their families would go unharmed after their executions but frequently no sooner had the Old Bolsheviks been executed than Stalin broke his promise and executed their relatives.

The man without mercy had already displayed his utter ruthlessness. In collectivizing agriculture, Stalin liquidated an entire class of Russian peasantry, known as the Kulaks, while the famine in the Ukraine that killed approximately 5 million people was the result of deliberate government policies. Historians now estimate that Stalin was responsible for the deaths of 15 million of his own countrymen during his 30 years in power.

Stalin married again in 1919. His second wife, Nadezhda Alliluyeva, gave him two children, a son and a daughter, but family life was strained and Nadezhda committed suicide in 1932 after a row with her husband.

Stalin lived entirely for himself and had no interest in founding a dynasty; his children were not favored. Yakov, his son by his first wife, also attempted suicide but missed; with typical callousness, Stalin merely tutted, "He can't even shoot straight."

Defining moment

The Young Revolutionary

1902

After leaving the seminary, Stalin embraced revolutionary politics and soon came to the notice of the Tsar's secret police. After organizing strikes and demonstrations against the Tsar, Stalin was detained by the police and spent a year in prison before escaping early in 1904. In 1907, Stalin masterminded a bank robbery to obtain funds for his revolutionary work. As this mugshot shows, Stalin deliberately chose a slovenly and unprepossessing appearance, marking himself as a man apart from the usually impeccably dressed Marxist intellectuals. Stalin was deliberately rejecting middle-class values and portraying himself as a man of the people.

TIMELINE

Birth

Stalin's birth was as unpropitious as Napoleon's. Born in Georgia into a poor family, a long way from the center of power and influence, nobody would have foreseen the impact he would have on history.

December 18, 1879

Marriage

For the first and only time in his adult life, Stalin lets someone else into his heart. When his wife, 'Kato' Svanidze, died on December 5, 1907, Stalin permanently closed himself to any future human vulnerability.

July 29, 1906

Climbing the Tree

When civil war broke out after the October Revolution that brought the Bolsheviks to power, Lenin appointed Stalin to a five-man Politburo alongside Trotsky. Stalin was now very near the center of power in the new Russia.

1917

Defining moment

Mastery 1924-1929

Lenin died on January 21, 1924. Stalin had maneuvered himself into being Lenin's likely successor, which enabled him to suppress Lenin's criticism of him in the final testament Lenin had prepared. During the next five years, Stalin gradually isolated and removed his rivals in the Central Committee. Leon Trotsky was expelled from the Communist Party and went into exile, while men like Zinoviev and Kamenev, who had helped him against Trotsky, were themselves expelled from the party and only allowed to rejoin after they had submitted themselves totally to Stalin. Stalin was now more master than the Tsar had ever been.

Stalin at the 14th Congress of the Communist Party in 1925. This was a gathering of delegates from the Communist Party, and was ostensibly the supreme governing body of the party, from which all policies were handed down

"THE YOUNG STALIN TOOK TO HEART THE LESSONS OF THE BLOOD FEUD: NEVER FORGET AND NEVER FORGIVE"

Yakov subsequently fought in the Soviet Army during WWII and was captured, dying in Sachsenhausen concentration camp. Vasily, his son by Nadezhda Alliluyeva, survived him but died from chronic alcoholism just before his 41st birthday, while his only daughter, Svetlana, eventually defected to the West, fleeing to America in 1967.

By the late 1930s, Stalin knew that he would at some point have to face a showdown with Hitler's Germany. But, preoccupied by internal politics and convinced that the pact his foreign minister, Molotov, had signed in 1939 would ensure German non-aggression, Stalin refused to listen to the increasingly agitated warnings of his military. When German forces rolled into Russia in June 1941, Stalin was caught completely unaware and was initially paralysed by indecision. But with the Germans pursuing brutal policies of ethnic cleansing, Stalin was able to rally the Russian people in what is known in Russia as the Great Patriotic War. In the great battles of Moscow, Leningrad and Stalingrad, Hitler's armies were destroyed, and the Red Army began its relentless advance westwards towards Berlin.

Defining moment

The Great Patriotic War

June 22, 1941 - May 9, 1945

Despite the Molotov-Ribbentrop Pact, Hitler invaded the Soviet Union with the express aim of destroying the country and ethnically cleansing vast areas of the USSR. After the initial shock, Stalin rallied the USSR in the Great Patriotic War. He relaxed some of his old sanctions, allowing many churches of the Russian Orthodox Church to re-open and rewarding his best generals. Unlike Hitler, Stalin learned to leave the management of the war to his generals.

With the Soviet Union bled white by its losses during the war, Stalin was determined to ensure that the countries the Red Army occupied became satellite states of the Soviet Union. At the Potsdam Conference in 1945, Stalin set out his terms and by 1946 Winston Churchill had learned enough to say that "an iron curtain" was being drawn across European continent. Stalin imposed communist governments on the countries of Eastern Europe, effectively drawing them under his control, while the former allies gazed with suspicion upon each other through the new curtain.

Communist sympathizers in America had passed enough information to the Russians for them to develop and build their own atomic bomb by August 29, 1949. With the Soviet Union now armed with nuclear weapons too, the first phase of the Cold War began. Stalin imposed a blockade on the Allied sectors of Berlin but the Berlin airlift ensured that West Berlin remained an exclave within communist East Germany.

Despite his absolute mastery of the Soviet Union, Stalin remained paranoid and in the early 1950s began another purge. But before it could begin properly, Stalin was struck down by a stroke early on March 1, 1953. He'd given orders not to be disturbed when he went to bed so his guards left him undisturbed until 10pm of that day. He was found lying by his bed, unable to move or speak, his pyjamas soaked in stale urine. The man who had killed millions of his own people spent his last four days on earth trapped in his own body. Then, according to his daughter, his eyes opened for the final time with "a terrible look – either mad or angry and full of the fear of death". Stalin died at 9.50pm on March 5, 1953.

Industrial Revolution
The Russia Stalin ruled was a largely pre-industrial country. Stalin was determined to change that, and began a process of centrally-planned industrialization organized into five-year plans. It eventually worked, but at a great human cost.
1928-1938

Collectivization
To force food production upwards, Stalin instituted a policy whereby smallholdings of peasants were consolidated into massive, state-run farms. When targets were not met, he identified the Kulaks, wealthier peasants, as his obstacle and liquidated them.
1928-1940

The Terror
Stalin's paranoid mind turned toward eliminating any possible rival. So he began the Great Terror, liquidating all the surviving Old Bolsheviks and as purging upper levels of the army and the party.
1934-1939

Molotov-Ribbentrop Pact
The Nazi and communist regimes, simultaneously watchful and fearful of each other, signed a non-aggression pact that also contained secret clauses carving up eastern Europe between them. Stalin invaded Poland 16 days after Hitler did.
August 23, 1939

Russia's bomb
The US was the world's sole nuclear power for just four years. Thanks to extensive infiltration of the Manhattan Project, Soviet intelligence was able to provide enough information to Russian scientists for them to create their own atomic bomb.
August 29, 1949

The end
After suffering a stroke on March 1, Stalin was left trapped in his body while his magnates, terrified he might recover, dithered over sending for medical care. The fear he inspired condemned Stalin to four days of agony before he eventually died.
March 5, 1953

END OF AN ERA

© Getty Images

MUSSOLINI'S DOWNFALL

Once the most powerful man in Italy, Il Duce met his fate while fleeing his country in disguise as the war neared its bitter finale

The hunched figure in the back of the German truck might not have merited a second glance had he not been wearing sunglasses. The Luftwaffe corporal, resting his chin on the sub-machine gun between his knees, was certainly not what the partisans of the 52nd Garibaldi Brigade were looking for. They were intent only on finding any fugitive Italians within the small column of German troops heading for home.

However, the sunglasses – worn on a cloudy day – attracted attention and a closer examination of the German corporal revealed the unmistakable features of Benito Amilcare Andrea Mussolini, former prime minister and dictator of Italy. It was April 27, 1945, and the story of 'Il Duce' ('the leader'), was coming to its conclusion.

The slow defeat

Mussolini had long sensed that his end was near. The war, never popular in Italy, had been going badly for some time. "From October 1942," he had commented, referring to the Allied victory at El Alamein, "I had a constant and growing presentiment of the crisis which was to overwhelm me."

In truth, it did not take a political savant to see that trouble was brewing. The Italian role in WWII had often bordered on the farcical. Very much a junior partner to the Germans, Italy had only declared war on France once it had been conquered. Subsequent military operations – including those in Albania and Greece – had been botched to the extent that German forces had been required to bail the Italians out.

A crossroads had been reached in May 1943, when the Allied victory in Tunisia removed Axis forces from North Africa. A difference of opinion divided the British and Americans at this point; the Americans favoring a concentration of force for the invasion of German-occupied France, while the British advocated delaying that and keeping the pressure on Germany through attacking its weaker partner.

The British plan prevailed, and Italy faced an uncertain future, but there was still hope that a destructive campaign on the Italian mainland might be avoided. As the first Allied strike began, against Sicily in July, one thing was clear: Il Duce's reign was over. At a meeting of his own Grand Council, in the sweltering heat of a late July day and into the night, Il Duce was voted out of office.

Realizing that he could ignore the vote of the council, he remained determined to hang on to power. His fate was sealed the next day, however, when he was arrested on the orders of King Victor Emmanuel III. Although the whole process was polite and peaceful, Mussolini failed to understand what was really happening.

On the day of his 60th birthday, Il Duce was in captivity on the island of Ponza, before

Mussolini was the figurehead of a cult of personality and represented the unifying force in Italian fascism

“MUSSOLINI HAD LONG SENSED THAT HIS END WAS NEAR. THE WAR, NEVER POPULAR IN ITALY, HAD BEEN GOING BADLY FOR SOME TIME”

being moved to an impressive suite at the Hotel Campo Imperatore, 5,900 feet up the Gran Sasso mountain in the Apennines. But the gilded cage would not hold the would-be imperator forever.

Italian surrender

Nobody, on either side, had any doubts that Italy would now try to extricate itself from the war. The critical factor in the tragic events that followed would be the German ability to act swiftly and decisively on that realization.

While the Allies bogged themselves down in negotiations with the new government – led by Marshal Pietro Badoglio – over the terms of an Italian surrender, the Germans were already quietly moving troops into Italy.

When the inevitable armistice between Italy and the Allies was announced, the Germans were ready with Operation Achse, which saw German troops replace Italians in southern France, the Balkans and the Aegean. They also immediately disarmed more than half a million Italian troops in their native country – a staggering 56 divisions of the Italian Army were simply dismantled.

The Allies had clearly miscalculated the German response, but worse was to come. Rather than digging in on a defensive line to the north of Rome, as expected, the Germans chose to resist the Allied invasion. Getting underway just hours after the declaration of the armistice, on September 9, the Allied landings at Salerno were fiercely contested from the start. Under Albert Kesselring, the Germans were prepared to make Allied forces pay for every inch of Italian territory they gained.

Mussolini was in a state of limbo at this point. Describing himself as, "a corpse whose death they hesitate to announce," he appeared to have lost the energy and passion that had marked out the early days of his career.

Under the terms of the negotiations with the Allies, he was meant to have been handed over when the invasion began, but the German response had been so swift that panic had struck the new Italian regime. Along with the King, Badoglio and the rest of the government had fled south from Rome on September 9, forgetting all about the deposed dictator, whose life and career was about to enter its final, humiliating phase.

Il Duce's control over Italy became absolute in 1925 when he dissolved the democratic government

Mussolini pictured with German and Italian troops in 1944. Units were receiving training in Germany to continue the fight against the Allies

The slaughter at Grotto Via Ardeatina was carried out by an SS unit as revenge for partisan activity

"UPON ITS SURRENDER TO THE ALLIES, ITALY BECAME NOTHING MORE THAN A SOURCE OF MEN AND MATERIALS FOR THE GERMANS, TO BE PLUNDERED AT WILL"

'Here are the liberators' – a propaganda poster demonizing the US for its part in bombing campaigns

"GERMANY IS TRULY YOUR FRIEND"

Turning their backs on Nazi Germany had devastating consequences for the Italians

Posters may have declared that the Italians had nothing to fear from their long-time partners in the 'Pact of Steel', but the truth was in fact very different – and darker.

Upon surrendering, Italy became nothing more than a source of men and materials for Germany, to be plundered at will. Factories were packed up and shipped out of the country, and Italy was even forced to pay 10 million lire per month as expenses. Even food was taken for German soldiers, leaving many Italians on the brink of starvation.

As well as the territory of the new Mussolini-headed government, the RSI, Germany also effectively annexed territories in the northeast of the country, which conveniently coincided with territory taken from Austria at the end of WWI. An 'adviser', Rudolph Rahn, was installed as German Ambassador to the RSI, further undermining Mussolini's power. The great leader was now little more than a puppet.

Twelve gliders, carrying over 100 German commandos, were dispatched to 'rescue' Mussolini, who was forced to leave his comfortable hotel in a dangerously overloaded Stork reconnaissance plane. Two days later, he was meeting the Führer. Hitler offered Mussolini a stark choice – either accept a position at the head of a new Italian government in northern Italy, or face the consequences. "Northern Italy," the Führer warned, "will be forced to envy the fate of Poland if you do not accept to give renewed vigor to the alliance between Germany and Italy, by becoming head of the state and of the new government." It was an unequivocal statement: acquiesce or be destroyed.

So began the last phase of Mussolini's career, as the head of a puppet regime. If he had felt like a corpse before, he was little more than a zombie now.

"PARTISAN GROUPS HAD SPRUNG UP SPONTANEOUSLY ON THE DECLARATION OF THE ARMISTICE WITH THE ALLIES, WITH AN ESTIMATED 10,000 CIVILIANS ARMING THEMSELVES AND FORMING LOOSELY ORGANIZED GROUPS"

The Allies creep closer

Many Italians had hoped that the armistice with the Allies would mean an end to their war. This was perhaps naïve, but few would have guessed that their struggle was just beginning.

Germany could not allow the Allies to occupy a section of Italy and use it as a launch pad for strikes against the Fatherland. The removal of the Italians as a fighting partner, however their abilities were viewed, was nevertheless a major blow and Germany would soon be fighting on three desperately hard fronts as the long-anticipated invasion of Europe neared.

Mussolini's popularity declined rapidly as the Allies advanced up the Italian mainland

A young soldier is comforted during an inspection of a paramilitary Black Brigade

Mussolini spent the last two years of his life as a puppet figurehead of the Italian Social Republic

THEATER OF NIGHTMARES

Italy was the setting for some of the most bitter fighting of the entire war, as well as the political intrigues behind the fall of Mussolini

01 Mussolini deposed

The path to Italy's eventual surrender to the Allies lies open following the ousting of Benito Mussolini. Taken into captivity at the Hotel Campo Imperatore, he is forgotten in the scramble to leave Rome in the face of the German advance upon the city and is rescued by German paratroopers.

02 The Allies invade

Just hours after the surrender of Italian forces to the Allies, landings begin at Salerno on September 9, 1943. The strength of German resistance surprises the Allies, who make slow progress and are then stalled by defensive works along the Gustav Line. A typically harsh Italian winter does not help.

03 RSI set up

Mussolini's only function from September 1943 is as the head of a puppet regime in northern Italy, effectively supported, organized and run by the Germans. Based at Salò, Mussolini has no power and virtually no influence left.

04 Anti-partisan operations

March 1944 sees an increase in the number and scale of operations against Italian partisans. Forces comprised of both German and Italian fascist units strike in a series of raids (known as 'rastrellamentos') in northern Italy, with partisan casualties often reaching the hundreds.

05 Breakthrough at Cassino

After three previous assaults on the area around Cassino fail, the Allies finally break through the Gustav Line, with II Polish Corps to the fore, in May 1944. Tantalizingly, it looks as if the entire German 10th Army (AOK 10) might be trapped, but the opportunity is lost.

06 The liberation of Rome

On June 4, 1944, just two days before the Normandy Landings on D-Day, the American 5th Army liberates Rome. Controversy still remains over the American commander's determination to reach Rome first, which may have cost the Allies the chance of bottling up AOK 10.

07 Mussolini's capture

On April 27, 1945, while attempting to flee Italy as German forces crumble under the Allied onslaught, Mussolini is captured by the 52nd Garibaldi Brigade, near the village of Dongo and the Swiss border. A day later, he is executed.

Mussolini giving his last speech in Milan, 1944, promising that German arms will turn the tide and condemning Bolshevism

"THE SITUATION WAS SELDOM CLEAR-CUT, WITH MANY YOUNG MEN CHOOSING TO JOIN AN ORGANIZED UNIT NOT THROUGH ANY POLITICAL OR IDEOLOGICAL CONVICTION, BUT SIMPLY OUT OF DESPERATION AND THE NEED FOR SOME FORM OF EMPLOYMENT"

The first Italians to wake up to the reality of the new situation were the soldiers themselves. More than 600,000 became prisoners of war, with the bulk of them shipped to Germany to work as forced labor, while around 200,000 took the alternative of joining the German Army.

Atrocities were common, most notably on the island of Cephalonia, where Italian troops made the mistake of resisting the Germans. More than a thousand were killed in the one-sided fighting that followed, and 5,000 survivors were then systematically massacred. The Allied offensive from Salerno made slow progress, but had driven the Germans back to a major defensive line by January 1944. Three assaults were launched on the town of Cassino, one of the keystones of the Gustav Line, but the German defenses could not be breached. The war had entered a brutal, attritional phase and the Italians found themselves bystanders caught between two destructive forces. For some, simply standing by and watching was unthinkable, but the understandable desire to do something to respond to the situation would lead Italy into the murky depths of a civil war.

Resistance erupts

Partisan groups had sprung up spontaneously on the declaration of the armistice with the Allies, with an estimated 10,000 civilians arming themselves and forming loosely organized groups. A two-day resistance was also staged at Rome until the Germans threatened to raze the city. Around 50,000 prisoners of war, mostly from Yugoslavia, were also thrown into the mix when the Italians guarding them simply left their posts. Many headed for the hills and the mountains to join partisan groups.

Such groups were small in number at the start of the war, possibly comprising as few as a dozen men. After the armistice was signed in September 1943, the number of active partisans in Italy would rise sharply. Following Mussolini's removal, previously banned political parties stepped out of the shadows to form partisan groups with fervent ideological grounding. Almost half of these groups were communists, known as 'Garibaldi Brigades'. The Action Party was the next largest faction, but there were also partisans fighting for the aims of the Socialists, Christian Democrats, Labour Democrats and Liberals, as well as some who spurned any sort of political affiliation at all, such as the Stella Rossa, the 'Red Star Brigade'.

The six major anti-fascist parties organized themselves into the Comitato di Liberazione Nazionale, or Committee of National Liberation (CLN), aiming to co-ordinate resistance to the German occupation and Italian fascist groups. Many of these had sprung up at the same time as Mussolini's new government. Fascist

ITALY'S PARTISANS

Organized resistance to the Germans and Italian fascists came in many forms

Parri was a militant anti-fascist and had been fighting Mussolini since the 1920s

Garibaldi brigades

With communist backgrounds, the Garibaldi brigades were the largest faction in the partisan landscape. Usually commanded by veterans of the Spanish Civil War (1936-1939), a brigade was nominally 100-300 strong, but numbers could be far higher and fluctuated wildly. Brigades actually lost effectiveness when numbers swelled, as too many recruits made them a bigger, slower target for anti-partisan forces.

Stella Rossa (Red Star Brigade)

One of the few partisan organizations to be free from political ideology, the Stella Rossa resisted outside influences and existed thanks to support and arms drops by the American-run Office of Strategic Services – the forerunner of the CIA. The Stella Rossa first became active, with just 20 members, in November 1943.

Giustizia e Libertà (Justice and Liberty) brigades

Backed by the Action Party, GL brigades had the lofty ambition of forming a sort of unified army rather than merely engaging in guerrilla warfare. They made up around 21 per cent of all partisan forces in Italy and received preferential treatment from the Allies, who mistrusted the communists. One of their leaders, Ferruccio Parri (pictured), would go on to become a prime minister of Italy.

militia, in the form of the Guardia Nazionale Repubblicana (GNR), worked to counter the partisans, aided by the Gestapo, the SS security service, the military-based carabinieri police and barely controllable gangs.

The situation was seldom clear-cut, with many young men choosing to join an organized unit not through any political or ideological conviction, but simply out of desperation and the need for some form of employment. Nevertheless, there were enough fanatics to ensure that fighting between the various factions was often savage.

Historians have long debated the effectiveness of the partisans, but there can be no doubt that they increased the scale of their activities as the Allied Italian campaign progressed. From less than 500 reported attacks in January 1944, there were more than 2,000 in March and more than 3,000 in June.

The attacks, especially when they targeted German soldiers, drew severe retribution. As a rule of thumb the Germans would execute ten prisoners or civilians for every German soldier killed by partisans. Perhaps the most notorious reprisal followed a bombing in Rome, mounted by the communist Gruppi di Azione Patriottica Centrale (GAP Central). A 40-pound bomb was detonated as a company of SS soldiers marched by on March 23, 1944, instantly killing 28 of them. A further five soldiers would succumb to their wounds the following day.

Furious, the Germans responded by rounding up Jews, communists, criminals and others that happened to be in the wrong place at the wrong time. The following day, in batches of five at a time, they were executed at the Ardeatine Caves south of Rome. Brutal enough to start with, the executions became more cruel as the day progressed and some of the victims were actually beaten to death. In total, 335 people were slaughtered by the vengeful Germans.

Inevitably, many groups turned their attentions away from the Germans and onto infrastructure – such as bridges and railway lines – or their fascist opponents, which did not draw such a strong response. The civilian population, warned by the Germans not to get

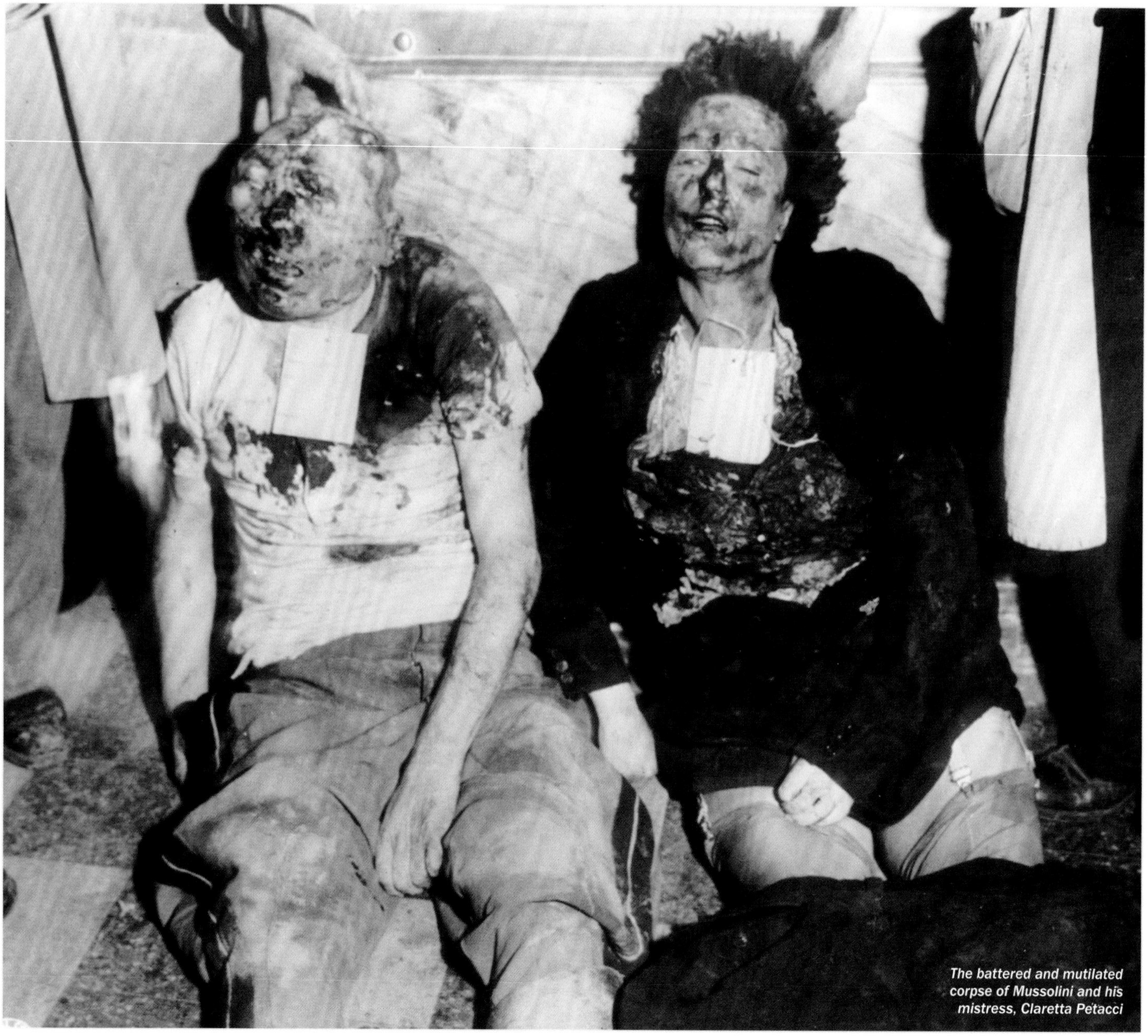

The battered and mutilated corpse of Mussolini and his mistress, Claretta Petacci

After executing the fascist leader, Italian partisans hung him, along with his retinue, in one of Milan's public squares

involved but encouraged by the Allies to do just that, entered a terrifyingly uncertain phase, where retribution for an act of resistance could be delivered at any moment.

Severe supply shortages, caused by the campaign raging within the country, also led to an explosion of black market activity. In many places the situation approached anarchy as armed gangs simply robbed people and houses in order to sell the proceeds.

The Allied forces, slowly inching their way up the country, also failed to deliver the level of provisions they had previously promised. Even worse, though, soldiers were known to indulge in the plunder and rape of the civilian population as they passed through.

The hamstrung leader

Mussolini despaired at the brutal nature of the German occupation, but his new government was toothless. Based, humiliatingly, at Salò rather than Rome, the Repubblica Sociale Italiana (RSI) saw its various offices scattered over a wide area in a deliberate attempt to limit its ability to function efficiently.

Heaping further humiliation on Il Duce, he was granted a new army of just four divisions, and the bulk of them would need to come from new recruits. Only 12,000 officers and NCOs were allowed to return from Germany and conscription was required to fill out the new army's pitifully meagre ranks. This led to a surge in partisan numbers, as many young men preferred to take their chances in the mountains rather than obey their call-up orders. Mussolini was not, however, a totally spent force.

Falling back on his early career as a journalist, he became a prolific writer once more, churning out propaganda pieces that referred to the Allies as 'Anglo-American invaders' and contrasted their habit of flattening Italian cities and towns with the way the Germans had left Rome intact after being driven out by the American 5th Army in June 1944.

The Allied campaign had progressed remorselessly – following success in the fourth Battle of Cassino in May 1944 – but there had been huge casualties on both sides as the Germans repeatedly fell back on new

Below: Italian partisans, aligned with the Action Party, patrol the streets of Milan after the city's liberation on April 25

Hitler and Mussolini's relationship deteriorated as the war continued

defensive lines. The diversion of German units from France to Italy in order to thereby aid the Normandy invasion (launched on June 6, just after the fall of Rome) was the stated Allied aim of the Italian campaign, but as many historians would later note, it was debatable who was actually tying down whom.

A desperate escape

By the end of 1944, Mussolini was little more than a recluse, but he still had a little fight left in him. He formulated a plan to launch a counteroffensive using his precious four divisions, but it predictably failed to make any lasting gains against the Allied advance.

In a final display of his old passion, Mussolini gave a speech in Milan in December, drawing rapturous applause from a packed crowd at the Teatro Lirico. It was little more than a last hurrah by a desperate man.

In February 1945, his German doctor declared that he was the "victim of a serious physical and moral collapse". Also crumbling was the German military position – on every front. The Allies broke through the Gothic Line in April at the same time as they approached Berlin from the West and the Russians approached it from the East.

On April 25, the partisan leadership met with Mussolini in Milan to thrash out the terms for the surrender of his fascist militia groups. His attempts to work out a deal with them rapidly collapsed, Mussolini unwilling to completely surrender while the partisans demanded that all fascist weapons were laid down before a deal could be struck.

Leaving Milan, at 8pm, Mussolini embarked on a desperate bid to escape the country. He made it to Como that night and by April 27 had fallen in with a column of German troops, wearily heading home after their exhausting campaign in Italy.

A partisan roadblock stopped the column, and after protracted discussions, the Germans were told they could continue their journey but that all Italians had to be left behind. The Germans were unconcerned about the fate of their Italian passengers, but they had agreed to allow Mussolini to travel with them in disguise. They'd even given him a greatcoat, helmet, sub-machine gun and the fateful sunglasses in a futile attempt to obscure the most familiar face in Italy. Their efforts were in vain.

Recognized quickly when the column was searched, Mussolini was arrested. He had fallen into the hands of the communists in the form of the 52nd Garibaldi Brigade patrol.

The final act

The communists were determined not to hand Mussolini or the other members of his retinue – including his mistress, Claretta Petacci – over to the Allies. A miserable few hours followed, in which Mussolini's fate was argued over and he was disguised once more, this time by the partisans as they attempted to keep him alive until they had decided what to do with him. The decision, when it came, was brutally simple. Alongside his mistress, Mussolini was riddled with sub-machine gun bullets on April 28, 1945. Although many claimed to have been the man to kill Il Duce, confusion still reigns over who pulled the trigger.

The remaining members of his retinue were also executed and the bodies, including those of Mussolini and his mistress, were unceremoniously dumped in the Piazzale Loreto in Milan. On the morning of April 29, the bodies were discovered and a mob quickly gathered to spit, kick and otherwise abuse the corpses. Mussolini, his mistress and others were strung up by their feet, their already stiffened bodies hanging grotesquely. The following day, Hitler committed suicide. Even then, however, Italy's misery was not over. Mussolini was gone but the partisans had plenty of other targets. An orgy of violence erupted as thousands of fascists, and suspected fascists, were summarily executed.

"MUSSOLINI WAS RIDDLED WITH SUB-MACHINE GUN BULLETS ON APRIL 28, 1945"

ADOLF HITLER'S BUNKER

BERLIN, GERMANY
APRIL 30, 1945

As battle raged on the streets of Berlin, Nazi Germany's Führer was 50 feet underground in his subterranean lair, the Führerbunker. Adolf Hitler was safe for now, but it wouldn't be long until the Third Reich's capital was overrun by the vengeful Red Army. Hitler's remaining allies had pleaded with him to escape south to the Alpine retreat of Berchtesgaden. However, the Führer, determined to be a martyr for the cause, stayed put. Now more mentally twisted than ever, he believed his presence in Berlin would inspire what was left of the Wehrmacht to hold out. There would be no humiliating armistice like in 1918.

Hitler's last few days were dominated by those he held in high regard deserting him. Heinrich Himmler attempted to make peace with the Allies while Hermann Göring appointed himself the new führer. It was only at the end of April that Hitler realized the game was up and made preparations for his passing. Under no circumstances would he be captured and suffer the same as Mussolini, strung up for the world to see. He married his long-time companion Eva Braun and dictated his final testament that, typically, was a tirade on how Jews were to blame for the war.

At 2.30am on April 30, Hitler bid farewell to those in the Führerbunker. That afternoon, he was found dead. A Walther PPK pistol was on the floor next to him and his new wife also lay lifeless after biting on a cyanide capsule. The bodies were burned until they were just charred remains. The Wehrmacht's guns soon fell silent and the tyranny of the Third Reich was over.

EXTRA THE STARS AND STRIPES EXTRA

HITLER DEAD

Fuehrer Fell at CP, German Radio Says; Doenitz at Helm, Vows War Will Continue

Churchill Hints Peace Is at Hand

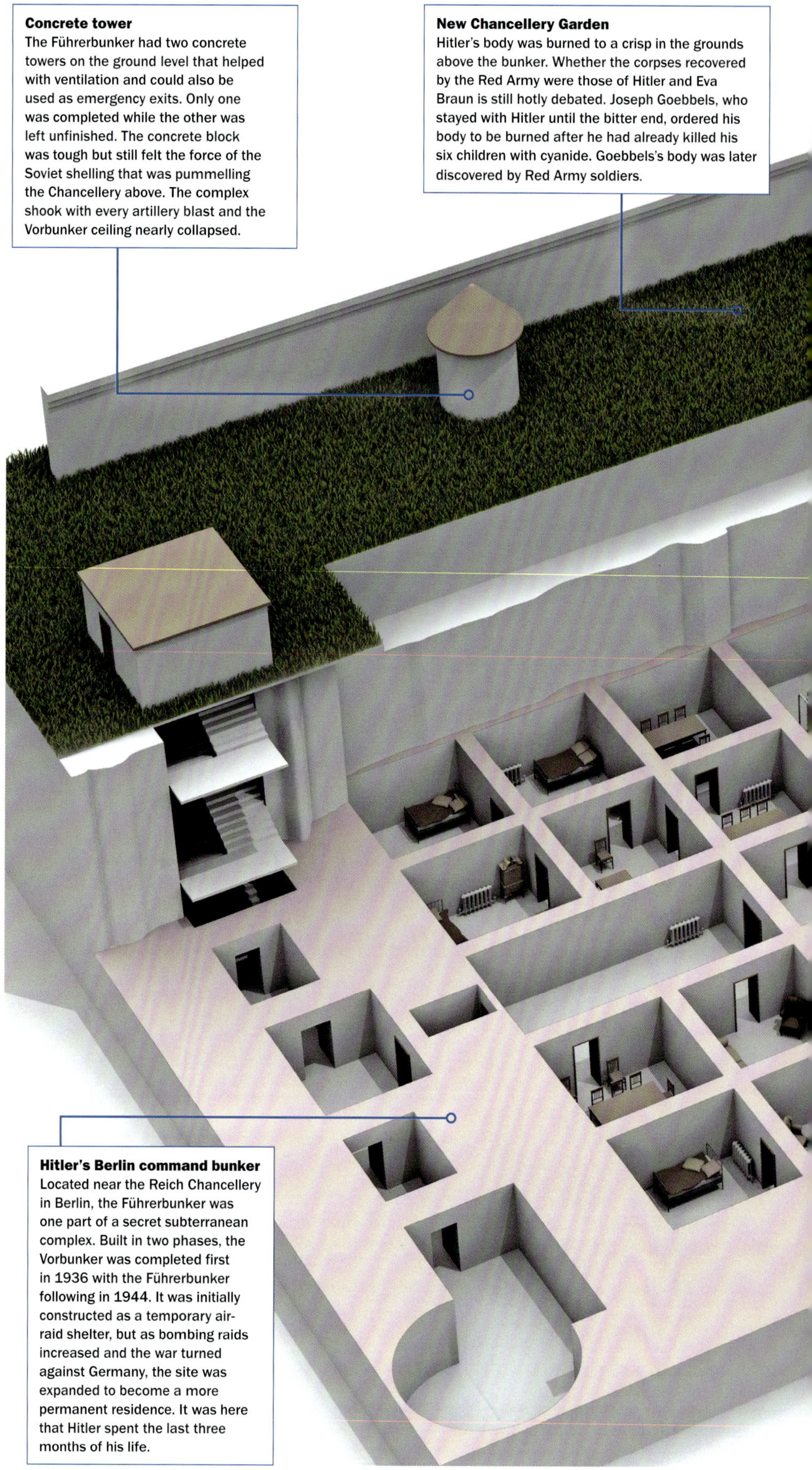

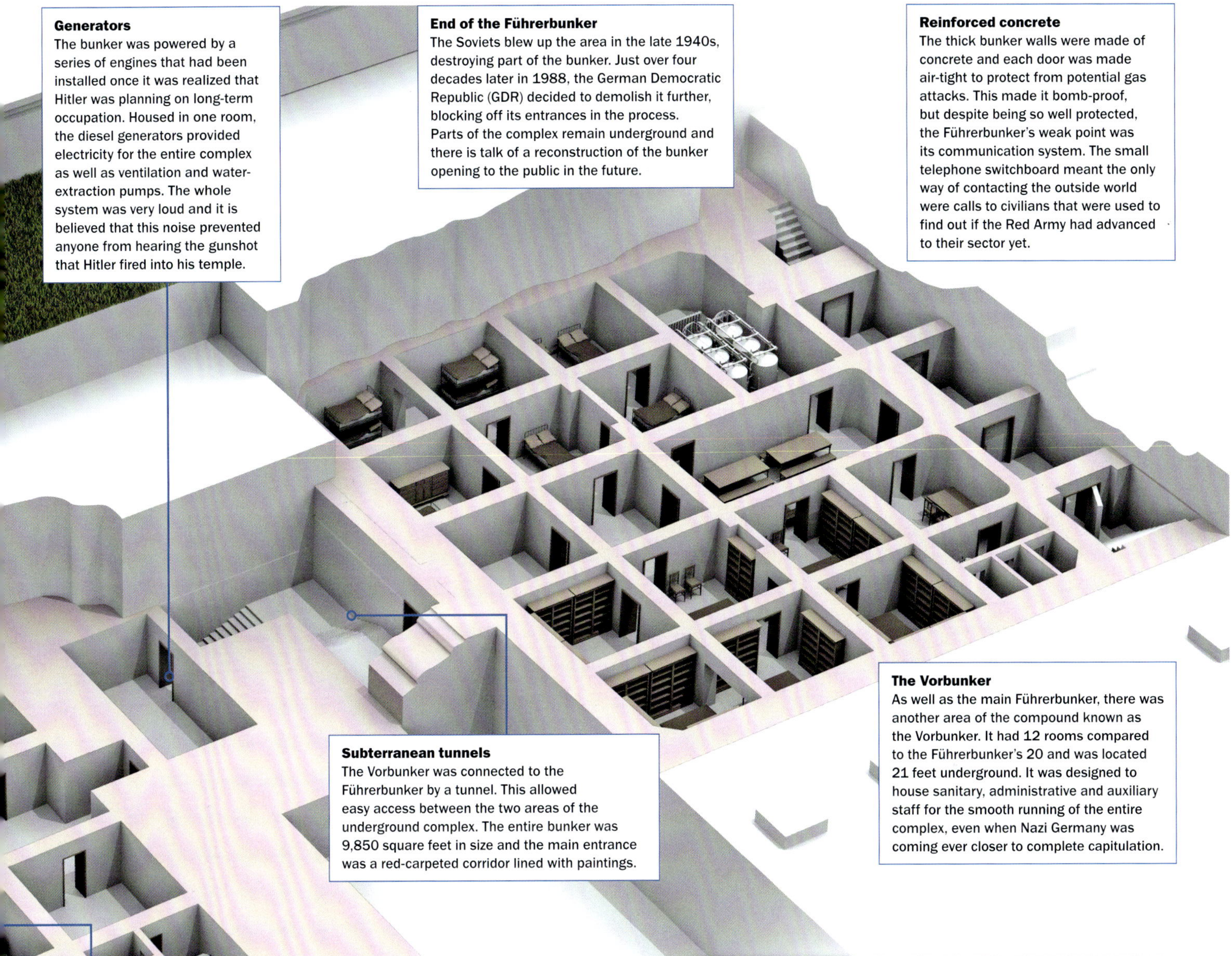

Generators
The bunker was powered by a series of engines that had been installed once it was realized that Hitler was planning on long-term occupation. Housed in one room, the diesel generators provided electricity for the entire complex as well as ventilation and water-extraction pumps. The whole system was very loud and it is believed that this noise prevented anyone from hearing the gunshot that Hitler fired into his temple.

End of the Führerbunker
The Soviets blew up the area in the late 1940s, destroying part of the bunker. Just over four decades later in 1988, the German Democratic Republic (GDR) decided to demolish it further, blocking off its entrances in the process. Parts of the complex remain underground and there is talk of a reconstruction of the bunker opening to the public in the future.

Reinforced concrete
The thick bunker walls were made of concrete and each door was made air-tight to protect from potential gas attacks. This made it bomb-proof, but despite being so well protected, the Führerbunker's weak point was its communication system. The small telephone switchboard meant the only way of contacting the outside world were calls to civilians that were used to find out if the Red Army had advanced to their sector yet.

Subterranean tunnels
The Vorbunker was connected to the Führerbunker by a tunnel. This allowed easy access between the two areas of the underground complex. The entire bunker was 9,850 square feet in size and the main entrance was a red-carpeted corridor lined with paintings.

The Vorbunker
As well as the main Führerbunker, there was another area of the compound known as the Vorbunker. It had 12 rooms compared to the Führerbunker's 20 and was located 21 feet underground. It was designed to house sanitary, administrative and auxiliary staff for the smooth running of the entire complex, even when Nazi Germany was coming ever closer to complete capitulation.

A variety of rooms
Hitler stayed in the bunker for 105 days from January 1945 until his suicide in April. The area was kitted out with a number of quarters to make the stay as bearable and functional as possible. The Führer had an office and a map room to plan military strategy in, as well as a bedroom and a bathroom and even a room specifically reserved for his dogs and bodyguards.

A little bit of luxury
The entire underground building was originally designed as a simple air-raid shelter but it became something much grander. The luxury of the Führerbunker may have been above a standard air-raid bunker but it was a world away from the Wolfsschanze (Wolf's Lair) where Hitler orchestrated his strategies during the war. The conference room in particular was cramped, but this was where the final military briefings of the German war effort were held.

A July 1947 photo of the rear entrance to the Führerbunker in the garden of the Reich Chancellery

THEODORE VAN KIRK

Having already served 58 missions in Africa and Europe during WWII, Theodore Van Kirk transferred to the 509th Composite Group. He was the navigator on the Enola Gay, which on August 6, 1945, dropped the first nuclear bomb ever used in war, on the Japanese city of Hiroshima. The last surviving crew member of the Enola Gay, he died on July 28, 2014.

> "I DIDN'T FEEL TOO GOOD ABOUT DROPPING THE BOMB - BUT I DIDN'T FEEL TOO BAD ABOUT DROPPING IT EITHER. IT COULD HAVE BEEN US..."

EYE WITNESS

THE FIRST ATOMIC BOMB, HIROSHIMA, JAPAN, AUGUST 6, 1945

Theodore Van Kirk, known to everyone as 'Dutch', was having trouble sleeping. It was a common affliction among soldiers before a mission, but then again Dutch and his fellow 11 crewmates stationed on the tiny Pacific island of Tinian had more reason than most to be suffering from insomnia that night. The date was August 5 1945 and tomorrow morning they were to drop the first-ever atomic bomb on Hiroshima.

To pass the time, some of the crew – including navigator Dutch, bombardier, Tom Ferebee, and pilot, Paul Tibbets, played poker. It was quite prophetic considering that in a matter of hours they would be gambling again – but this time with much higher stakes.

Sure, the US had successfully detonated the first nuclear device the previous month during the Trinity test in New Mexico, and Dutch, like all the crew, had several months' intensive training at Wendover Airbase in Utah under his belt. Nevertheless the fact remained that what they were about to do had never before been attempted in warfare. Indeed, Dutch recalls, "One of the atomic scientists told us we think you'll be okay if the plane is nine miles away when the bomb detonates." When challenged on his use of the word think, he levelled with them: "We just don't know."

Dutch had been hand-picked to join the 509th Composite Group – the unit tasked with deploying nuclear weapons – by his former commander: "I flew with Paul Tibbets all the time in England. We flew General Dwight Eisenhower [later to become US president] from Hurn [on the south coast of Britain] down to Gibraltar, for example, to command the north African invasion. Then we were all separated and doing various things – I was at a navigation school, for example, teaching other navigators. Tibbets was picked to take command of the 509th group and that's when he looked up some of the people he'd worked with in the 97th [Bombardment Group]."

The history books often paint a picture that the US government and other Allied powers were hand-wringing right up until the final hour over the decision to use the A-bomb. However, although Japan was presented with an ultimatum to surrender on July 26 – which they rejected two days later – Dutch personally felt it was always a foregone conclusion: "I knew that I was going to drop the atomic bomb from February of that year [1945]. It didn't come as a surprise. We were posted to the US airbase at Tinian for about a month prior to dropping the bomb, just keeping in shape."

Around 10pm, the crew were called from the barracks to have an early breakfast before one last briefing and final checks of the Enola Gay. Dutch remembers they had pineapple fritters because he hated them, but Paul Tibbets loved them. While he might not have seen eye to eye with his commander when it came to breakfast, he has only praise for the man that piloted the specially modified B-29 to Hiroshima – and back again.

"He was an outstanding pilot. His skill saved all of the crew's lives a number of times in Europe and Africa. When he got in an aeroplane, he [became] part of it. When you flew with Paul Tibbets you didn't have to have your shoes polished or your pants pressed – and all that sort of stuff – but when you got in the plane, you better damn well know what you were doing!"

It's hard to imagine what the mood on the Enola Gay must have been like as it took off at 2.45am, but from Dutch's perspective this mission was the same as any other. "We were going a long distance over water, using Iwo Jima as a checkpoint on the way. Now if you got lost between Iwo Jima and Japan, you really were a sorry navigator! Everybody on board was doing his own thing. Ferebee took a nap, for example, [while] our radio operator, as I recall, was reading a whodunnit about some boxer. Everybody was making sure they did what they were there to do, and that they did it right."

While the Enola Gay and Bockscar (the plane that dropped the Nagasaki A-bomb) are the two that have gone down in history, Dutch is keen to point out that the operation was a lot wider than that: indeed, seven aircraft were involved in Special Bombing Mission #13 to Hiroshima on August 6. Three were observational planes that flew ahead to ensure conditions were right, Top Secret was a backup to the Enola Gay which landed on Iwo Jima, while the other two aircraft – The Great Artiste and Plane #91 (later

TIMELINE

July 16, 1945

5.29am ● **First detonation**
US scientists successfully detonate the first nuclear device at the Trinity test site.

July 28

● Japanese government rejects surrender terms put forward in the Potsdam Declaration.

August 5

2pm ● **Calm before storm**
Having been told they have the go-ahead to drop the atomic bomb, Van Kirk and the rest of the crew try to get some sleep.

3pm ● The Little Boy bomb is loaded onto the Enola Gay.

6pm ● Struggling to sleep, Van Kirk, Ferebee, Tibbets and others play poker.

10pm ● The crew gets up to prepare for the flight to Hiroshima and eat breakfast.

August 6

12am ● Van Kirk and the crew make their way to the Enola Gay, after a final briefing.

1.37am ● **Weather report**
Three weather planes leave North Field Airbase on Tinian to confirm conditions are favorable.

2.45am ● The Enola Gay takes off, followed by three other B-29s taking part in Special Mission #13.

5.52am ● **Little Boy armed**
The planes fly over Iwo Jima island, where the Enola Gay's backup, Top Secret, lands. The Little Boy bomb is armed.

7.30am ● With the all-clear from the weather planes, the Enola Gay, The Great Artiste and #91 head for Hiroshima.

8.13am ● Pilot, Paul Tibbets, hands over control to the bombardier, Tom Ferebee, to make the bomb run.

8.15am ● **Payload dropped**
Little Boy is released and it detonates 43 seconds after, about 1,900 feet above the city of Hiroshima. The Enola Gay experiences a shockwave moments later.

3pm ● **Mission complete**
The Enola Gay touches down on Tinian, its mission successfully completed. Paul Tibbets receives the Distinguished Service Cross.

Seven of the Enola Gay's 12-man bombing crew stand before the aircraft; Dutch is third from the left, looking down, next to pilot, Paul Tibbets

named Necessary Evil) – accompanied the Enola Gay for the full operation.

"The Great Artiste had instruments that were to be dropped at the same time as we dropped the bomb. If you were to ask me the name of them, I couldn't tell you; I just always called them 'blast meters' because that's what they were measuring.

"The other aircraft [Plane #91] was flying about 20 miles behind with a large camera to get pictures of the explosion. Unfortunately on the day the camera didn't work. So the best pictures we got were from the handheld camera of the navigator on that plane."

The three aircraft arrived at Hiroshima without incident around 8am. The city had been chalked as the primary target for several reasons. There were a great number of military facilities and troops there, as well as a busy port with factories supplying a lot of the materials that would be used to defend Japan in the event of an invasion. Beyond these factors, Hiroshima had never been previously targeted by Allied forces, so any damage recorded later could solely be attributed to the nuclear bomb. Tragically for the citizens of Hiroshima, it also meant the Japanese authorities had very little reason to suspect an attack there – even when the tiny squadron of three B-29s was no doubt spotted approaching...

The North Field Airbase on Tinian played host to 15 modified B-29s and their crews

On the actual bomb run, Tibbets relinquished control of the Enola Gay to bombardier and close friend of Dutch's, Major Tom Ferebee. As the Little Boy bomb (which actually was not so little, weighing in at 9,700 pounds was released, the plane experienced an upward surge, but Tibbets managed to stabilize the B-29 and beat a hasty retreat.

"We made the 150-degree turn that we'd practiced many times and pushed down the throttle to get away. All people were doing was holding on to something [in preparation for] the turbulence that was sure to follow. A loose person or a loose anything in the plane was going to go flying, so we all made sure we were in position and wearing our goggles." They were about nine miles away when the bomb exploded, 43 seconds after it had been released. "We couldn't hear a thing over the engines, but we saw a bright flash and it was shortly after that we got the first shockwave.

"When we turned to take a look back, all we could see of Hiroshima was black smoke and dust. The mushroom cloud was well above us at about 40,000 feet and still rising. You could still see that cloud 300 miles away." What the crew of the Enola Gay couldn't have known at that point was just how destructive the atomic bomb had been. Underneath all that smoke and dust nearly 70 per cent of the city's buildings had been laid to waste and 80,000 people were dead – and that figure was set to rise with the much-underestimated effects of radiation.

Unlike The Great Artiste with its faulty camera, as far as Dutch was concerned on

The destruction wreaked on Hiroshima by the A-bomb was on an unprecedented scale

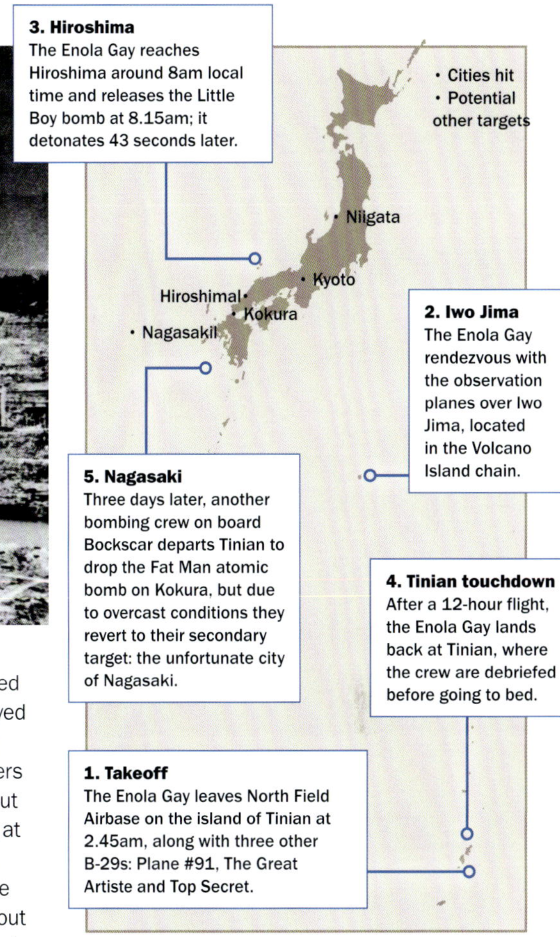

board the Enola Gay "everything had gone exactly according to plan. The weather was perfect; I could probably see Hiroshima from 75 miles away. My navigation was only off by six seconds," he says with pride. "Tom put the bomb exactly where he expected. We got a lot of turbulence, but the plane did not break up, which it could have done, and we got home. Now, as for the second mission to Nagasaki, everything went wrong. They had a lot of luck on that mission…"

Indeed, three days later on August 9, a different bombing crew on Bockscar almost didn't make it to Nagasaki due to a combination of bad weather and logistical errors. However, they managed to salvage the mission; the result of their success, or 'luck' as Dutch describes it, was the instant obliteration of another city and at least 40,000 of its inhabitants. Less than a week later Emperor Hirohito made a radio announcement to his subjects, declaring Japan's surrender due to "a new and most cruel bomb, the power of which is incalculable, taking the toll of many innocent lives."

A few weeks after the bombings, Dutch Van Kirk was part of the crew transporting scientists to Nagasaki to measure the devastation of one of these 'new and most cruel bombs' first-hand. "Having picked up some scientists in Tokyo from the Japanese atomic program – they were also working on atomic bombs, you see – we flew down to Nagasaki; we couldn't land at Hiroshima at that time. We landed on a dirt field and the Japanese commander of the base came out, looking for someone to surrender to. We were given old cars – 1927 Chevrolet models, or similar – to drive to the city center, but they all broke down three times before getting into Nagasaki.

"There wasn't really anything that shocked us, though there is one thing [that has stayed with me]. The Japanese military was being broken up at the time and one of the soldiers arrived on the bus looking for his home – but it had been destroyed. I remember looking at Tom Ferebee, and saying, 'You know, Tom, that could have been us if the war had gone the opposite way.' I didn't feel too good about dropping the bomb – but I didn't feel too bad about dropping it either. This was one man among many that were saved by dropping the bomb" – because it had precluded a full-scale invasion of Japan. "It was very important we saw that, and we both recognized how lucky we were."

Along with all the other Enola Gay crew, who have since passed away, Dutch Van Kirk has no regrets about dropping the atomic bomb, seeing it as the lesser of two evils. Asked whether he believes the result would have been the same – i.e. WWII would have been forced to end – if things 'had gone the opposite way' and Japan had dropped an atomic bomb on America first, there's a long pause, before Dutch responds, "No, I don't think so. I think we would have been more resilient."

But underneath the assured bravado of his reply, there's no getting around how long he had hesitated before he answered – or the fact that, like that atomic scientist who couldn't offer any certainties on Tinian back in 1945, he had used the word 'think'.

If you'd like to read more about Dutch Van Kirk and his missions, *My True Course: Northumberland to Hiroshima* (by Suzanne Dietz) is available from www.amazon.com.

ORIGINS AND AFTERMATH

The US started developing the nuclear bomb following a warning from Albert Einstein and other physicists in 1939 that the Germans were close to constructing their own. Project Manhattan got underway in 1941 and by July 1945 had successfully detonated the first-ever nuclear device in the Trinity test. By this point Germany had already surrendered so the Allied forces' sights were now trained solely on the last remaining Axis power: Japan. Having refused an ultimatum to surrender in the Potsdam Declaration, the Allies felt they were left with two options: a full-scale invasion or the use of nuclear bombs. They opted for the latter. It remains one of the most controversial military decisions ever taken, yet many argue that invading Japan would have claimed many more lives in the long term.

Little Boy produced a force equivalent to around 15,000 tons of TNT

BRINGING THE NAZIS TO JUSTICE

The Allies wanted to punish the Nazis for their crimes. The Nuremberg Trials became the greatest court cases in history

In 1943, Soviet leader Joseph Stalin met his British and American counterparts Winston Churchill and Franklin Roosevelt in Iran. The Tehran Conference, as it became known, had been called to discuss how best to defeat Hitler, but the conversation soon turned to vengeance. Stalin proposed that, once the war was won, 50,000-100,000 German staff officers should be executed in retribution for Nazi atrocities. Roosevelt – perhaps only half joking – said that perhaps 49,000 would do.

As the war worsened, this appetite for revenge grew. When it was over, one senior US politician Henry Morgenthau even advocated obliterating Germany's industrial base and sending the country back to the Dark Ages. Others, however, such as US Secretary of War Henry Stimpson, called for a more measured approach. Yes, those responsible must be brought to justice, but they needed to be tried fairly both to demonstrate the importance of the rule of law and create a historical record of the crimes committed.

Stimpson's argument won the day. On May 8, 1945, US President Harry Truman appointed lawyer Robert Jackson as Chief of Counsel. His mission was to get the US, Britain, France and Russia to agree on how such a trial might work, as well as decide who should face prosecution. The trouble was, the scale of the crime was so vast that it eventually became apparent that not everyone involved could possibly face justice. A huge list of those responsible was collated, and although there would be later prosecutions for less well-known Nazis in the military, judiciary and medical professions, the first and most significant case was that brought against the Nazi leadership.

Although many top Nazis, including Hitler and Himmler, were already dead, other kingpins – including Hitler's successor Herman Göring, armaments minister Albert Speer and deputy Führer Rudolf Hess – were in custody. These men, it was decided, would be among the first to answer for the millions of deaths the Nazis had caused. Not that it would be that easy.

First, no international court or suitable laws existed at this time. Second, how was guilt to be proved? These leaders may have signed the orders, but none had actually pulled a trigger. Once an agreed system of trial was worked out, the challenge, then, was to bring a case against them based on complicity. It was case that would eventually be built around what one of Jackson's team – Murray Bernays – called his 'conspiracy theory'.

Bernays argued that the Nazi Party was a criminal conspiracy that'd plotted to steal the land of Germany's neighbors, to steal their wealth and to commit racially motivated mass murder. As such, the men who'd issued the orders were ultimately culpable. Accordingly,

Seated beside the guard clutching a baton behind his back, Göring listens to the proceedings keenly

TIMELINE

Tehran Conference
The Big Three (Stalin, Roosevelt and Churchill) meet in the Iranian capital to discuss defeating Hitler. The subject of bringing about post-war criminal proceedings was also on the agenda.
November 28 - December 1, 1943

London Charter
The London Charter of the International Military Tribunal is issued. This decree set down the laws and procedures by which the Nuremberg Trials were to be conducted.
August 8, 1945

The Nuremberg Trials begin
The prosecution's case is put forward by US attorney Robert Jackson in a damning and deeply moving speech which leaves a profound impression on both the court and the public.
November 20, 1945

Jackson's opening speech
In a speech delivered at Harvard University, US Secretary of State George Marshall announces a $13-billion aid package to help Europe recover from the devastation.
November 21, 1945

Pre-meditated aggression is proven
Jackson presents the Hossbach Memorandum – evidence of a pre-war conference at which top Nazis had discussed waging war against Germany's neighbors in order to create greater 'lebensraum', or living space.
November 26, 1945

these individuals could be charged with three categories of crime: waging aggressive war, war crimes, and crimes against humanity.

It was decided that judges rather than a jury would preside over a military tribunal, who'd pass sentence based on the arguments presented by teams both prosecuting and defending the accused. Nuremberg, meanwhile, was selected to host the trials. The city's sports stadium had been the venue of annual Nazi rallies throughout the 1930s, and Nuremberg's Palace of Justice was less than five miles away. It was seen as a fitting location to end what had largely been started in a place many considered to be the Nazis' spiritual home.

Göring, Speer, Hess and 20 more of Hitler's surviving henchmen were now incarcerated in the court's cellblock as the final preparations were made. Prosecution teams representing Britain, France, the US and the USSR were assembled: Attorney General Hartley Shawcross represented the British, Chempetier de Ribes the French, and General Roman Rudenko the Soviets. It would be Jackson, however, who would lead from the start.

Fearing a paucity of evidence he'd initially planned to use a series of witnesses to substantiate his case. But as scrupulously kept records of the Nazi slaughter flooded in, he changed tack. With 47 crates of documents, files, and films at his disposal, he began building a meticulous case.

For their part, Göring and co were defended by some of the finest legal minds in Germany. Lawyers immediately went on the attack, questioning the very validity of the main charge – that of 'waging aggressive war'. No state in history had ever faced such an indictment, they argued; there was no juridical basis for the charge. The men in the dock could not be held culpable for state policy; after all, they were just following orders passed down to them.

The prosecution countered, arguing that men had committed these crimes, not some faceless, unimpeachable state. Evidence was now produced. Minutes of a secret meeting from 1937 between Hitler and his top advisors showed them discussing the need to expand Germany's borders– a goal that could only be achieved by force. Further documents and witnesses followed, proving the Nazis had plotted to attack Germany's neighbors.

The prosecution then painstakingly traced back a deliberately forged chain of criminal acts: the burning of Germany's parliament – the Reichstag – the crisis that'd allowed the newly elected Hitler to declare martial law; the subsequent clampdown on the Reich's political opponents; the establishment of the concentration camps. Jackson showed how the conspiracy had caused the war to spread throughout Europe. He revealed, too, how Germany never declared war, opting instead to break treaties to attack without warning.

The defense lawyers responded by producing a mountain of paperwork of their own. It was a tactic designed to drain the moral authority from Jackson's case. Proceedings were slowed down, too, by the judges, who, keen to make sure that justice was seen to be done, allowed the defendants almost total freedom of speech. The more eloquent among them, such as Speer, seized the opportunity to charm the court. Others used it to give sermons on the merits of National Socialism. When Göring was given the floor, he delivered a rabble-rousing diatribe that went on for two and half days.

Although Jackson had been keen to avoid sensationalism, when the Nazi defendants began to hijack the headlines he called on key witnesses whose testimonies would once and for all damn those in the dock.

The stand was now busy with those who'd carried out the orders of the accused, and their evidence shocked the world. The trial continued for 11 long months until on September 1, 1946, the court adjourned for the tribunal judges to consider all of the evidence.

A month later, verdicts were given and sentences passed. Of the 22 surviving defendants (one had committed suicide), 11 – including Göring – were condemned to death, nine were given sentences of between ten years and life, and three were acquitted. With all appeals refused, the executions were set for the night of October 16.

By going after the Nazi leadership, Jackson had established a precedent that stands even to this day – that all humanity would be guarded by an international legal shield, and even a head of state could be held criminally responsible for their aggression and crimes against humanity. Göring, however, would remain defiant to the last. The night before his execution, he swallowed cyanide that had been smuggled into his cell. He was found dead on his bunk the next morning, dressed in blue silk pyjamas, a coward to the very end.

Death squad leader testifies
Otto Ohlendorf – the former head of the mobile SS paramilitary death squad Einsatzgruppe D – is put on the stand. He casually admits to having overseen the shooting of around 90,000 Jews.
January 3, 1946

Holocaust survivor testifies
Marie-Claude Vaillant-Couturier takes to the stand to give testimony. The former French resistance fighter had been imprisoned at Auschwitz where she'd witnessed the genocide of both Roma Gypsies and Jews.
January 28, 1946

Herman Göring takes the stand
Hitler's former right-hand man insists he's merely a military man who'd followed orders, that he isn't anti-Semitic and that he'd had no control over the actions of others.
March 13-22, 1946

Albert Speer takes the stand
As armaments minister, Speer had used 400,000 slave laborers to reach his production targets, thousands of whom had died. Sensing that contrition might save his life, Speer atones.
June 20, 1946

Nimitz Affidavit
Admiral Dönitz, whose U-boats had terrorized shipping in the Atlantic, presents an affidavit from America's Admiral Nimitz that the US Navy had used identical tactics in the Pacific against Japan.
July 2, 1946

Verdicts given
The verdicts are given over two days. The trials' findings form the basis of the Nuremberg Principles drafted in 1950. These set out guidelines for criminal culpability under international law.
September 30 - October 1, 1946

Sentencing is passed
Göring is sentenced to death. Speer escapes with a 20-year sentence, while Dönitz gets just ten years. Hess gets life imprisonment. He dies in Berlin's Spandau Prison 41 years later.
October 1, 1946

Executions
On the temporary gallows in the court's gymnasium the executions are botched; necks don't break immediately. Von Ribbentrop takes 17 minutes to die, General Jodl 18, Field Marshall Keitel 28.
October 16, 1946

Doctors Trial
Part of the Subsequent Nuremberg Trials, this successfully prosecuted 16 Nazi who'd been involved with human experimentation and mass murder under the guise of euthanasia. Seven defendants were subsequently executed.
December 9, 1946 - August 20, 1947

Judges Trial
Also part of the Subsequent Nuremberg Trials, the defendants in this case were 16 judiciary officials responsible for implementing the Nazis' eugenic and race laws – ten of whom were successfully prosecuted.
March 5 - December 4, 1947

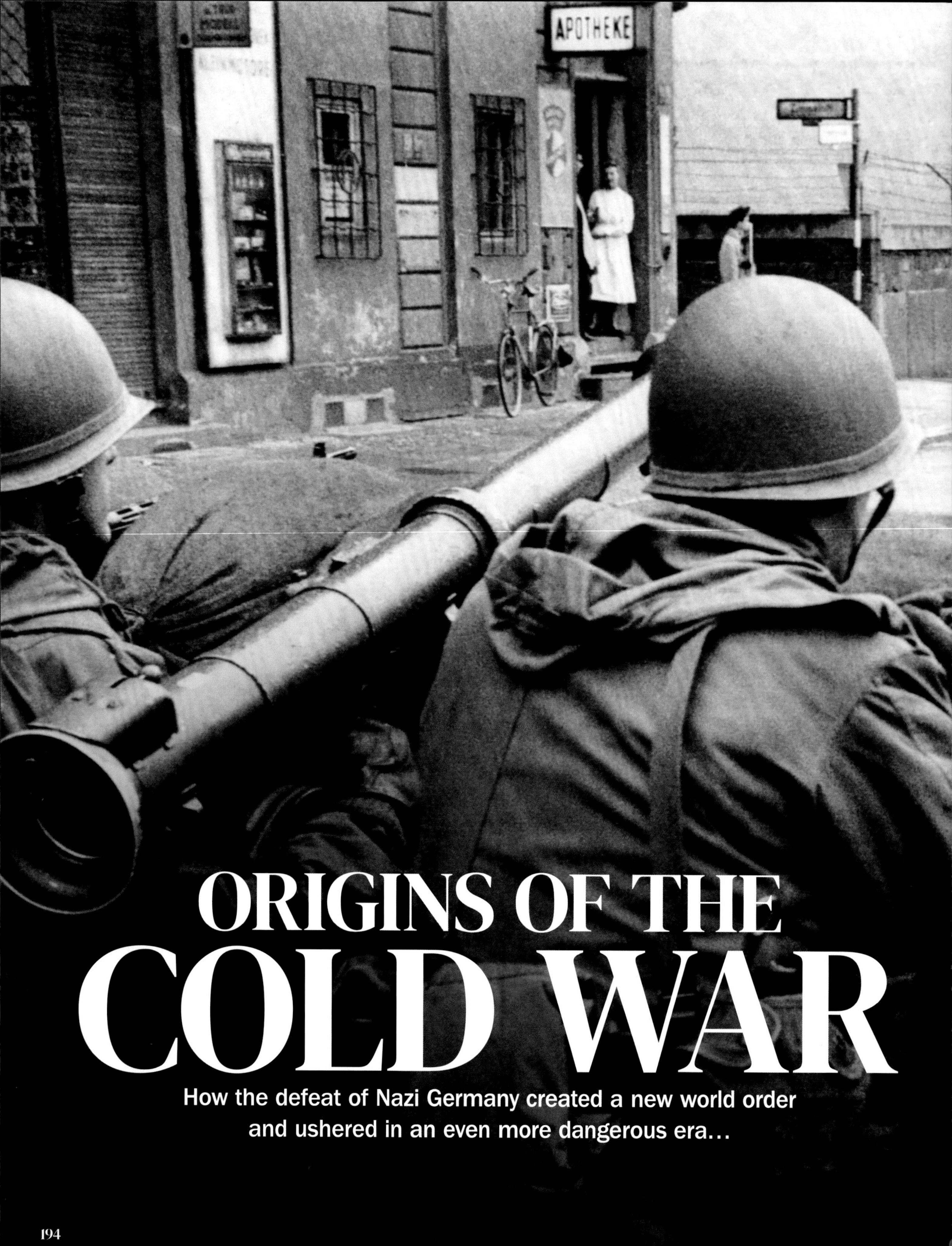

ORIGINS OF THE COLD WAR

How the defeat of Nazi Germany created a new world order and ushered in an even more dangerous era…

The Nazi movement's last showdown came in May 1945, when the Soviet Army finally crushed it during the Battle of Berlin. It was one of the costliest encounters of WWII, claiming 1.3 million casualties in just nine days of fighting. Before it was even over, however, British Prime Minister Winston Churchill was already plotting to attack his ally – the USSR – and drive its vast army out of Eastern Europe.

Operation Unthinkable – as he codenamed his plan – even sought to rope in what remained of Germany's army to ensure victory. 'A tide of Russian domination is sweeping forward,' wrote Churchill. 'After the war is over, the territories under Russian control will include the Baltic provinces, all of eastern Germany, Czechoslovakia, a large part of Austria, the whole of Yugoslavia, Romania and Bulgaria. It's to a showdown with Russia that we must now turn our hopes.' The attack was planned for July 1, 1945. On May 23, however, Churchill was obliged to call a general election. Perhaps fortunately, it was an election he didn't win.

Operation Unthinkable was, of course, top secret, but by 1945 the Russians had so successfully infiltrated British intelligence that Joseph Stalin knew all about it. Indeed, by the time of the Potsdam Conference of July-August 1945 – which was intended to sort out the shape of post-war Europe – the Allied nations that had defeated Nazism were already splitting into two factions: the capitalist governments of Britain and the US on one side, the USSR's communist regime on the other.

At a previous conference in Yalta in February 1945, Stalin had agreed to free elections in lands his army had occupied across Eastern Europe. Suspicious about his allies' intentions, however, he now reneged on his word. The USSR needed 'friendly states' on its Western borders, he insisted. After all, hadn't Russia been dragged into the war when former ally Nazi Germany had invaded without warning?

Moscow would therefore install communist governments in Poland, Bulgaria and Romania, while occupying East Germany – as agreed at Yalta – with the rest of the country divided up into separate zones controlled by Britain, France and the US. The Grand Alliance that had won the war was now dead. "An iron curtain has descended across the continent," Churchill famously declared the following year, describing the irreconcilable rift between the capitalist West and the communist East that now existed.

It was a phrase that would stick. Churchill's comments made public what the Western Allies had already discussed in private. In February 1946, George Kennan, a US diplomat in Moscow, had sent a telegram to Washington arguing for a 'containment policy' towards Russia. Kennan insisted that the USSR was determined to extend its influence around the world – its oppression of the Ukrainian nationalist movement and imposed puppet governments were evidence enough of this. Its leaders, though, were risk-averse. When faced with determined opposition, particularly from the US – he claimed – they would back down.

The earliest test of this theory came in spring 1946 when a communist insurgency took on the British-backed government in Greece, just as Turkey was coming under increasing diplomatic and economic pressure to allow the Soviet navy access to the Mediterranean. Previously, Britain would simply have flexed its imperial muscles, but six years of war had left the country bankrupt and its empire crumbling. So it was left to America to play the role of world policeman. Within a year, US

American and Soviet soldiers meet in Germany as the Nazi regime collapses. Little did they suspect that they'd soon be enemies

Railing against the oppressive Soviet regime, East Berliners pound a Soviet tank with rocks during riots that erupted in June 1953

TIMELINE

The Potsdam Conference
Britain's new PM Clement Atlee, the US President Truman and the USSR's Marshal Stalin meet on the outskirts of Berlin to discuss how post-war Europe is to be organized.
July 17 - August 2, 1945

Korea divided
The Korean Peninsula is split along the 38th Parallel as Soviet troops drive imperial Japanese forces out of the north of the country, while the US invades from the south.
August 10, 1945

Kennan's containment telegram
Diplomat George Kennan's 'Long Telegram' from Moscow advocates a policy of containment against the USSR stating that the US should, 'regard the Soviet Union as a rival'.
February 22, 1946

Churchill's iron curtain speech
"From Stettin in the Baltic to Trieste in the Adriatic, an iron curtain has descended across the continent," Churchill tells an audience in Fulton, Missouri. The phrase becomes a Cold War trope.
May 5, 1946

The Marshall Plan
In a speech delivered at Harvard University, US Secretary of State George Marshall announces a $13-billion aid package to help Europe recover from the devastation of WWII.
January 1, 1946

The Truman Doctrine
In a speech remembered as the Truman Doctrine, the US's President Truman pledges American assistance to any nation threatened by communism, establishing the containment theory as policy.
June 5, 1947

President Harry S Truman had secured $400 million from Congress in military and economic aid for Greece and Turkey, after citing the US commitment to backing free peoples against armed aggressors or outside pressures. This policy, which became known as the Truman Doctrine, appeared to work.

By October 1949, the Greek communists were defeated, while Turkey's economy was strong enough to resist Russia's overtures. Although the defeat of Hitler brought peace to Europe, it had left the continent in chaos. It smashed infrastructure and created continuing hardships that now fuelled support for the communist cause as people called for a fairer distribution of national wealth.

The US, keen to smother communism and smelling the opportunity to make a buck, came up with the Marshall Plan. Named after US Secretary of State George C Marshall, who devised it, it saw America channel $13 billion into 18 war-ravaged economies between 1948 and 1951. This significantly accelerated the reconstruction of Western Europe, creating jobs and new markets for American-made goods in the process. A similar offer of aid was made to countries in the USSR's sphere of influence. Unsurprisingly, it was turned down.

In June 1948, the bizarre game of tit-for-tat that came to characterize the Cold War took a new twist when Britain, France, and the US began merging their zones of occupation into the unified state of West Germany. Stalin responded by blocking all access to Berlin, which, while deep inside the Russian zone, had been similarly divided into four sectors.

Stalin's aim was to either force the Western powers to end their plan to unify West Germany, or leave Berlin. Truman now ordered a massive airlift to supply the 2 million Berliners under Anglo-French and American control, and an armada of aircraft flooded the city with food, clothing and fuel. As a further show of strength, he also sent B-29 bombers, the only planes then capable of carrying an atomic bomb, to bases in Britain. Outmaneuvered, the Russians lifted the blockade in May 1949, having achieved nothing except exacerbating an already precarious situation. By now the West had firmly closed ranks against its former ally.

In April 1949, the North Atlantic Treaty Organization (NATO) was formed, creating a new military alliance between the US, Canada and ten other European countries. It was clearly a bulwark intended to contain the USSR and when the old enemy (West) Germany was invited to join the club in 1955, Moscow responded by forming the Warsaw Pact – a military alliance with the countries under its control. The Cold War was rapidly taking on global proportions.

As had been agreed at Yalta, the USSR had declared war on Imperial Japan in the dying days of WWII. Its troops had then driven the Japanese out of the northern Korean Peninsula while US troops had liberated the south. By 1948, though, the tensions between the USSR and the US saw Korea effectively split into two separate regions – the communist-run People's Democratic Republic of Korea, north of the 38th Parallel, and the US-supported Republic of Korea to its south. Both sides claimed governmental legitimacy, and in June 1950 things hit crisis point when the North Korean Army marched south.

Under the flag of the newly created United Nations, the US sent a mighty force to fight the North Koreans, who were backed by Mao Zedong's new communist regime in China. By the time the conflict ended in 1953, more than 1.5 million US troops had served in a war that ended not in peace but with an uneasy truce that still stands to this day. The border was re-established almost exactly where it had been three years before and here, as was happening elsewhere around the globe, an almighty stare-down between two incompatible political systems would now dominate for decades.

The Berlin Airlift
The US launches Operation Vittles – aka the 11 month-long Berlin Airlift. Planes supply the west side of the city day and night for nearly a year.
June 26, 1948 - September 30, 1949

East Germany founded
In response to the formation of West Germany, the USSR declares the formation of the German Democratic Republic under the rigid leadership of a German communist named Walter Ulbricht.
October 7, 1949

Berlin blockade begins
After the US, UK and France effectively unite their three zones of occupation by introducing a common currency (the Deutsche Mark) the Soviets sever road and rail access into Berlin.
June 24, 1948

NATO is formed
The US and Canada join ten European allies in a formal anti-Soviet military alliance that extends the deterrent threat of the US's nuclear weapons to cover Western Europe.
April 4, 1949

First Soviet A-bomb
The USSR successfully tests its first atomic bomb at Semipalatinsk desert in Kazakhstan, its nuclear program having been greatly aided by its network of atomic spies.
August 29, 1949

Chinese-Soviet Alliance formed
Chinese leader Chairman Mao Zedong visits Joseph Stalin in Moscow to negotiate an alliance between the Soviet Union and China. The Sino-Soviet Treaty of Friendship, Alliance and Mutual Assistance is then signed.
February 14, 1950

North Korea attacks South Korea
North Korean troops cross the 38th Parallel to 'liberate' the southern part of the peninsular from the anti-communist government under Syngman Rhee in Seoul.
June 25, 1950

US troops sent to South Korea
The newly formed United Nation's Security Council recommends that all UN forces sent to Korea be put under US command. Ninety per cent of all the soldiers who serve in the conflict are American.
July 7, 1950